MESSAGES...
and How They Have Failed Us

Deidra Y. McCarty

Edited by:
Jim Murphy
Charles O. Burton
M. Oates

PublishAmerica
Baltimore

First printing

At the specific preference of the author, PublishAmerica allowed this work to remain exactly as the author intended, verbatim, without editorial input.

ISBN: 1-4241-6373-0
PUBLISHED BY PUBLISHAMERICA, LLLP
www.publishamerica.com
Baltimore

Printed in the United States of America

Dedication

This book is dedicated to the many souls who have willingly shared their stories inclusive of rejection and abandonment issues, bouts of depression, anger, grief and loss, deprivation and a myriad of unnamed abuses. Their stories, disclosed in therapeutic offices, family and social gatherings, church meetings, workshops and seminars produced tears from friends, colleagues, family members and both counselor and counselee. And to the many men, women and children who were destined to enter my life and assist me on my life's journey towards revelation, honesty and discovering the many MESSAGES that failed me.

"Our steps are ordered of the Lord"

INTRODUCTION

"How Frog Feels About It"

I'm green and

Gold

In this bright sun

This warm wet stone is just my size

I uncoil my

Tongue. Surprise

Some flies

Green and gold and still as stone

I sit

Listening

Grass whispers a

Warning and I

Leap

Into the glistening

Muck of the pond

Sunned

Sated

Safe

Why should I want to be kissed?

Why should I want to be a prince?

—Lillian Moore

The poem above taken from a children's book depicts the way many of us live our lives. Like the frog sitting comfortably on his lily pad we too are convinced that we feel "sunned, sated and safe" seemingly satisfied with our present life and the status quo. We accept life as is with little or no desire to reach our full potential and at minimum explore our purpose and passion. A life filled with mediocrity, complacency, daily routines and an occasional social gathering prohibits us from examining the true longings of our soul. And just as the frog we are content to catch a few flies now and then. Why do we settle for so little despite the many MESSAGES that suggest "we can have it all...be who we want to be...live where we want to live...and attain immeasurable heights?" The reasons are as varied as the individuals themselves. But more often the reasons have at their source, feelings of guilt, worthlessness, anger, resentment or inadequacy. These feelings are the results of well-meaning parents, teachers, priest, pastors and other individuals who convey subtle yet pervasive MESSAGES that dictate and influence our thoughts and behaviors.

As you begin your personal journey in an attempt to uncover the many MESSAGES that have failed you consider the fact that many books have been written in time past that list your weaknesses and failures. This book goes beyond the predictable in that it brings to light the whys and wherefores of much of our dissatisfaction that reside within. As you explore the how, why and origin of who you are, the words within this text will serve to encourage and aid you as you revisit and censure many of your childhood, adolescent and adult MESSAGES.

Further, this book does not profess to have all the answers neither will it guarantee a life lived in a perpetual state of happiness. But it can provide you with sufficient guidelines which if followed will enable you to be the person you were intended to be. Learning to appreciate yourself without having to measure up to the standards of another will ultimately reduce anxiety, enable you to enjoy fulfilling relationships, and take you more than halfway to where you want to be. As you read and reflect on the following comments, quotes, and stories of wounded individuals much like yourself be prepared to gain a measure of hope as you discover the many MESSAGES that have failed you.

And so...the journey begins

During our formative years, the most impressionable time of our life, we receive MESSAGES that suggest that the key to happiness requires you to mirror the behaviors you observe, obey, accept, and go along with the demands and requests of others and negate any semblance of your own curious nature. The result, we regularly experience feelings of guilt when someone communicates verbal and behavioral MESSAGES that we interpret as one of disapproval, inadequacy and failure. In summary, due in large part to the seemingly subtle MESSAGES given in our homes, places of worship, employment, social settings, or academia we find ourselves rejecting the "who" of who we are.

Our reticence to accept life's predictable developmental stages stem from a myriad of negative MESSAGES that we have heard, seen and incorporated into our daily lives. MESSAGES so powerful that they can, and do have the ability to alter the view we have of ourselves which entails our emotional, intellectual and physical make up. From whom and from where do these MESSAGES originate? Sadly, they have as their origins words and actions from people with whom we are most connected. From the words of a mother who demeans and humiliates to a father who is just not available, the MESSAGES make for fertile soil producing addictions, promiscuity, depression, anxiety, people pleasing, and other negative feelings and behaviors. Additionally, these feelings impact our behaviors throughout life as we bear witness to the actions and hear the words of teachers, peers, and society at large. They continue to wreak havoc in our lives leaving us distrustful of others, performance oriented, prone to bouts of depression, struggling with issues of low self-esteem or withdrawing from the simple pleasures life has to offer. How then can we learn to establish or maintain meaningful relationships when the MESSAGES from the very people that influence and mold us, have miserably failed us?

Throughout this book you will be encouraged to first identify, thoroughly examine and then challenge the MESSAGES that have prohibited you from pursuing your hopes, dreams, and passions.

As we regularly receive MESSAGES from the sources noted above they can and do influence the following: What it means to be male or female; our choice of friends, associates and perhaps later in life a mate; our thoughts and reactions to subjects that include everything from child rearing, politics, religion and education; our perception of the perfect body weight, height, hair and eye color; and more commonly our views regarding death and the here-after.

These well-intended MESSAGES are both implied and overstated yet paradoxically influence our decision making skills (or lack of) and often leave us frustrated and confused. Picture yourself dutifully carrying various MESSAGES into your daily life that you received during early childhood and your adolescent years. You will soon discover that these same MESSAGES that you have relied upon for your survival and ability to cope with life's challenges have ultimately failed you.

Within these pages you will find individuals struggling with unexplained feelings and behaviors that upon investigation had their origins in subtle yet pervasive MESSAGES. From the many stories told by individuals in the office of their therapist to the open dialogue in workshops and seminars, several truths emerged.

The first truth addresses unexplained feelings and behaviors that are in reality glimpses of that period in our lives when as children we unknowingly embraced MESSAGES that produced emotionally, spiritually and developmentally impoverished adults. A tragic accounting of the many mass murders and suicides among young children and adolescents affirm this truth. Today's research suggests that the number and frequency of "unexplained executions" had their origins in the minds of emotionally, physically or sexually abused and neglected children who unknowingly were waiting in the wings for a place to express their anger and self-loathing.

The second truth suggests that negative MESSAGES are generally communicated without malice or evil forethought. Instead, they were in fact thought to be the MESSENGER'S "right of passage" that they too received from the generations that preceded them.

The third and final truth espouses that these powerful MESSAGES can be likened to an individual collecting and carrying rocks of all shapes and sizes in a knapsack that continue on with him throughout his life's journey. In his mind these precious rocks will serve him during times of need and uncertainty. However, when he reaches for sustenance, comfort and direction, each rock, no matter the shape or size, is a hard cold reminder that not only is he ill-equipped to fulfill his purpose…he is wrongly equipped.

To successfully move from complacency and the comfort of the familiar, we must revisit both MESSENGER and MESSAGE to determine the meaning behind each MESSAGE relayed from our past and yes even their influence in our present and future way of living. In doing so you will soon discover that the benefits are unparalleled. As you recount the MESSAGES that fail you will gain;

> —Knowledge and awareness of your specific MESSAGE(S) (positive and negative) and their corresponding impact on your life.
> —The ability to identify and communicate thoughts, feelings and emotions relative to the MESSAGES you received that are critical to the healing process.
> —An understanding of the importance of identifying and ultimately to experience feelings of liberation from the negative MESSAGES that once enslaved.
> —The skills and "tools" that serve to differentiate between MESSAGES that benefit and those that hinder.
> —An understanding of the concept of the "The Paradoxical Gateway," or the necessity to be "born again."

In essence, this book written during times of introspection and personal encounters, in addition to listening to the stories of others, is intended to bring explanation, hope and resolution, not excuses for the longings and failings of our souls fashioned by MESSAGES that have failed.

CHAPTER ONE

The Rattle of Chains

Picture yourself, standing in line at the supermarket. Suddenly you hear raised voices two isles over. From other shoppers you learn that someone was in the 15 item checkout line with 20 plus items. The result, words are being exchanged between two customers leaving the cashier frustrated and bewildered. Perhaps you too have responded to a seemingly innocent remark, minor infraction or gesture that produced tears, confusion, anxiety, uncontrollable rage, acts of violence, or extended periods of depression followed by days of isolation. In the above scenario an elderly woman assaulted another customer who stepped in front of her at the checkout counter with more items than the sign "plainly read."

As you consider yet another scenario ask yourself what MESSAGE was the young man responding to when he raised his weapon and shot an innocent passenger on the interstate after someone blew their horn. In still another scenario you may have been shocked by the headlines that report the murder/suicide of a husband and wife only to hear on the late night news the statements of neighbors who speak of a very happy and presumably compatible couple. Like those observers you too have been left wondering "what happened?" Although the actions that led to the final acts mentioned above went undetected and without a single warning, in the minds of each perpetrator the clock was ticking well beyond the eleventh hour.

When we ask "why" we may be searching for some reasonable explanation. Attempts are made to explore the event or events preceding the disturbing actions. Later on what we discover is that the person had experienced the proverbial straw that broke the camel's back. The elderly lady who assaulted the customer was not reacting to a single occurrence but a series of events fastened together like links of a chain. Although each link represented a different time, place, or event, in reality they are all interconnected.

The elderly lady, like so many of us that "suddenly" respond with behaviors "unlike ourselves," was in actuality transported back in time. Remembering when someone cut in front of her in the junior high school lunch line, the time when a sale item was snatched by a rude shopper, or the time she was falsely accused and punished by a parent for a deed undone. The hurt and anger return because of earlier MESSAGES or events that she assumed had been long forgotten. Instead of, "he stepped in front of me," her actions were reminders that "You don't matter", "You are worthless", "You don't have rights," "You are not important," "I don't believe you." Our lives are much like the link/chain phenomenon in that every link details an event, rule, promise, situation, failed relationship or disappointment.

The attainment of a good education is assumed to be a positive MESSAGE when relayed to us throughout our formative years. However, if your family placed unrealistic emphasis on the importance of education that very MESSAGE may influence the decisions you make throughout life, determine your view of the less educated or perhaps produce guilt or a sense of inadequacy if you failed to fulfill the academic goals that met their expectations.

It has been a painful reminder of my own upbringing as I reflect on the distinction made between those who attained college degrees and those who did not. The degreed family members are touted to be the symbol of success despite their indulgences in drugs, promiscuity, and various compulsions and addictions. The remaining faction of the family was encouraged to be more like…your brother, cousin, etc. without first examining the individuals true passions or desires. This mindset has created small pockets or groups within the family separated by those who continued their education and those who did not. The segregation between family members has resulted in resentment and produced subtle MESSAGES that suggest you are less than but because you are family we (the educated) must at best be civil. The example here is not to minimize the importance of education but instead to reveal the how and why of our reactions to old MESSAGES without examining the rationale or reasons behind our responses.

The painful reminder of our gender, marital status, race, or ethnic background has the ability to rattle similar chains from the past that evoke feelings of betrayal, anger, victimization and inferiority. Further, remembrances of similar events have the power to set an endless number of links in motion. Once we recall past events, the question becomes what action should I take now. Ignoring or dismissing painful words brings to mind the old adage that "sticks and stones may break my bones but words will never harm me." This saying relayed to us as children was an attempt to aid us in combating hurtful words. In truth words do hurt and often result in physical and emotional maladies. Once again this presumably well meaning advice has conveyed the wrong MESSAGE. Words **can** be painful because they do indeed influence our thoughts, emotions, view of self and determine our corresponding responses.

As a mental health practitioner I regularly refer to this occurrence as the "link/chain" phenomenon. During the prescribed fifty minute counseling session, individuals relay stories of abuse, rejection, abandonment and feelings of despair and hopelessness. In more practical terms, what is seen, felt and heard are accounts that describe physical, sexual and emotional abuse that would unnerve even the most apathetic. The results are individuals living lives that entail the following; A level of rage, whether manifested inward or outward, that has resulted in self-destructive behaviors i.e. drugs, alcohol, hedonism, overeating, unprotected sex and other indulgences. These indulgences are meant to stop if not minimize the pain. Others may choose to isolate themselves certain that they can only find safety and solace inside their own homes. Some experience outbursts of anger or tears of grief with the simple mention of a name, place or event. And frequently, a client may become overwhelmed following an honest assessment of his current situation or feel revulsion at any words that hint at his positive attributes suggesting that he has the power to change his present situation. And finally discussions with educated, articulate, intelligent individuals fixated on suicide because salvaging their life has not been deemed to be an option.

In summary we all are purveyors of people who unknowingly respond to MESSAGES from the past that now dictate their daily activities and determine the level and frequency of their interpersonal relationships. And as noted earlier, some MESSAGES are akin to responding to the constant noisy rattle of heavy chains. When you experience a moment of quiet repose you too may hear the loud clanking of your own chains or through observation perceive the sounds and sighs made by another weary soul.

The paradox is that we often fear liberation from the MESSAGES that have failed because we have found **comfort** in what we accept as the tried and the true. We carry the yoke of bondage unwilling to trade it for a life replete with inner peace and options. Further, MESSAGES given to us and carried out as children, whether implicit or explicit, that state "be responsible for your siblings," "meet my (the adult's) needs" "pull yourself up by your booth-straps," help us to maintain equilibrium and keep us connected to the familiar.

As you explore your own MESSAGES be reminded that the goal is to acquire insights that will ultimately liberate you from the shackles that are comprised of links that have been collected over time. Links that detail MESSAGES that hurt, hinder, and in fact fail.

Despite the years of research and periods of observing human behavior I found even during the writing of this book that I too experienced emotional assaults that regularly had me staring at a blank computer screen. The numerous MESSAGES shouted…There are enough self help books on the market…, People have heard it all, what makes you such an expert…? Take God out of it and you may have a best seller…, Don't share your own experiences, you may hurt your siblings and other family members...What will they think of you? And the list continues.

In summary, the many MESSAGES noted above have failed many of us because they have left us vulnerable, defenseless, without discernment, lacking relationship skills and believing that this is all life has to offer. The MESSAGES vary but the results are the same.

As you re-visit the MESSAGES from your past decide what those MESSAGES meant and more critically what they mean today. To begin the journey toward wholeness you are encouraged to list the MESSAGES that have circumvented the process designed to lead you to treasured life experiences, passion and purpose and valued relationships.

CHAPTER TWO

What Messages?

Defining the Message(s)

For most, the word MESSAGE evokes varying definitions and visual images. For some, MESSAGES are simply thought to be a combination of words written on a slip of paper and passed on to an individual so that he may respond appropriately and in a timely manner. For others MESSAGES are the colored message pad or post-it that is a standard tool in most offices. Others view MESSAGES as the verbal or written words we receive on our answering machines, the Internet or voice mail so that we may retrieve, delete, or simply ignore at our leisure. Still others speak of the MESSAGE that was imparted during their religious services. However, the most pervasive MESSAGES are frequently and distinctly non-verbal. They include looks of disdain, rejection or disapproval from the sender be it mom, dad, friend, teacher or boss. These looks infer that you should…shouldn't…are…belong…and require a response that affirms that the MESSAGE has been received, interpreted and promptly acted upon. The simple raising of an eyebrow or clearing ones throat may convey a MESSAGE. But no matter how subtle, we do "get the MESSAGE." The many expressions and gestures conveyed by the sender are so powerful that a frown or quick glance can and does influence and force many of us to choose or avoid certain behaviors despite obvious negative and long term consequences.

One dictionary defines a subtle MESSAGE as perceptions of stimuli too weak to be noticed yet strong enough to influence behavior. As you reflect on this definition consider the various individuals in your life who have made statements, sent signals or displayed behaviors that were also too weak to be noticed by others, yet strong enough to influence your behaviors or responses even today.

General Messages

From birth to adolescence and continuing into adulthood there are familial, societal, academic and for many of us, religious MESSAGES that continue to influence our thinking and the corresponding reactions to those thoughts. Regrettably, these MESSAGES, given with the intent to "make us better citizens," often produced the opposite results. Recall if you will one MESSAGE that was conveyed to you in either words or actions. What comes to mind? Can you pinpoint the MESSAGES that sent you down the feeling paths of hopelessness, ambivalence, anger or behaviors that defy explanation? These MESSAGES or inquiries are the basis for this chapter. Listed below are a few of the MESSAGES whether overtly given or subtly conveyed that affect our present behaviors. They serve as the first stepping stones of our journey along the above-mentioned feeling paths. And in truth the MESSAGES below were shared by clients, family members, colleagues, and friends. After examining them you are encouraged to add your own and the corresponding responses to them:

MESSAGES that state you **SHOULD** (be)
- thin
- happy

- beautiful
- hard working....and then you will be successful
- a mother
- have a man
- have a woman
- quiet
- expressive
- nurturing
- a caretaker
- responsible
- reasonable...which means you should agree with me
- right
- liked (by everyone)

...under any circumstance and at all costs.

MESSAGES THAT STATE YOU **SHOULD NOT** (be)
- so successful that you lose sight of what is important; therefore you should not be successful
- dissatisfied
- without a man
- without a woman
- angry
- trust yourself
- set boundaries for yourself or others
- motivated by the success of others
- self-serving
- Responsive to the needs of your own body, mind and soul
- look deep inside for reasons and resources
- Too...
  strong
  weak
  forceful
  confident

These MESSAGES regularly invade our thoughts and can produce feelings of hopelessness and helplessness.

Messages from the family

During childhood and adolescence, the MESSAGES above presumably go undetected. Consequently, for many of us we are not aware of their impact until later in life, and for others the impact is never realized. They can be likened to a tattoo that requires a surgical procedure to remove it.

There has been an increase in the number of individuals donning tattoos, from one small butterfly to complete body coverings. Analogous to the tattoo is the branding iron used by cattle owners. But unlike the tattoo or brand used by ranchers to identify their herd, the distinct MESSAGES we received are invisible to the naked eye. The rancher or cattleman is confident that once his brand is burned into his steer's flesh, no matter how far it wanders from the familiar to explore the unknown, it is easily identified, eventually rounded up, prodded home and forced to return to its "safely" fenced pasture. And much like our families, the ranchers' MESSAGE is clear, you belong here and any attempt at finding your own path will be met with humiliation, isolation, confinement and punishment. To some degree we too don certain brands that serve to help identify our family traits. However, eye or hair color, height, body type, and "personality" are not the only outward signs that distinguish the family tree of which we are a part.

For the majority the "should/should not" MESSAGES listed earlier have their origins in the first formal institution known as the family. It is here that we first learn the meaning of indoctrination and compliance, adherence to the rules of the most influential MESSAGE givers and begin to collect the first links in our chain. How many of us have heard the words "You should be more like your sister...see how outgoing she is?" or "Why can't you get good grades like your brother?" "Act your age!" "Big boys don't cry." As you continue through the following chapters hopefully you will be prompted to discover and begin to relish your own uniqueness. Each of us has been given unique gifts and talents. But it is often our parents who ignore the fact that our uniqueness should be affirmed and encouraged. And in many instances we may serve only as the fulfillment our parents' sense of failed accomplishments or unfulfilled goals and dreams. Even Scripture espouses the importance of directing a child towards his particular passion and penchant. It states, "train up a child in the way he should go; and when he is old, he will not depart from it." Although this scripture is often misinterpreted, "the way he should go" is actually defined as the child's bent or purpose. According to Matthew Henry's Commentary this verse should be applied as our parents encourage our capabilities "with a gentle hand." It is imperative that as children we are allowed to venture into areas that meet our need to contribute to society while bringing a sense of value to ourselves. This may entail the fine arts, sports or human service. But the early MESSAGES from parents and others frequently undermine the view we have of ourselves and our capabilities.

During my early years as a counselor I counseled a client who required a variety of interventions to gain insight into his view of self. Despite personal, academic, financial and career successes he constantly struggled with what has been labeled as the "impostor phenomenon." This syndrome introduced and coined by Joan Harvey and Cynthia Katz in their book *If I'm So Successful Why Do I Feel Like a Fake?*, lists the three signs of the impostor phenomenon or IP.

> The sense of having fooled other people into overestimating your ability.
> The attribution of your success to some factors other than intelligence or ability.
> The fear of being exposed as a fraud.

Harvey and Katz further note that it is important not to confuse the impostor phenomenon with low self-esteem. "The two concepts are separate and distinct from each other." In the case of an impostor, one MESSAGE received during childhood, adolescence and astonishingly in late adulthood can create an individual who does indeed feel like "the great pretender." If we learned very early that our authentic self is not acceptable then we may be inclined to spin a web of deception. Trying on and changing various masks to "fit in." The obvious result is a lost soul, embittered, harboring resentments from events of the past and regularly disassociated from his feelings.

Societal Messages

In our contemporary society brand names have become commonplace from the kind of jeans we should wear to the make and model of the automobile we should drive. And may I add that each brand has its own significance or status symbol. Akin to the above we don specific emotional and familial brands just as visible as the branded steer or manufacturer's product. These brands forced upon us during our developmental years can ultimately inhibit us from trusting ourselves, taking the initiative to try new things, experience real autonomy or engage in healthy relationships.

As mentioned earlier, it has long been accepted that our height, shoe size, hair and eye color have been predetermined through heredity, now known as our DNA or genetic code. For all of us, our DNA or genetic code, though invisible to the human eye, is passed along and manifested to varying degrees in the anatomy of our offspring. Colored eye contacts, face lifts, hair or breast implants, provide general cosmetic improvements, but time alone is a reminder that the results are temporary at best.

Conversely, there are seemingly covert behavioral and verbal MESSAGES that have left scars that negatively influence our thoughts and responses. The MESSAGES relayed have been passed along as part of the social, familial, or religious culture that began as innocent and earnest attempts to provide us with a predictably easier or enlightened path. In reality the foundation that was built with these various MESSAGES, deemed to be the basis for a fulfilling life, produced feelings of inferiority, self debasement, and in many instances, guilt when attempts were made to depart from these MESSAGES.

Compare the restrictive nature of a single MESSAGE to the two bedroom starter home that was everything the newlyweds could have hoped for but is now a source of frustration and undeniably a place fraught with tension as the couple brings home its third child. The good news is that the small starter home need not be totally demolished. It does indeed have historical and memorable significance. Instead we may consider some carpentry work, add a little paint, carefully plan the rearrangement of furniture, utilize unused space and perhaps employ an architect or interior decorator. These changes may provide the couple with their dream home without a substantial financial commitment. We too must recognize that demolishing our past is not a viable alternative however time spent analyzing, accessing, revisiting, and ultimately preserving the MESSAGES that are most beneficial will serve us best.

From personal experience and stories shared by others the fact remains that the tasks involved in any renovation may prove to be difficult, overwhelming as well as time consuming, but, unlike our blood type, height and shoe size, the possibilities are endless.

Don't Touch that Dial…Another Message from Society

Although the family has the greatest influence we also receive MESSAGES from the astute marketer who is first trained to conduct research and then relay MESSAGES that entice us to respond to various stimuli. The choice is no longer **when** to respond, but **what** to buy, **how** much to pay or **where** to go to make the purchase. In the early days of television, advertisers deemed it to be in poor taste to make blatant negative statements about another manufacturers' product. However, the advertisers' desire to gain the larger market share has turned what was once a gentleman's game of competition into war-like strategies, embellishments and divisiveness. Part of the strategy included the removal of the average Jane or Joe from the commercial replacing them with glamorous, convincing, well known and recognized actors/ actresses, sports figures and politicians. Obviously, times have changed. We are no longer shocked when we see our favorite actress endorsing a particular product. The MESSAGE implies that you can be like…look like…live like…or have kinship with this well-known person if you use this product.

In a marketing class taught by a delightfully mature professor well beyond retirement age, he noted that today's consumers are fickle, easily intimidated and willing to purchase items for the sole purpose of having the latest, most expensive and/or that carry a particular brand name. This statement has proven to have merit as we sit blankly in front of our television screens unconsciously absorbed and frequently entertained by the many commercials encouraging, imploring and seducing us to "buy! buy! buy!."

In our world of high tech we receive MESSAGES via e-mail, fax, the Internet, cellular phones, fiber optics and the list is being added to on a daily basis. We now have the ability to send and receive MESSAGES across the street, the city, the country, and around the globe. However, relative to the most persuasive form of advertising, the impact of the television commercial presents astounding statistics. According to W. Russell Newman, in the U.S., ninety-eight percent of all households own one or more televisions. He further adds;

> In a typical week, nine out of ten citizens are exposed to radio and television, and in the average American home the television set is on about 7 hours each day…Between the ages of 2 and 65 the average American will watch 72,000 hours of television-at 24 hours a day, a total of 8 full years. The daily average is about 4 hours. The heaviest viewers are housewives and senior citizens. Children watch the same amount of television as do adults; teenagers watch about an hour less per day.

Newman's data further purports that considerable time is spent "watching the ole' tube." His data confirms the fact that television has the power to transmit various highly influential MESSAGES via the thirty second commercial. Additionally, the MESSAGES that the sponsors and television producers convey during the short story line, talk show, reality television show, sports event or special presentation are generally presented with full knowledge that the quality of the products, situations or images are embellished if not blatant lies. Their purpose is to convince the viewing audience that life's major problems can be solved within thirty minutes, love is just around the corner, sexy people will follow you if you choose this brand of alcohol, and all family members love and relate to each other on a reasonable level. And so when you fail to solve your minor problems, family and otherwise, the subtle yet convincing MESSAGE is obvious, you the viewer are emotionally unstable, your family is dysfunctional and you are incapable of sustaining a loving stable relationship.

Today, parents are provided with ratings that determine the entertainment value of various media (movies, videos, compact discs and cassettes) that are supposedly appropriate for our adolescents and under-aged children. The purpose of the rating is to assist in the decision-making process and help parents quickly assess then accept or reject films, cartoons etc, with violent or explicit sexual themes that in all probability influence the minds and behaviors of their children. Once again the censors are the privileged few who relay the MESSAGE that they know best and without question can decide what is appropriate for our children. The producers, censors, and most certainly the advertisers have little concern for their viewing audience. In truth their objectives are to take full advantage of the majority of us who click the remote or turn the dial to find a program that will appeal to our various senses. They also conclude that we as viewers will watch almost anything until we are lulled into a coma-like state. With constant exposure to the innumerable products marketed with impressive slogans, jingles and respected individuals, how can the viewer choose wisely or determine what products to purchase and use or what images to emulate?

In addition to the varied television commercials there are other vehicles used to influence the consumer resulting in billion dollar profits for the advertising industry. They include radio, magazines, newspapers, catalogs, bill-boards and the home shopping network, a vehicle targeted towards those who choose to shop without leaving the comfort of home. In concert with these more boisterous approaches of marketing, advertisers have also used a more subtle almost subversive method of promotion.

During the early fifties an advertising hoax or manipulation was used and discovered in a number of movie theaters. While showing a movie the advertiser strategically inserted film clips of, hot buttered popcorn, plump juicy hot dogs, ice cold soft drinks and other refreshments available at the concession stand. Unaware of these subtle MESSAGES viewers would suddenly become desirous of nourishment or feel the need to visit the concession stand. These subliminal MESSAGES were outlawed because of the impact they had on moviegoers. The periodic insertion of a film clip showing an ice cold drink was just as our definition stated "too weak to be noticed but strong enough to influence" the viewer. From every radio, television and cable station we are bombarded with MESSAGES of varying degrees and intensity. And with the advent of mass media scrupulously using familiar songs and slogans, favorite sports figures and catchy phrases, how does one disseminate and then make reasonable choices regarding products that provide the greater benefit?

I noted earlier the purpose of the pink message pad, the Internet and now the advertising industries blatant forms of chicanery that influence and determine the MESSAGES we are exposed to. Affably the good news is that the choice still remains with us. With the various commercial mediums we can use our prerogative to "turn off the set," "change channels" or simply employ the mute button on our handy dandy T.V. remote. As adults it is incumbent upon us to examine and monitor more closely the powerful MESSAGES imparted to us via mass media.

But even as adults we need the guidance and counsel of the Holy Scriptures. In God's word he provides us with instruction in terms of what we should see, hear and how our time should be spent. The book of Proverbs, written by what was and is known as the wisest man that ever lived, King Solomon, provides us with thirty-one chapters of wise sayings that if followed can and will minimize the negative outcomes of the

MESSAGES we have received. The verses below are examples of the use of or failure to use wisdom and the consequences that follow:

> A man who flatters his neighbor spreads a net for his feet.
> If a wise man has an argument with a fool, the fool only rages and laughs, and there is no quiet.
> Ponder the path of your feet; then all your ways will be sure.
> A fool gives full vent to his spirit, but a wise man quietly holds it back.
> Be not wise in your own eyes; fear the LORD, and turn away from evil.
> Trust in the LORD with all your heart, and do not lean on your own understanding.
> In all your ways acknowledge him, and he will make straight your paths.
> Book of Proverbs—English Standard Version

Auto Pilot

Ivan Pavlov, a Russian physiologist, conducted a well-known study whose research and findings theorized that certain stimuli presented in concert with a reward produced measurably predictable results. The experiment was later coined "Pavlov's Dogs." Essentially, his research deduced that once the subject (the dog) was programmed to receive a reward when certain stimulus (food) was introduced, the dog's response would continue despite the removal of the "reward." To prove his theory Pavlov sounded a bell each time the dog was to be fed. In summary the sound of the bell caused a predictable flow of saliva, that later persisted even when no food or reward was provided.

Scientists generally agree that the human response to certain stimuli is also determined as a reflex action. From the smell of fresh baked bread to the screeching sound of tires, we respond in a myriad of ways. However, consider the fact that just as Pavlov's dog failed to wonder why the bell was ringing, who was ringing the bell, and what reason they had for ringing it, we too negate the rationale behind our behaviors and respond automatically to external and even questionable stimuli.

Do I have a choice?

Most theorists suggest that animals lack the ability to reason. That is, even the most well trained animal lacks the knowledge of the "why" of its actions. It only "knows" to respond to its basic needs (food and shelter) and training that has been introduced and reinforced. This knowledge is at the root of an important question that asks how many of us, as a matter of course and as the result of consistent and pervasive MESSAGES, fail to use our precious gift of reasoning? For example, when certain stimulus fails to attract our attention or satisfy our need(s) many of us simply turn our attention to something or someone more provocative oftentimes without examining the **why** or the consequences of our choice and corresponding actions. And like Pavlov's dog, we ignore the fact that although the bell may be ringing real nourishment will not be provided. Further, because we **can** choose alternatives to satisfy our cravings we blindly and resolutely choose stimulants, depressants or more frequently the comfort of a "warm body" without investigating the individual's character, goals or core values. This statement by no means is meant to minimize the importance of intimacy found in meaningful relationships. It is a simple reminder that our ultimate goal may be to seek out a person, place or thing that is **guaranteed** to make us feel better, be it a warm body, food, a brand name gym shoe, drugs or that shiny new car that invariably proved to serve as a temporary fix. Through trial and error some of us discover that our adherence to MESSAGES from the past failed to satisfy and so we venture out in search of any stimulus that will.

The popular song of the mid-seventies *I Can't Get No Satisfaction* personifies the mood of the day. The words we remember most (because of their constant repetition) are MESSAGES unto themselves. "I can't get no satisfaction…I can't get no satisfaction…I tried and I tried but I can't get no satisfaction…"

Consider the times when we too have tried and tried to find fulfillment but the end results only led to more dis-satisfaction. In a later chapter the adverse results produced by the search for *satisfaction* through our involvement in relationships with predictable consequences will be discussed.

It is reasonable to agree that relationships are part and parcel of the human existence. But for now consider the value of spending quality time with yourself, a period of time known as introspection, recognizing that it is mandated before we can fully enter into the life or lives of another. This may seem to affirm the earlier MESSAGE that one should be with a man/woman. On the contrary, the vital MESSAGE here is that without time for introspection we are left with feelings of anger, betrayal, or rejection yet constantly in pursuit of another relationship that eventually fails. The tragic outcome is that each time we experience another disappointment the likelihood of rattling links in our chain increase exponentially…only this time with a vengeance. And I may add that in this instance the clanking metal is a positive MESSAGE attempting to warn of the dangers, consequences and to further serve as a reminder of previous experiences that became the impetus for feelings of worthlessness, inadequacy and low self-esteem.

When we do hear and acknowledge their rattle our desire is to quiet the noise or kill the pain. We attempt to do so by establishing rigid boundaries, arming ourselves with self-protecting behaviors, indulge in self destructive behaviors, or when all else fails return to old habits that keep us occupied. Over time and with the discovery that another warm body fails, we make one last attempt at finding comfort. We may move from isolation to more socialization. We may even seek out a new watering hole (known as happy hour) and carry on a façade with actions and words that say, "I'm really happy by-my-self." Convinced that whatever our choice, it must be done quickly because too much time spent alone may evoke MESSAGES, images and thoughts too painful to consider.

Without question there are advantages to the quick fix in that it permits us to temporarily operate in a state of auto-pilot or perform our daily routines. In this state of existence we decidedly choose one or all of the following options:

-We half-heartedly let go of our feelings of disappointment, anger and/or unforgiveness.
-We may pretend to be carefree.
-We skirt the "right now issues of life" by spending time in one of two realms, yesterday or tomorrow.
-We may go through the motions like a programmed robot conducting various tasks.
-We engage in the necessary activities required from friends and family so as to appear unscathed by the misery and pain of our existence

Our actions merely carried out in anticipation of our "next fix" are generally done in secret. Depending on the level of pain and other deep seeded emotions we, we move from "the fix" to auto-pilot and then back again. What occurs is a simple repeat of the cycle with temporary and minimal results. Over time it becomes evident that only more (food, clothing, money, drugs, etc.) will suffice. The reasons we choose to numb ourselves and activate the auto-pilot button may vary. Experiences shared by a number of clients suggest that the desire to numb themselves from life's painful existence include an unconscious and in some instances a conscious desire to remove or minimize the ache of old yet pervasive MESSAGES.

One example of this numbing affect was revealed in the case of a fifty-three year old client, married and the mother of two adult children. From the MESSAGES received from her parents and particularly the church she had learned to be high functioning. For her, meeting the basic needs of others was pleasurable despite her own feelings of inadequacy and self-hatred. Friends and family viewed her as outgoing, humorous and self motivated. Despite her enviable life, she complained of a gnawing sense of sadness and hopelessness and on occasion thoughts of suicide. Further, although she could not identify one specific complaint or symptom her physical condition prevented her from full employment as a nurse. It was only after numerous sessions in my counseling office that the truth was revealed. She like many of us had been programmed to become detached from her true feelings. Initially she was unable to connect the events of her past with her present feelings. Unaware of the impact that childhood MESSAGES had had, she cavalierly expressed the emotional unavailability of her father, the frequent physical abuse of her mother, and years of sexual molestation and rape. Even the tragic death of her closest friend and confidant left her unscathed. She further managed to dismiss the numerous times she needed to be heard by her mother or anyone when the issues of adolescence and incest became overwhelming. She was however willing to admit to "some" angry feelings as she reflected on the times she was compared to other siblings. (In a later chapter, common themes associated with being the first born, the middle child and "the baby" will be explored). This client is just one of the many individuals who in terms of connecting their present feelings with past events had received varied yet powerful MESSAGES relative to the advantage of being grateful to God, obedient, self-sacrificing and a dutiful church attendee and tither.

As the sessions progressed the overall MESSAGE became more apparent…"to thy own self be [untrue]." In our list of should and should not MESSAGES mentioned earlier it was discovered that the MESSAGE that had the greatest influence on her feelings was that she should not be responsive to the needs of her own body, mind and soul.

Where's that Remote?

Consider now the covert and blatant MESSAGES we receive from parents, teachers, priest, ministers and society at large. At what level and during what time period do we have the freedom to ignore or initiate the mute button to dispel negative MESSAGES communicated by these authority figures? Have they too used more subtle yet similar

MESSAGES to control, influence and yes even send us down the path of self-destruction?

Obviously as children, relative to our most valued relationships, we have certain developmental and emotional limitations that prevent us from changing the channel or employing the mute button. Conversely, as adults we can actively listen, disseminate the MESSAGES and when the words, images or story line convey visuals that repulse and cause the links of our chain to reverberate we can first assess the MESSAGE then trust ourselves to choose responses that are in our best interest. Inevitably, wrong choices will be made but faux pas does not indicate total failure.

It is now necessary to examine and monitor more closely the significant MESSAGES imparted or relayed not only through various mediums but as you will note later the authority figures we encountered from birth through adulthood. Without question the process of first hearing then actively listening then interpreting and finally deleting or modifying the MESSAGES that fail may take years to master. And so you are encouraged to BEGIN NOW! With full knowledge that failure to do so will continue to produce MESSAGES that can indeed become self-fulfilling prophecies.

CHAPTER THREE

The Origin of the Messages

The Flint, the Spark, the Fire

It is remarkable how frequently we experience unexplained feelings of sadness, depression, anger and a wide range of other emotions. The reasons behind these feelings are generally buried deep inside leaving us with little or no clue as to their origin, at least on a conscious level. It is during those times that we find ourselves behaving in ways that defy all explanation. The truth is that these uncharacteristic behaviors may in reality be responses to memories of past events. For example, we may attempt to suppress feelings of resentment, anger or hurt when a friend, co-worker or mate makes a simple remark or statement. However, simple remarks left unaddressed may be reminders of past events that cause us to withdraw from others or exhibit behaviors that later leave us saddened or questioning "why did I respond to…? What was I thinking?"

In another example, we may find ourselves overcome with grief as we observe a father embrace his toddler-aged son or daughter. In the first case, the perceived hurtful words may remind us of the demeaning statements made by a mother, father or older sibling. In the second case, observing this tender moment between father and child may stir the longings we had (and still have) as a child to be nurtured or simply to be held.

On a regular basis we receive and respond to MESSAGES that have little to do with events that are happening in the here and now. Instead our responses are from the past that carry pervasive MESSAGES given during the most impressionable time of our life. Unfortunately it was during this time that the only language we had was the language of feeling unaware that appropriate analysis may only be attained in the future.

Our responses to hurtful MESSAGES can be compared to a raging fire whose origin began with a tiny spark. Recalling historic times, once the flint was struck, producing the necessary spark, it could then be used to start a fire that would provide warmth and reduce the risk of harm from wild animals. On the other hand that same fire could reveal its destructive power by ravaging an entire forest. It is critical that at this time we focus on the latter with full knowledge that emotional, physical and spiritual healing can only begin when we confront the MESSAGES that may destroy us and possibly innocent bystanders.

That Gnawing Feeling

Surprisingly, we receive our first MESSAGES while in the safety and warmth of our mother's womb. During this time we are developing legs, arms, fingers and toes and other essential body parts. Numerous studies have been conducted that suggest that during pregnancy the mother should play and listen to soothing music, read children's stories aloud and reside in and maintain a tranquil state of mind. Further, only positive statements should be made regarding the fetus. The reasons outlined in the studies reveal several advantages.

The first advantage suggests that for both mother and child the birth experience will be much easier. Second, the child will experience fewer physical and emotional maladies later in life. And finally positive

MESSAGES conveyed like "we love you," "you are wanted," "we want the best for you," begin the affirming process.

One client spoke of never feeling wanted or loved by either parent. When the client was urged to explore his thoughts associated with these feelings he stated that he was the youngest child of four and that shortly after his birth, his father abandoned the family. Years later during a serious discussion with his mother he was told that his father's last words to her were "every time I take my pants off you get pregnant." During the session waves of guilt resurfaced as the client attempted to resolve his feelings of rejection and abandonment. In his mind he was responsible for the break up of his parents and the financial difficulties his mother later suffered. He further concluded that every attempt he made from early childhood to the present to gain love and attention from his mother, siblings, friends and other family members resulted in efforts that were dismissed, ignored or went unnoticed.

The result was a young man regularly performing and people pleasing in hopes of gaining the love and attention he so desperately needed and deserved. Further exploration into his belief system coupled with the words and MESSAGES relayed to him by his mother created several distortions that were the basis of what is known as our "Worldview."

Though foreign to some of us we are all guided by a worldview that dictates our thoughts and influence our behaviors. There are several questions that arise when one speaks of a worldview. The first and most obvious requires a definition of a worldview. Second, does everyone have one? Third, how is a worldview formed? And finally what purpose does it serve? The answer to the first question is that a worldview is based on five principles noting that each is determined or influenced by the MESSAGES that we **hear, see** and **respond** to. The first element of any worldview entails our belief relative to the existence of God as supreme. The second includes beliefs about ultimate reality, i.e. what is the relationship between God and the universe? Did an eternal personal omnipotent God create the world? Are miracles possible? The third component asked whether knowledge about the world is possible and can we trust our senses. The fourth principle is the basis for our moral judgments and ethics. The fifth and final principle addresses whether human beings are free to make their own choices. This principle includes the question of death and the hereafter.

Whether or not we are consciously aware of our worldview, in the terms stated above, each of us does indeed possess one that guides our beliefs and behaviors toward God, self and others.

The young man mentioned earlier believed that he was merely a victim of his environment and that God, although he existed, was not personally involved in his life. His thoughts and corresponding feelings were without question the results of the many MESSAGES that formed his worldview. Further, his struggle with a distorted self-image plagued all areas of his life, relationally, emotionally and spiritually. His worldview was based on a belief that God was not involved in world events or for that matter his personal life. Careful probing revealed that he embraced a belief known as Deism. The word Deist is derived from the Latin word for God *"Deus."* Deism involves the belief in the existence of God, on purely rational grounds, without any reliance on revealed religion or religious authority. Additionally, Deists;

> Do not accept the belief of most religions that God revealed himself to humanity through the writings of the Bible, the Qur'an or other religious texts. Disagree with Atheists who assert that there is no evidence of the existence of God.

And finally Deists regard their belief as a natural religion, as contrasted with one that is revealed by a God or which is artificially created by humans. They reason that since everything that exists has had a creator then the universe itself must have been created by God. Thomas Paine, author of *Common Sense,* the impassioned pamphlet that helped ignite the American Revolution concluded a speech shortly after the French Revolution with *"God is the power of first cause, nature is the law, and matter is the subject acted upon."*

Like many others we too have distinctive views (or a worldview) regarding everything from the meaning of life, love, marriage, child rearing practices, to the truth about life after death. Our views and often time our distortions may become manifest in a variety ways. In his book

Feeling Good: the New Mood Therapy, David D. Burns, M.D. lists and defines ten "Cognitive Distortions. He further purports that these ten distortions are the result of our early experiences [or MESSAGES] and "do cause many, if not **all** of [our] depressed states." They include; All-Or Nothing Thinking, Overgeneralization, Mental Filtering, Disqualifying the Positive, Jumping to Conclusions, Magnification or Minimization, Emotional Reasoning, Should Statements, Labeling and Mislabeling and Personalization.

For purposes of clarity the following define Burns' ten distortions;

All-Or-Nothing-Thinking: You see things in black and-white categories. If your performance falls short of perfect, you see yourself as a total failure. Overgeneralization: You see a single negative event as a never-ending pattern of defeat.

Mental Filtering: You pick out a single negative detail and dwell on it exclusively so that your vision of reality becomes darkened, like the drop of ink that discolors the entire beaker of water.

Disqualifying the Positive: You reject positive experiences by insisting they 'don't count' for some reason or other. In this way you can maintain a negative believe that is contradicted by your everyday experiences.

Jumping to Conclusions: You make a negative interpretation even though there are no definite facts that convincingly support your conclusion.

Mind Reading. You arbitrarily conclude that someone is reacting negatively to you, and you don't bother to check this out.

The Fortune Teller Error. You anticipate that things will turn out badly and you feel convinced that your prediction is an already-established fact.

Magnification (Catastrophizing) or Minimization: You exaggerate the importance of things (such as your goof-up or someone else's achievement), or you inappropriately shrink things until they appear tiny (your own desirable qualities or the other fellow's imperfections).

Emotional Reasoning: You assume that your negative emotions necessarily reflect the way things really are: 'I feel it, therefore it must be true.'

Should Statements (my favorite): You try to motivate yourself with shoulds and shouldn'ts as if you had to be whipped and punished before you could be expected to do anything. 'Musts' and 'oughts' are also offenders. The emotional consequence is guilt. When you direct should statements toward others, you feel anger, frustration, and resentment.

Labeling and Mislabeling: This is an extreme form of overgeneralization. Instead of describing your error, you attach a negative label to yourself. 'I'm a loser.' When someone else's behavior rubs you the wrong way, you attach a negative label to him: 'He's a *%$**# louse.' Mislabeling involves describing an event with language that is highly colored and emotionally loaded.

Personalization: You see yourself as the cause of some negative eternal event which in fact you were not primarily responsible for.

After spending time observing, recording, and making numerous attempts to understand the emotional and physical complaints of clients, it became evident that the majority of us struggle with a minimum of three to four of the ten cognitive distortions noted above. Cognitive distortions are the end results of our responses to the many MESSAGES received during our formative years. Although Dr. Burns' premise does have some validity, as does other psychologist, psychiatrist and other theorists in the field of mental health, I am reminded of the following scripture; simply stated; "man is born in sin and shaped in iniquity."

Since man's fall in the Garden of Eden we are and will continue to operate and be influenced by our sinful nature that began in the womb and for that matter "from the foundations of the world." In summary at conception we were shaped in iniquity. And at birth the cycle continues with abstract and then concrete thinking, then feeling, and finally the choices we make. Our thoughts dictate how we may respond to the many MESSAGES that we receive throughout our lifetime. Even scripture is a testament to this truth "As a man thinks [and believes] in his heart so is he." To feel any and all emotions and then act accordingly thoughts must first enter our minds.

The Eight Stages of Life

Erik Erikson, a prominent theorist, studied, recorded, and concluded that from birth to older adulthood we respond to the many MESSAGES we receive adding that we will choose one of two opposing "crises." He proposed that there are eight stages of development and regardless of race, gender or ethnicity we are destined to progress through each stage. Erikson further proposed that these eight stages are identified as Psychosocial Crises and they are the sum and substance of us from our birth through late adulthood. These eight crises are further defined as a series of crises that occur in response to demands that are placed on us as we develop and conform to adult expectations about self-expression and self-reliance.

Based on his research Erikson also concluded that each stage or crisis prepares us to live life either confidently or follow a path that may lead to some form of self destruction. At this juncture it is vital to note however that parents or caregivers are the first persons who through their actions determine whether the crises will be life giving or destructive, validating or demeaning, and produce individuals who live life as an optimist or pessimist, introvert or extrovert.

Although the term crisis suggests an emotionally significant event or radical change of status in a person's life, Erikson's definition of crisis is more in line with the Chinese philosophy that views a crisis as a period of time that offers "danger or opportunity." In summary we find ourselves responding to MESSAGES that have their origins in one of the two crises that determine our decision to see life's challenges as dangerous and harmful or an opportunity to "carpe diem" (seize the day).

A case in point, if we received MESSAGES that produced shame and doubt about our gender, skin color or level of intelligence we may become individuals who have little or no confidence in who we are and the perfect being that God created. Conversely, MESSAGES that encourage autonomy, self-reliance and celebrate our capabilities, are likely to create in us a sense of eternal optimism producing an individual who exercises his independence and sees opportunity at every turn.

Erikson's eight stages are as follows:

Age	Stage	Focus
Birth-1 ½ years	trust vs. mistrust	social support
1 ½-3 years	autonomy vs. shame and doubt	establishing independence
3-6 years	initiative vs. guilt	developing self-care skills
6-12 years	industry vs. inferiority	mastery of culturally relevant skills
12-18 years	identity vs. identity confusion	definition of self
Young Adulthood	identity vs. isolation	establishing meaningful relationships
Middle Adulthood	generativity vs. stagnation	caring for others
Older Adulthood	integrity vs. despair	life evaluation; seeking of self-fulfillment

Upon examination, you will note that each stage has differing results. For the older adult the final stage of life may leave him with a sense of accomplishment regarding the various choices he made during his lifetime or produce feelings of despair filled with regrets as he revisits his yet unfulfilled dreams.

What if any thoughts come to mind when picturing an elderly grandmother who always has a kind word versus the old witch next door whose face is permanently disfigured from constant frowns? Each stage builds on the other much like the foundation of a building and its successive floors. However, emphasis should be placed on the foundation because in every situation it is the foundation that determines the buildings stability and figuratively speaking our footing, stability, longevity and usefulness.

Finally if at every stage of our development we experience the positive crises [or MESSAGES], we will most likely attain emotional, relational, and spiritual health. Conversely if we fail to receive affirming MESSAGES the results may give rise to behaviors denoting immaturity, issues with regard to trust, poor or non-existent relationship, and emotional and physical maladies.

Erikson concludes that throughout our developmental stages we consistently make attempts to respond to adult demands before we are ready. And if these demands are placed on us as children, adolescents and young adults we will with certainty find life and our corresponding relationships difficult, oppressive or non-existent.

Consider now Erikson's first four stages of development that occur during our formative years, age zero to approximately age twelve. It is during these critical years that the MESSAGES sent and received have the potential to create havoc or provide the necessary sustenance for a meaningful life. For example, based on the initial MESSAGES that occur during stage one (birth to age 1-1/2 years), the general consensus is that the infant will be viewed as a precious vessel readied to become a giver and receiver of many trusting relationships. It is during this stage the infant learns whether or not the world is friendly and can be trusted to meet his needs. If when the infant cries for nourishment or to be attended to and the caretaker responds accordingly in a timely manner and on a consistent basis, those times when the caretaker is unavailable the infant has the ability to wait for his need to be met. Without thought or struggle the infant's daily experiences affirm that eventually someone will be here to meet my need(s). The MESSAGES are, "I am important," "I was wanted," and "my needs are reasonable and will eventually be met

In his book, *The Road Less Traveled*, M. Scott Peck concurs adding that our ability to "delay gratification" works in concert with our decision to trust or mistrust others later in life. This principle also serves as the foundation for establishing relationships and obviously acquiring the patience to reach our desired goals. A definition is now needed too insure an understanding of and the significance and power of delaying gratification. Peck offers the following;

> [to delay gratification is] A process of scheduling the pain
> and pleasure of life in such a way as to enhance the pleasure
> by meeting and experiencing the pain first and getting it over
> with. It is the only way to live.

This definition suggests that the person who has the discipline, insight, and fortitude to delay gratification will ultimately be compensated on a much larger scale. Ask yourself what MESSAGES you received about having your needs met and/or the benefits of delaying gratification? Were you affirmed relative to your uniqueness, gender, gifts and talents? Or did you experience rejection and abandonment (no matter how subtle)? Your answers to these questions are the basis for trust in a world where deception is generally the norm.

In my counseling office, clients of all ages, race, ethnicity and gender reveal various emotional struggles they have endured when attempts were made to ignore the benefits of delaying gratification. Instead, the MESSAGES they received early on were "get it while you can," "where you can," and from "whom you can." In essence the level of consistency and trust that was and is expected from your caregiver simply does not exist. Painfully these very MESSAGES are the impetus for greed, hedonism, substance abuse, promiscuity, apathy, depression and anxiety.

Many of us struggle with issues relating to trust that influence our relationships with others. The pervasive mood or theme is "my goal is to feel good at all cost." This entails numerous sexual encounters, spending sprees, verbal attacks on peers in the workplace, family feuds, or acts of manipulation and exploitation. However, if we have learned to trust ourselves as well as others we are more likely to "schedule the pain...of life," and even expect it. We can endure the painful process of obtaining an education, saving for retirement, involve ourselves in menial labor with optimism relative to future employment, hear, acknowledge and respond to our inner voice and trust the sometimes lengthy process involved in establishing a lasting relationship.

Trust is the fundamental building block for our survival. For just a moment ask yourself who if anyone, you trust and why? And more significantly, do you generally trust yourself? Do you trust yourself to make decisions? To set boundaries? To establish relationships? To be vulnerable? To express your true feelings? To take risk? In this instance risk is not some event planned well in advance with certainty of the end results, instead real risk is defined as doing something that will allow you to lose. Each time a negative MESSAGE is given followed and reinforced, particularly in the area of trust, we may find ourselves withdrawing from the simple pleasures of life, i.e., freedom of expression, freedom to enjoy another, freedom to grieve a loss and even freedom to fail. The tragedy is that when we numb ourselves to feelings of pain we also numb ourselves to feelings of pleasure. We learn to suppress the excitement of seeing a close friend or to express feelings associated with accomplishments and success, and finally to savoir the feelings evoked with the purchase of that new car, suit, dress or home, to smell a flower, to watch a sunset or simply just to be.

Erikson's second stage of development entails experiencing autonomy versus shame and doubt. This stage occurs between the ages of two and five and its primary focus is to establish independence. Many have labeled this time as the terrible two's or the terrible three's. Picture an impatient father trying desperately to dress his 3 year old who struggles from his arms making every attempt to dress himself, tie his own shoes or pour milk in his cereal bowl. In these situations the statement often heard by the frustrated child is "daddy I can do it by myself." But on each occasion that he is prohibited from exploring his small world and more disconcerting his own capabilities, shame and doubt rear their ugly heads. Alice Walker in *The Drama of the Gifted Child* notes the following;

> In an atmosphere of respect and tolerance for his feelings, the child in the phase of separation, will be able to give up symbiosis with the mother [or father] and accomplish the steps toward individuation and autonomy.

Without permission to separate from the caretaker or a safe environment, the MESSAGE whether implied or overstated, may create in the mind of the child words like obstinate, helpless, incapable or inadequate. Today we choose to call it low self-esteem or learning disabled. Both of which may lead to clinical depression, suicide, substance abuse, migraine headaches, ulcers, panic disorders and various mental and/or physical maladies.

Erikson continues with six additional stages but only a brief description of four of those stages (three, six, seven and eight) and a more in-depth rendering of stages four and five will be provided here. Be reminded that each stage builds upon the other or as he designates, "the principle of hierarchic integration." Stage three (ages 3-6) entails developing self-care skills. Here we learn initiative versus guilt. Stage six focuses on establishing meaningful relationships, further defined as identity versus isolation. And stages seven and eight encourage generativity [generosity] and integrity, respectively. Erikson's principle of hierarchic integration purports "if the psychosocial development of trust is not met during birth to age one year, one's ability to trust self and others will be incorporated in to and influence the remaining developmental stages."

Some years ago Shell Oil marketers produced commercials encouraging car owners to buy the best gasoline products (Shell Oil of course) to guarantee a maintenance free car. The commercial ended with the following reminder "you can pay now or pay later." This statement summarizes Erikson's theory on the stages of human development. Without foundational principles in place the results will be an individual making some form of payment later in life. The payment may entail loss of financial stability, loss of hope, loss of self-esteem, loss relationships, or a premature loss of life.

Stages four and five, thought to be the most challenging between parent and child, include ages 6-12 and 12-18. They encourage industry versus inferiority and identity versus identity confusion respectively. Dr. Estes, a renowned Jungian psychologist and author concurs with Erikson's premise. In *Women Who Run with the Wolves*, Dr. Estes notes "that the stealing of [one's] soul-skin is very easy, so much so that the first theft occurs somewhere between the ages of seven and eighteen." Unfortunately, it is during these critical stages that the individual's focus is mastery of relevant cultural skills and a definition of self. If the soul is stolen between the ages of six and eighteen, a most vulnerable period, what impact will this theft have on the young adult, the adult in midlife and the adult in his senior years?

Recall your years in both middle and high school. If you find this task too challenging, locate a school that will permit you to observe teacher/student and student/student interaction. Despite the changes in today's world of academia, that places less emphasis on extracurricular activities, and more emphasis on computer literacy and gender mixing during sports activities, surprisingly you will observe similarities between student interaction today and from times past.

Predictably these youngsters, just as many of us, struggle with what is socially and culturally acceptable without sacrificing who they are. After your mental or physical exercise, ask yourself what obvious MESSAGES you received from the sources mentioned earlier e.g. mass media, academia, parents and society? Does this exercise stir emotional distress or bring a smile to your face?

Peek-a-boo...I see me

People regularly enter my office resolved to dismiss the relevance of their early years. But their words and behaviors of protest only signal a past too painful to revisit. Their fears are heightened when asked to list the social and cultural norms they continue to uphold or attempt to remove from their daily, weekly and/or monthly routine. Questions like, is Saturday always laundry day? Can you miss Sunday church services without feeling guilty? Is Sunday dinner a mandate in your home? Is mom or dad **always** right? Do you continue to feel responsible for your younger siblings? Are groceries always purchased on Saturdays? Do you have large family gatherings during the holidays (although you dread them)? More in depth questions reveal astounding truths. When asked one or more of the following questions our façade may become evident vis-à-vis; Do you find it difficult to initiate conversation with strangers? Do you frequently compare yourself to others? Do you feel uneasy when a subject is discussed that you know little or nothing about? Can you handle criticism without feeling attacked? Can you spend quality time alone? Do you readily change your plans to accommodate others? Is the thought of confrontation frightening to you? Is it imperative that you receive approval from your best friend, mother or sibling before making a decision? Every response to the questions above provides us with knowledge that aids in a tedious process known as "chaining."

In the chaining process the client is first provided with strips of colored construction paper cut from full sheets of paper. They are then directed to prepare a paper chain similar to the ones some of us created to decorate a Christmas tree. Each day they are instructed to record on the strips of paper events, thoughts or feelings that evoked a noteworthy response. Finally, they are asked to bring their chain, made as long as they choose, to the following session.

During the counseling session the client is invited to review his remarks written on each link. After several sessions and many links later, the client begins to recognize common themes and his reaction to them. For example, if during his developmental years he experienced rejection, abandonment or any form of abuse, with the aid of his chain, he soon discovers that he fears commitment and intimacy, rationalizing "that's just how I am." For this client each experience of rejection, real or perceived, gives him another reason to continue to physically and emotionally isolate himself. Some links are added on a conscious level while others are as subtle as the advertisers film clip inserted in a motion picture.

The client ultimately recognizes that various MESSAGES were delivered with words of contempt. If small endeavors, like the first attempt at writing his name, was demeaned and criticized, all future negative comments have the potential to launch the now full grown adult into a state of self-hatred, feelings of inadequacy, or failure. As the sessions proceed the client produces a lengthy chain comprised of countless MESSAGES fashioned of one or two words or complete sentences. Ultimately the chain offers insight to the client and predictably the motivation to alter and hopefully overcome his response to the many powerful MESSAGES that began as early as his first day on earth.

Soren Kierkegaard in his writing Either/Or presents the following;

> ...I wish to show here an inward picture which does not become perceptible until I see through the external. This external is perhaps quite unobtrusive but not until I look through it, do I discover that inner picture which I desire to show you, an inner picture too delicately drawn to be outwardly visible, woven as it is of the tenderest moods of the soul.

His statement suggests that we must first see through the external or the MESSAGES we received that prohibited us from revealing our true selves. These MESSAGES may be likened to the Wizard in the film The Wizard of Oz whose persona "appears" fiery and fierce. However, once the curtain was pulled aside and the Great Oz is exposed, [remember Toto?] we as viewers found a transparent, frightened isolated individual whose energies were directed towards the preservation of the illusion. The paradox is that once we too expose this hidden being that we so desperately try to conceal we gain the advantage. We can now be fully accepting of our vulnerabilities, our creativity, our fears and "the tenderest moods of [our] soul." Additionally, once we gain this knowledge, on more than just an intellectual level, we allow ourselves to unashamedly enter into relationship with another.

Before we march off with information regarding the chain exercise that details the MESSAGES that failed we must be reminded that on this journey the old cliché that "the longest distance between two points is the head and the heart" does seem to ring true. Soren Kierkegaard's statement although profound was best expressed by a client who while on the road to self-discovery wrote the following;

ONE DAY
One day soon I'll meet me.
Not the me that's me, But the me to be.
There will be no sound; there will be no color
Just two different people who are just like each other.
One fighting to live
The other fighting to die
One day soon
I will look me in the eye.
A cornucopia of dreams and hopes
But I wonder if me will be able to cope?
I've met him once before in one time past
But I wasn't ready for me so the relationship didn't last.
This time though, I know the way
Maybe even one day has met this day.
It's hard to tell in a room like this
Maybe, just maybe, I and me never did separately exist.
—Troy W.

The evasive "Me," lecherous and confounding, that this writer was in search of existed from the beginning, hidden behind a façade that rendered him confused and fearful. Additionally, he lacked knowledge of the real "Me," or the benefit of connecting with others.

At some level we all have the desire to be known by and in union with another. Our deepest desire is to reveal our true selves and to experience intimacy. An intimacy defined as a desire for someone who willingly "Into-Me-See," without repulsion, rejection, judgment or criticism. What we in fact desire is another with the ability to See-Into-Me with compassion, unconditional regard, acceptance, affirmation and love. But the repeated negative MESSAGES from siblings, peers, parents and other authority figures, highlighting our inadequacies, produce identity confusion, stagnation, mistrust and ultimately prohibit us from ever attaining real intimacy.

When apprised of this reality one client stated that she refused to be seen, to be vulnerable or to be at the mercy of another. After solicitous yet careful probing, coupled with substantive support, the client admitted that being seen meant enduring more rejection and abandonment. Because of her resistance, she was encouraged to reflect on early man and woman who were completely naked in the Garden of Eden, yet unencumbered by their nakedness. During an intervention that involves visualization she was carefully guided to picture both man and woman reveling in emotional, spiritual and physical freedom. It was only then could she imagine the freedom and advantage that complete openness offered.

Interestingly a similar desire to attain a measurable level of freedom is pursued in nudist camps. Reportedly, the participants return to their respective homes and places of employment changed for the better. Free, more open and less inhibited. By no means am I suggesting that you join a nudist camp, conversely, I implore you to simply recognize the similarities in the concept and attainment of freedom through emotional vulnerability.

"That's not my ugly baby"

A few years ago a local news station carried a story about a mother who adamantly denied that the child given to her by the hospital staff was not hers. In a brief news interview the mother was quoted as saying "that's not my ugly baby." The rationale she used was that "it" did not look like her other children. Research was conducted and as we all held our breath the results revealed that the baby did indeed belong to the indignant mother. If this tiny infant was rejected purely on looks alone and compared to its other siblings what MESSAGES will "it" receive during "its" formative years? Even now we should all hear the chains rattling. In addition to the need to be nurtured in a secure, dependable and loving environment how will these negatively overt MESSAGES encourage "it" to delay gratification, trust self and others, take initiative and establish "its" unique identity? Note the use of the word "it" in reference to this infant. The purpose is to denote that "it" may ultimately lack sexual identity or gender, uniqueness, worth or value. "It" was and will always be an object without definition. Further, every MESSAGE sent by mom and "its" siblings will undoubtedly create the most destructive feeling, the feeling of self-hatred. It is unlikely that this infant will feel secure during any time of its developmental years. Instead, the fundamental MESSAGE received is "I am not wanted." Translation, perform! perform! perform, in hopes of gaining time, attention and approval from my mother and sadly in adulthood anyone who enters my life.

According to Maslow's theory of the Hierarchy of Needs first necessitates food and shelter. Once these needs are met the next levels entail security/job, relationships/belonging, esteem and the energy to bring change, known as self-actualization. It is however doubtful that this individual will ever attain a feeling of belonging, esteem or self-actualization. For this child bargaining, begging, seduction or at worse manipulation will be the only way to get "its" needs met. Further, delaying gratification will never be considered. "Its" objective will entail fulfillment of its own needs and by any means necessary.

Our entry into the world "The Lion King"

In Walt Disney's animated movie, *The Lion King*, Simba, the main character is received not only by his proud parents but the entire animal kingdom. The celebration and dedication moves the most stoic. But what of the child whose entrance into the world is met with resentment, bitterness, and hostility? At this juncture these two extremes require examination.

Unlike the celebration and reception of Simba many of us have learned that we were a footnote, an afterthought, another mouth to feed or a "mistake." We were not welcomed into this world or our families with sustained vigilance or a commitment to provide all of our needs and some reasonable wants, but rather with the same interest as a new toy, passionate but short-lived. Relative to this phenomenon, experiments have been conducted to discourage teenage pregnancy. The teen is given a hand held gadget or in some cases a doll that without warning begins to cry. The teen lacks the knowledge of what the infant needs…feeding, changing or just to be held. They must simply respond to an annoying noise similar to a real baby's cry or a beep or buzzer that demands that some action be taken…NOW!!! The results of the study revealed that over a short period of time and in some instances just a few days, resentment built and even physical abuse was observed and noted.

Based on further studies of actual teen mothers we can only surmise that the infant noted earlier will feel distant from the only person he has ever known and at a time when there should essentially be no boundaries between parent and child. This child, on some level, recognizes and understands that his presence (much like the teen/infant experiment) is an annoyance that on occasion should be responded to. The results, he may be forced to adopt his mother's or caretaker's disdain relative to his own existence. And like all truth perceived or real, his self-hatred resounds not only throughout his lifetime but also through the generations that follow. The delegation of the child to the unwanted corner of the family's life gets repeated over and over again until the "you are and were unwanted" MESSAGE becomes words that for him carry infallible truth.

The classic picture is painted in the hospital on the post-delivery unit. As the physician enters the patient's room the mother casts a brief glance of acknowledgement of his presence. Beside her in either the bassinet or the bed is her baby that she is attempting to feed. There is a phone to her ear and the television is tuned to her favorite talk show, you know the one with all the fighting. Certainly mothers can not afford to be singularly focused. The art of mothering requires that you run several trains on several tracks if you are going to have a successful outcome that day. The consensus is that this mother lacks the tools, knowledge and experience to choose selflessness. Even the ability to activate the "maternal instinct" is missing. This capacity has been diminished by years of similar MESSAGES. Isn't it rather strange that this time in the hospital with no laundry to do, no bottles to wash and professional help around the clock that mothers make the choice to fill their time with distractions **away** from their new infant? Once again the question that must be asked is what if any affirmations did this mother receive relative to her uniqueness, femaleness or value? Obviously, it is difficult to model that of which you have no knowledge. It is virtually impossible to assign a person value without first receiving the MESSAGES "You are important" and "I am available to you." Consequently, the negative MESSAGES received during her formative years are undoubtedly passed on to her offspring.

The new mother does not focus her attention on the baby because she too has not experienced appropriate child rearing from the cradle to the present. She like so many others was the first grader who was not sent to school, but got herself up, fed herself and got to school the best way she could. At a surprisingly tender age she was essentially the adult in a house without guidance often caring for her younger siblings and making every attempt to manage both mom and dad's physical and emotional needs.

What actions does she take when she concludes that in this house **her needs** will never be met? And what emotional struggles will she encounter once the knowledge that she has never been cuddled or held to satisfy her "skin hunger?" The answers to both are as predictable as the sunrise. She plots a course designed to meet her own needs...immediately.

Consequently, her choice to delay gratification will never be considered. In terms of meeting her (perceived) needs the MESSAGES to herself include; "I don't expect...so..." "I will never have...so..." "Why wait for..." And if the need real or imagined requires a "thing" outside of herself...SO BE IT!!! What could possibly fill the giant hole that pervades her every thought and action?

Limitations and Capabilities

Admittedly various negative MESSAGES can and do influence our thinking and behavior, additionally, without debate the majority of us lack certain innate skills, gifts or qualities that limit us to some degree. For example not all of us have been gifted to write, sing, run a business, compete athletically, perform on stage or enter a field for which we have neither skill, desire or ability. Forcing a child to participate in an activity for which he is not qualified or for the appeasement of the parent may on the surface appear commendable. But in reality waylay the child's true passion. In other words, it is not **always** a negative MESSAGE that prohibits. Conversely, one positive MESSAGE that aligns with the child's desires can create a sense of faith and optimism that makes success possible on many levels.

During a counseling session a client shared an example of a negative MESSAGE that had the potential to prohibit her pursuit of advanced studies. At her place of employment, she was told by her boss that her writing skills were substandard. Her belief in his MESSAGE, meant to demean, produced what she called "writing phobia." Her fear of writing became so overwhelming that she would frequently call in sick when required to prepare a simple report or letter. After being passed over for a number of promotions she considered enrolling in school to obtain a degree in education. However, she regularly postponed enrollment consciously aware of her fear of writing. Finally through the encouraging words of her peers and others she registered for two classes. Through commitment and "burning the midnight oil" she received B's in both classes. The following semester she decided to take a required course in philosophy. Instructed to read *Plato's Republic* and write an observation paper she was determined to be more creative than what was required.

Instead of a regular paper she wrote a short play summarizing her thoughts. The professor, known for his lofty standards, gave her the highest compliment she had ever received. She was asked to share her paper with her classmates. As with all great stories her writing continued to reveal her personal and creative style. Perhaps you have had a similar experience that may or may not have ended on a positive note. Be assured that there are individuals much like you struggling to overcome one negative MESSAGE that influenced and prohibited the flow of their creative juices.

My opportunity to observe and counsel clients with various psychological and emotional maladies provided me with data that I found to be noteworthy. I discovered that despite the varied backgrounds that include ones socio-economic status, race, ethnicity and/or religion, in most instances the emotional and behavioral responses were much the same. Note one example. A common practice among teens from families, regardless of their socio-economic status, often led to unprotected sex and more often the announcement of "an unplanned pregnancy." It was revealed later that this event occurred when the teen felt abandoned by one parent or another. The reasons for this unplanned event varied but the rationale frequently cited was that the pregnant teen viewed the birth of her child as a means to receive and maintain unconditional love. They were wholeheartedly convinced that this "being" would provide them with the unconditional love they so desperately needed with a promise to never leave them.

Blue for Boys…Pink for Girls

Throughout this book you will be encouraged to examine a variety of similar MESSAGES sent and received that can and have held you hostage, suppressed your dreams and visions, produced self-destructive behaviors and negatively influenced the attainment of your desired career/relationship goals and accomplishments.

As noted earlier, the transmission of one MESSAGE can be very subtle. Specific examples are the MESSAGES transmitted and received merely by our position and gender within the family. Kevin Leman, author of *The Birth Order* and *Unlocking the Secrets of Your Childhood Memories*, identifies the expectations and roles that children play in the family. He describes the various labels and tasks given to the first born, middle and baby or last born child. He further details the expectations that are imposed upon children relative to their gender. Great demands and expectations are generally cast upon the first born child sending MESSAGES that often present challenges that prohibit creativity and spontaneity. Note just a possible few: Your worth (and ours) is based on your performance and accomplishments. You must be responsible and set a good example for your siblings. If you fail you will make me (the parent) look or feel bad.

For the middle child the most pervasive MESSAGE is that you are not as special as your older sibling. One commercial depicts a mother preparing for the arrival of her first born child. The room is decorated and painted with bright colors, mountains of toys, and plush teddy bears are lined against the wall. As the commercial suggests mom, without question, purchases the most expensive disposable diapers. Some time later a homemade video shows the mother struggling with more children using the economy or less popular brand name diapers.

Frequently in a therapeutic session the client will respond to a request to bring pictures and other memorabilia of his early childhood. More often than not the first and last-born child will have little or no difficulty responding to the request. However, the middle child is taken aback by the few items available to display. Why is it that there are several albums detailing the first child's every move, stage of growth and activity? When the parents are questioned they may without malice or forethought relay to the child one of several MESSAGES. "By the time you came along we were having marital, financial or emotional difficulties and after Mary or Jimmy the birth of our children became routine." These responses have the capacity to send several negative MESSAGES to the child. Was I wanted? Did I create the difficulties? "Is that what you and mom argued about? "So I really wasn't special?"

In reality their individual stories ring true and support Leman's premise. The responsible oldest is performance oriented and feels angry and resentful. The middle child is "lost" somewhere in the family, but has tremendous needs leaving him vulnerable and needy. And the youngest child is generally irresponsible and dependent upon others to fulfill his needs and desires.

Bookstores are replete with self-help books that attempt to improve one's self-esteem through cognitive insight oriented therapies, reframing, meditation, journaling, hypnosis and a plethora of interventions and techniques. In truth, each theory offers some relief and further insights. But to truly gain insight relative to our present behaviors it is imperative that we re-visit and examine the MESSAGES we received during our formative years. Not only MESSAGES from parents or caretakers, but as you will note in the following chapters, MESSAGES from society, academia and religious institutions. These MESSAGES and others like them are presented without malice or evil intent. They are, for some, the rights of passage that are carried in the unwritten language of the generations.

Early on you were introduced to the chain/link concept and its significance to our present behaviors. We may or may not understand the origin of the MESSAGE on each link, however, and at this juncture it really does not matter. It is vital that we become aware of the subsequent links and their connection with our present moods, motivations, relationships, and view of self and others.

Making daily choices is all part of our life experiences. This entails choices as simple as what suit, tie, or dress to wear to what route I should take to my place of employment. Throughout the scriptures God reminds man of the choices he is given. The choice began in the Garden of Eden with Adam and Eve who were privy to numerous fruit bearing trees. Additionally, in the book of Deuteronomy God makes it clear to his people that they have free will or the ability to choose. Note the explicit words of the writer; "I have set before you life and death, blessings and curses. You **choose** so that you and your seed will prosper." However, based on the MESSAGES that we received early in life our choices may be limited. Choosing will most likely be what is most familiar. Oswald Chambers adds;

> Until we are born again, the only kind of temptation we understand is that mentioned by St. James—'Every man is tempted, when is drawn away of his own lust, and enticed.' But by regeneration we are lifted into another realm where

55

there are other temptations to face, viz. the kind of temptations Our Lord faced…Satan does not tempt us to do wrong things, he tempts us in order to make us lose what God has put into us by regeneration…Temptation means the test by an alien power of the possessions held by a personality…He went through the temptation 'without sin,' and He retained the possessions of His personality in tact.

Negative MESSAGES leave us vulnerable and ripe pickings for evil influences. But in our defense the Apostle Paul reminds us that our struggles are not with flesh and blood but with forces that reside in high/heavenly places. Fighting this emotional battle requires more than just pure information or as the term psychology is defined "the science [and understanding] of behavior and mental process" Before we can address the MESSAGES that pervade our behavior and mental processes, knowledge of God's unconditional love and the powers that oppose Him must be understood.

Thus far the names of three renowned individuals have been cited; David Burns a behaviorist, Erik Erikson a developmental psychologist and Pavlov a physiologist and Nobel laureate. Although their theories approach man's condition of despair from a different perspective each espouse that the developmental years are the rootstock of our present thoughts, feelings, responses, choices and behaviors. More succinctly, all agree that MESSAGES received from birth and early childhood can and do influence the paths we choose later in life.

The study of human behavior is intriguing and because of man's quest for answers to the "whys" of our existence, this so named pseudo-science has evolved over several centuries. Without the usual renderings of blood letting, transfusions, frontal lobotomies and electro-convulsive therapy whose practice originated in decades past as well as the horrendous conditions of early mental asylums, the integration of psychology and theology is mandated to produce a sense of wholeness. Although psychology does provide some insights and truths it is important to remember that all truth is God's truth despite the content or originator.

Without God's compassionate hand, grace and unconditional love we experience partial healing at best. And so the journey continues, in search of the numerous yet varied MESSAGES that fail us.

CHAPTER FOUR

The Earliest Messages

It was Christmas Eve and mother and daughter were in the kitchen preparing the usual dinner fixings. And just as years past the focus was on the main entree, the traditional Christmas ham. As the daughter pulled her roasting pan from the cabinet and proceeded to place the large smoked ham inside, she paused remembering to carve several inches off her perfectly shaped ham. While navigating her way through the cold slippery ham watching her mother busily preparing the candied yams, the thought occurred to gain an answer to a question that had intrigued her for several years. Cautious and fearful of appearing dumb she casually approached her mom. "Mom, why is it that during the preparation of the Christmas ham we remove several inches off of a perfectly lean ham?" Her mother responded with a concerned but quizzical look, "You know honey I really don't know, it's just something your grandmother always did and I learned it from her, I guess you should ask her." Later that evening as the young mother prepared her children for bed she remembered the discussion she had had earlier that day with her mother. Although it was rather late she remained somewhat curious. She decided to call her grandmother and simply pose the same question. She picked up the telephone and dialed the number. Her grandmother, now approaching her 80th birthday, responded with the usual enthusiasm in her voice when hearing from her grandchildren. After sharing with her grandmother what the following day's menu entailed, the young mother posed the pressing question. "Grandma, mom and I were talking earlier today about preparing the Christmas ham and the question was raised as to why we always carved several inches off the ham before placing it in the roasting pan." She could hear her grandmother chuckle and then pause before responding. Finally, her grandmother let out a hearty laugh attempting to speak at the same time. "Oh honey the reason I carved a few inches off the ham before placing it in the roaster was because my pan was too small."

This seemingly innocent yet wasteful act carried on for more than fifty years through two generations is a humorous look at the MESSAGES that we receive and act upon that are now obsolete. This example also communicates the influence mothers have in terms of modeling certain behaviors, whether explicit or implied. They influence our choices to obtain an education, to have children, to choose an appropriate mate, to exude confidence or as noted in the scenario above to mindlessly continue a ritual that lacks relevance.

Why, Mom, why?

Clients frequently complain about the discipline and other actions of their parents, particularly their mother, only to discover that despite their insistence during adolescence to "be and do things differently," they find themselves following in great detail the same actions meted by their mother. One client complained of what is now ascribed to in the psychological world as Chronic Fatigue Syndrome. In summary, this disorder is defined as the inability to terminate a behavior that is ritualistic in nature. Further, it creates marked distress and significantly interferes with the individual's relationship with others. In medical terms Chronic Fatigue Syndrome (CFS) is said to produce such tiredness or fatigue that the patient can not perform daily activities as he did in the past. There are other symptoms but fatigue that lasts 6 months or more is described as the primary. Most experts now believe that it is a separate illness with its own set of symptoms. However, some doctors negate this theory. There are no tests that can confirm a diagnosis of CFS. Because of this, many people have trouble accepting their disease or convincing their friends and family that they are not just struggling with depression.

Some clients battle CFS for years yet the disease is not well understood. Doctors don't know what causes CFS. Sometimes it begins after an illness such as the flu, but there is no proof or any connection. Despite the lack of scientific explanation some doctors do concur that it is likely that a number of factors or triggers come together to cause CFS.

One female client came to my office complaining of anxiety, fatigue, moodiness and depression. She was 38 years old, married, with three adolescent girls from a previous marriage and one 7 year old male child from her present marriage Based on her age coupled with a few minor complaints her sister recommended that she schedule a complete physical with her primary physician. Her results revealed normal ranges for her cholesterol, estrogen and thyroid levels, admirable heart functioning, and blood pressure. Additionally, her tests proved normal kidney functioning, blood sugar levels, and her body's adequate intake and use of vitamins and minerals. Following her medical examination her doctor encouraged her to schedule an appointment with someone from the mental health profession. After sharing her symptoms the next step was to examine the frequency and severity of her complaints. She was then provided with a chart that required daily and hourly monitoring of specific symptoms from mild to severe. Several sessions later the client willingly shared her chart adding that she was amazed by her constant lack of energy during her daily and even enjoyable activities. The client charted her symptoms and feelings i.e., restlessness, inability to concentrate/focus, insomnia or hypersomnia etc. for thirty seven days adding that she experienced ruminating and pervasive thoughts that she was unable to "turn off." Her moodiness, feelings of angst and fatigue prompted me to explore areas in her life that she had been hesitant to visit and disclose. It was soon discovered that during childhood she had suffered emotional abuses that she successfully learned to dismiss or minimize. Despite a sense of foreboding she was reminded by her siblings that they all had a fairly good childhood and that she was "just too sensitive." When she shared her feelings with her deeply religious aunt she was instructed to read her Bible and focus less on the past and more on her wonderful life and numerous blessings. Although she could not recall physical or sexual abuses she could recall subtle MESSAGES that of late appeared to impact her emotional well being. She spoke candidly about the demands her mother placed on her and her seven brothers and sisters to maintain a clean almost medicinal house. Regardless of her railings about various demands relative to the completion of chores on a designated day and time, she was locked into the same pattern. However, without the external stimulus from her mother she in fact had become self-demanding, critical of her accomplishments and ritualistic in terms of keeping her house "spotless."

As we explored the dynamics of the demands noted above it became apparent that revisiting her past and the corresponding MESSAGES was exceedingly painful. It was further discovered that when others spoke of the horrendous environments in which they lived she dismissed or minimized their stories of abuse thoroughly convinced that she was a loving mother unscathed by her formative years. Her belief system was firmly in place; protect your mother at all cost.

Several months in to therapy she willingly journeyed back in time and shared the following story: It was her mother's habit to do laundry every Monday regardless of other activities or emergencies. She recalled pleading with her mother to allow her to attend a school function that was being held, obviously on Monday evening. Promising to complete the laundry if she had to remain up all night, her pleadings went unheard and she was denied the privilege to participate. Tears rolled down her face as she continued. Here I am an adult, happily married, raising four children and working full time yet I can still hear the scolding voice of my mother. She further disclosed the following story;

It was Monday evening and although I had worked a full day I scurried about gathering my laundry. My husband resting on the sofa observed my agitated mood and behavior and suggested that I wait until the following day or perhaps even the weekend to complete my chores. She was both appalled and stunned by his seemingly uncaring, senseless words. In fact she shared during the session "I nearly lost it," thinking how could he even suggest such a thing, after all it was Monday evening? But his wisdom prevailed and after a heated debate she realized that she was following a rule so deeply ingrained that the possibility of other alternatives seemed ludicrous. Despite the painful remembrances of not being able to attend a school activity, a paradox existed. What she experienced years past as a "no" to a simple request left the client confused, frustrated and exhibiting compulsive behaviors when tasks were not completed routinely and in a timely fashion. Just like her mother, the client continued to tell herself "no" when she considered deviating from her schedule. Why was the client so fearful of breaking a tradition that kept her relegated to time? There are no simple answers. However, please note that the powerful MESSAGES from our mother whether positive or negative, particularly during our formative years, are often mindlessly repeated without examination.

Over the last ten to fifteen years observing clients fixed in behaviors and rituals that cause them harm and while conveying mixed signals in many of their relationships have become common occurrences. And in many instances individuals become defiant, resistant and even hostile when more reasonable options are suggested.

To understand the impact and influence that mothers have on both their sons and daughters I felt the need to further explore this phenomenon. My research led me to the definition and power of the word imprinting. A number of studies have been conducted on imprinting, which is defined as "an instinctive behavior pattern by which the young of a species rapidly learn to recognize and follow a member of their own species, typically the mother." According to E. H. Hess:

> This phenomenon takes place early in life within a specific period. This instinct is considered to be the basis for a long-lasting dependence on the mother; if the mother is not present within this period, the responses are oriented toward another object, usually a living organism.

Hess further asserts that imprinting is not limited to visual stimuli, ones tone of voice, pitch, and intensity also play a significant role. Imagine a child hearing the verbal sounds of a distraught, frustrated, angry, or frightened mother. During this crucial stage the child may feel responsible for his mother's emotional state and attempt to "fix" or nurture his caregiver. Although his studies dealt primarily with ducks, geese, chickens or members of the Aves family, he observed that the length of time involved in the imprinting period, regardless of species, did vary and that the time period for imprinting to take place was relatively restricted. "Ducks have an imprinting period lasting only hours in length with peak effectiveness about thirteen to sixteen hours after hatching. [However], this sensitive period possibly ends either with the natural loss of the following tendencies; maturation or with the development of fear responses to strong stimuli."

We too have the ability to recognize our mother figure whether it is through our olfactory perception, the high pitch of the female voice or a more primitive remembrance of the beating of the heart. Further, it has been theorized by one Harvard study that we know our mother by the seventh day of life.

Based on Hess' study I now pose the following questions; what occurs if a child's earliest experience with its mother is one of rejection, fear, abandonment, disappointment or intolerance? What feelings will be "imprinted" upon the newborn? Will the child sense these feelings and respond accordingly? Unlike the results in Hess' experiments with ducks and geese, current research suggests that bonding does not automatically occur between mother and child. How long will it take for the young mother with the "ugly baby" to bond with her child if at all? In reality did the depressed mother of four establish a bond with her children? Recall Erikson's statement regarding the importance of establishing trust between mother and child. Trust, bonding and imprinting all play significant roles in the mother-child relationship. Without them, just as Hess suggests, the child will follow any living organism. As early as one week the child may adopt a general feeling of rejection or fear of abandonment. Furthermore, the child may turn its attention towards another and painfully seek in a word "satisfaction."

As an aside be mindful that the imprinting process is so compelling that children living in homes where parents subject them to all forms of abuse will literally fight to the death to remain with the abusive parent. Professionals employed in protective services can attest to this phenomenon. Despite living conditions that entail garbage strewn about, lack of clothing and daily assaults, physical, emotional and verbal abuse, the imprinting MESSAGE states I am not willing to leave my mother, father or caretaker.

I too am witness to what I deem as the ultimate abuse suffered by children from infancy to ages ten and above. During my internship at a boys' residential facility I recall one case in particular. A thirteen year old resident had been severely burned over seventy percent of his body. His face had received the most damage and was disfigured to the point that most felt compelled to look away. Even now I shudder as I reflect on this young man. As I conversed with my colleagues, obviously curious about his disfigurement, I discovered that this young man's mother had set him on fire for reasons even today are unknown. However, when weekend visits were scheduled he would beg the caseworker to allow him to see the only person he truly felt connected and love for…his mother.

John Bradshaw in his book *Homecoming* states that frequently the child will sense that he is not wanted. Throughout the child's developmental years the aloofness that both mother and father may exude because the child is not a boy or girl can be felt. The ultimate negative MESSAGE decries; "who and what I am is not acceptable." After hearing this MESSAGE throughout the child's formative years, attempts may be made to please mom or the caretaker that can lead to a role reversal. You may have witnessed or personally experienced the efforts of a now adult-child caring for his parents' emotional and financial needs coupled with the need to serve as companion and confidant.

Other cases have resulted in the child's failure to develop his or her own sexual identity. In many of these cases unnatural requests were made of these children to serve as either a surrogate husband or wife. Consider the child who is encouraged and rewarded for consoling, nurturing, acting as confidant and even sharing the most intimate secrets that occur between mom and dad. Case study upon case study revealed angry adults who were confused, promiscuous, and in some instances asexual. Other examples revealed children who were encouraged and rewarded for taking on the role of the absent parent either physically, sexually and/or emotionally.

In *Conjoint Family Therapy* author Virginia Satir uses the term "parentified" defined as a period of time when a child becomes the listening ear and confidant for one or both of his parents. In the situation between mother and offspring, the child unknowingly loses itself and the desire to have his own needs met. The results, the desire for normal separation is not attained. Consider the number of children who never leave home, physically or emotionally. There are countless reasons to remain or to return to the safety of the familiar be it financial difficulties, a need to collect oneself, a struggling marriage, imaginary fear for the safety of the parent and the list continues. Please be aware that separation entails more than just being physically removed to prevent possible enmeshment, it is a mandate to allow the healthy development of our sexual and self-identity.

Erik Erikson suggests that between the ages of twelve and eighteen adolescents are constantly evaluating themselves and measuring themselves in terms of the reactions of others. During this stage he or she either forms a solid definition of self identity or faces the opposing crisis; identity confusion.

Many of us continue to struggle with negative MESSAGES we received from birth through this stage of development. In essence we may recall MESSAGES that we unconsciously respond to or act upon. Several clients spoke of being called stupid, weird, lazy, ugly, fat, skinny, clumsy and other demeaning names and labels. To affirm these labels (a self-fulfilling prophecy) these clients involve themselves in self-destructive behaviors, unaware that they are responding to the MESSAGES they unknowingly embraced during their formative years.

One client came to her initial session filled with tears. Her complaint was that she frequently struggled with feelings of depression and isolation. As we began to explore what is known in the field of mental health, her core issue, she disclosed that the MESSAGES she received from her mother had literally imprisoned her to self destructive behaviors. She had bore three children, none of which shared the same father, was currently in an abusive relationship yet feared being without a man in her life. Her mother's early repetitious MESSAGES were; you will never amount to much, followed by the words and you will probably be pregnant before you reach your sixteenth birthday. She in fact heard the MESSAGES and responded accordingly. Her attempts to disprove her mother's words resulted in sexual relationships intended to affirm her worth. Conversely, her many attempts to find love and approval had the opposite effect.

Numerous articles, journals, books and the like broach the subject of motherhood with caution. Is this a cultural phenomenon passed on from previous decades through our present generation? As I begin to counsel clients regarding "mom" some became resistant, defensive and protective to the point of aggression. There responses were in reality attempts to avoid any semblance of mom's failings or abuse. Several examples come to mind. A forty year old female client shared her childhood which was fraught with physical and emotional abuse including having her sexual organs harshly examined with a hair brush. This brutal act, performed by her mother to discourage her from sexual activity, went beyond the boundaries of an invasion of privacy and sexual abuse. The results, the inability to experience sexual pleasure that stemmed from the painful parallel drawn by her mother. And from a medical standpoint the diagnosis of Vaginismus, which is the uncontrolled spasm of the vaginal muscles that render coitus impossible. In a word she experienced severe pain each time coitus was attempted. This case is indeed extreme, however, for other clients this cyclical occurrence can only be broken when they recognize that most often it is not just the act alone but the partner whom they despise. This MESSAGE has at its roots a mindset that suggests sex is dirty and serves one purpose, to provide pleasure only for the male. In light of this mindset, the wife or expectant mother will feign discomfort during sexual intercourse.

Another female client was determined to have her story vindicated by suggesting to her gynecologist that her husband "be with me during my pap test." Due to the number of sexual harassment suits this request has become more common, generally understood and followed by most in the medical profession. However, the client further requested that the insertion of the specula or vaginal instrument be closely observed by her mate. It was at that time that the doctor recognized a theme associated with this so-called common request. Labeled as marching backwards, the doctor's insight revealed that despite the many strides made by women in the last thirty plus years, fear prevailed when the issue of sexual compliance was denied. For the husband the blatant MESSAGE sent was denial of sexual intercourse is acceptable only if **I** am allowed to affirm your discomfort. For the wife, the MESSAGE is "**I** am not permitted to determine for myself when and if my own body feels discomfort."

Aside from the issues of gender and sexuality noted here, that effect and prohibit one from defining who they are, many physical and emotional abuses alter our individuality and who-ness. The varied accounts of such abuses preempt normal growth in areas of intimacy, individuation, self-acceptance and esteem. One client was reportedly tied to a chair head covered with a pillow case and a smoking rag was introduced in an attempt to force her to "tell the truth." Numerous accounts of being beaten with extension cords, forced to sit in closets for hours, deprived of food and water, experiences of sexual molestation by older siblings, family members, neighbors, step and biological parents, generally evokes rage even among the most apathetic.

A surprising number of clinicians suggest that physical and emotional abuses are more damaging than sexual abuse, arguing that sexual abuse is done under the auspices of love, however, additional research reveals that any form of abuse, particularly combinations of, carry their own consequences. Abuses, particularly by the mother produce adult-children who carry rage, guilt, low self-esteem, co-dependency, a strong need for control and inability to establish healthy relationships and intimacy.

Once again these examples may indeed appear extreme to some but even subtle failings and powerful MESSAGES leave clients depressed, lonely, anxious, fearful and isolated. As mentioned in an earlier chapter looks of disdain, parentification, love based on performance, prohibition from self-expression and creativity or simply put that discourage self exploration to determine "who you are," leaves us confused and floundering. Additionally, little or no involvement in our daily lives as children can be just as damaging.

We are a nation of individuals who have been taught to forgive the unforgivable especially acts perpetrated by mothers. It is an unspoken rule in many cultures that to demean ones mother justifies vengeance up to and including a sentence of death. We ask ourselves why we go to such lengths to protect mom. Why are self help books replete with a preface that begins with "this is not a book about parent [mother] bashing?" Even the most immoral will remind him or herself of the biblical statement that says "honor thy father and thy mother." But have we bothered to explore in what context that scripture was written? Author Donald Sloat in his book "Growing Up Holy & Wholly" submits

> Churches and parents often depict the Christian life as a program for living based primarily on rules of behavior, and they emphasize that one must keep the rules in order to remain in God's [and mom and dad's] good graces.

But does remaining in God's good graces suggest that the child dismiss and more often ignore his emotions to adhere to the MESSAGE that mother knows best? Why is it then that later in life when the mother who has controlled, prohibited individuation, manipulated, created an environment that often times left her child unprotected to be used as a sexual sacrifice for lover, friend, neighbor and painfully, her husband, allowed to utter the words that state "I did the best I could.?" But in reality did she do the best she could? Did she make any attempt to protect the child that she bore from misuse and abuse whether from the family or society at large? I make no apologies to mothers for the damaged children who suffered in silence while they chose to use them as scapegoats and sacrificial lambs for their unfulfilled dreams, poor choices and fear of abandonment.

Alice Miller in *The Drama of the Gifted Child* adds;

> It is one of the turning points in analysis when the narcissistically disturbed patient comes to the emotional

insight that all the love he has captured with so much effort and self denial was not meant for him as he really was, that the admiration for his beauty and achievements was aimed at this beauty and these achievements, and not at the child himself...Does this mean that it was not really me whom you loved, but only what I pretended to be? What became of my childhood? Have I not been cheated out of it?...From the beginning I have been a little adult. My abilities were they simply misused?

I further offer no apologies to the mothers who attempted to create their children in their own image. The cookie cutter child is generally viewed and embraced with pride. But what happens when it is discovered that ones offspring can and does speak different words, think different thoughts and have dreams and visions distinctly independent from mom and therefore have access to limitless possibilities and choices? The answer, pride turns to shame, jealousy, anger, even hatred and ultimately rejection, particularly when the child's decision to separate is made manifest.

The rationalization of "I did the best that I could" is used to explain I didn't get what I bargained for which was the friend that has eluded me, the absence of a champion to help me right the wrong, the confidant or the she or he that should have been. Unbeknown to her what she really got was better. If the truth is examined with scrutiny you will find that the child emerged, triumphant, stronger, and more insightful than genetics would predict.

It is not with a cavalier attitude that I have written the words above. In fact this chapter was the most difficult to write. Admittedly, the process was both tedious and painful as I too was forced to de-mystify my mother's and my own predilections toward motherhood. As I reflected on my own experiences as well as those of clients I felt a sense of betrayal to all mothers, even my role as mother to my now thirty-nine year old son. As I conducted research on this sensitive topic I first asked what and how would mothers feel after reading this section? Would the words appear as an indictment regarding the role of motherhood? What would prospective readers truly gain by exposing the failing MESSAGES that they continue to receive from their mothers? And finally, what should one do who had a similar experience(s) with the very individual who carried them in her womb, providing the necessary nourishment for life? After years of discussion with family and friends, clients and colleagues coupled with intense anxiety and an attempt to evade the entire subject, my inner voice affirmed a louder more pervasive MESSAGE that stated…truth must prevail.

For those of you who feel wounded, offended and undergo a sense of betrayal by the above renderings I ask only that you ask yourself "why." For those who experience a sense of liberation and validation you are encouraged to further examine your mother child relationship, listen carefully to your "soul sentinel" (the part that is vigilant over your soul) and ascertain additional MESSAGES given to you by your mother. Revisit the very MESSAGES that failed you both past and present.

Up to this point you have been provided with partial information relative to the question "why mom why?" Part of the answer is based on the negative MESSAGES communicated by the mother that entail mistrust, rejection, unmet needs and failure in the area of modeling or imprinting. A fair analysis requires examination of the **other half** of the "why?"

The term post-partum depression is indeed a reality but not because of obsolete explanations. Great expectations are cast upon the expectant mother. First, societal MESSAGES suggest that the expectant mother is suppose to enjoy watching her body become shapeless, covered with stretch marks and walk with swollen feet. Second, she is suppose to rejoice in the fact that it takes effort to tie her shoes, bend over, take a bath, and even find a comfortable position to sleep. Third, she may experience rejection and even repulsion from the father of the child because she is no longer sexy. Fourth, a smile should be her permanent facial expression denoting pleasure when the oohs and aahs are made over this tiny infant even though her body is still experiencing hormonal changes that regularly produce anxiety, depression and a general sense of fatigue. Struggling with a number of mixed MESSAGES the mother feels misled, disappointed and may even view the entire experience as anticlimatic. And although she is cognizant of her thoughts and their corresponding feelings, how can she relay positive MESSAGES upon this helpless infant?

In her article entitled the Mother Wound Dr. Jane Myers Drew offers the following;

> No one had a perfect mother. Each mother is a complex woman who had her own history and aims. As a child you were only part of your mom's life, which was filled with many other relationship challenges. Your mother had an existence that in many respects was separate from you. It's often difficult to accept this emotionally, because your mom was so very important to you at the time…Your mother, like many mothers may have lacked the ability to satisfy her own inner emotional needs. This made it difficult, if not impossible for her to give you what you needed emotionally.

To my surprise many of my clients view of motherhood as one that entails perfection and any hint at mom's shortcomings is grounds for early termination of the session and perhaps cancellation of future counseling sessions. In their eyes even the words mother, mom, mommy are considered sacred as the word God.

Some years ago I met with counselor shortly after the death of my mother. I announced that there was no need to revisit my past and I was only there in search of interventions that would guide me through the grieving process. I do however recall feeling torn between the idealized picture of my mother preparing daily meals, involving herself in her children's education, registering me to participate in religious activities versus the horrific emotional and physical abuses she inflicted upon me and my siblings. Still I was unwilling to delve into the origins of feelings of rage, deceit, and abandonment. Admittedly I carried these feelings for many years unaware that they were in fact directed toward my mother.

Within certain cultures so sacred is the idealized depiction of mom that negative words and/or comments that even hint at her failings are cause for the offended individual to threaten or do bodily harm to the offender.

I frequently aid clients in the preparation of two instruments known as a Genogram and Eco-Map. These instruments are similar to a family tree; however the difference is that they provide a historical accounting of longevity, issues surrounding poor mental health, including addictions and other familial issues. As their names imply, both serve as visual aids and provide data relative to understanding the mother and father dynamic and other family members. These instruments are vital as clients explore issues that are part and parcel of their family of origin. Dr. Drew further adds;

> Your mother also had her own mother, who greatly influenced Her and—for better or worse—was her model for how to be a mother. Sins and tragedies typically pass from generation to generation. Often I hear that a troubled client's mother's, mother died at an early age or was an alcoholic or abusive to her child. We can all benefit from investigating our family's histories. Learning about your mother's parents and grandparents can help increase your tolerance for her failings. It's difficult for mothers to give more than they received. Knowing this, [makes] it easier for you to look at her not only as your parent, but as a human being who repeated what she learned and did what she felt she had to do. She was a link in a generational chain of dysfunction. Ultimately, it's important for you to accept your mother as someone who had strengths, limitations, and inner wounds—similar to yours.

Mommy! There's That Man Again

Unlike ones mother who by all accounts establishes a natural bond with her unborn child, the beginning stage of bonding between father and child is not so easily determined. Where mother represents a sanctuary of tenderness, compassion and coddling, father is often the stoic pillar of security that is appreciated but rarely understood. Hence it is not until the child's phase of life known as the toddler years (and perhaps before then), that he can fully assess the significance dad's "presence" or dad's "absence" played in his development. Nevertheless, a father does influence his growing child through various MESSAGES and in most instances the child maintains an undying loyalty to this so-named "silent provider."

When Earl Woods, father of the renowned golfer, was asked how his son Tiger responded to his "pushing" while growing and learning the game of golf, he responded with one of the most profound yet provocative statements. His reply was that there were two things he was proud of relative to the raising of his son. First, he stated that he never "pushed" Tiger nor forced him to practice. Second, he simply exposed him to the game and was **there** for support. Now Tiger will go down in history as the most prolific golfers to ever play the game. We can assume that Earl Woods never wore a Superman cape or leaped tall buildings in a single bound; He was simply **there.** We will never know or be able to enumerate the number of "I love you, Tiger" expressed by Mr. Woods. Nor will we ever know the number of amateur contests Mr. Woods missed during Tiger's career. However, we can be certain that there was a bond and mutual reliance that was fostered between this father and his son that played a major role in creating what appears to be a gifted and self-assured man who happens to be a golfer. The MESSAGE, dad does not have to be a dashing, ex-marine fighter pilot who now works as a double agent for the CIA. He merely has to be **there** in order to model the many facets of manhood and provide the necessary MESSAGES to instill trust, autonomy, and self-identity and man/womanhood.

But what exactly does "**there**" mean? I surmise that the heart of this question takes on a more dynamic meaning to the male child than it does for the infant girl. Or does it? Little girls generally develop into women who develop unfathomable strength, leadership qualities and possibly compassion. This is to say that father's availability does influence the character of daddy's girl.

But what of the father who is unavailable and/or abusive toward both or either son and daughter? Sadly, the influence of a mother serves as a modest or mediocre respite against the most negatively influential father. As you explore the following scenarios consider the Biblical stories that depict the relationship between father and child that was first established by Adam then inherited by Abraham, King Solomon and their contemporaries.

The passage from boyhood to manhood is one that must inextricably be coaxed by the "tribal head"…dad. Herein belies the answer to why in even the most ancient cultures some exemplar of rite of passage is inherent. After a period of grooming, testing and molding, the man-child is qualified ceremoniously as a man. On the other hand, in most cultures the breeding, child rearing and even cohesive attributes of the female are counted as common-place—even taken for granted. Were the warrior-leaders of the ancient Mayans or Incas overbearing, abusive, lazy drunkards who were just "there?" Is there any wonder that the children of our so-named Generation-X have no problem calling women, even their own mothers) "b---hes," "sluts" and the like? No, this is not the example that was set by men as diverse in culture and ethnicity as John McEnro Sr. and Earl Woods. Somewhere between the fetal bond and narcissistic obscurity lies the answer to the question of "where is there?"

There…?

Maybe he is the product of the timeless, rural, deep South where, "I love you" is reserved for and after a knock-down, drag-out brawl or after being assuaged of a liquor bottle (if even then). Or maybe he is from upper-crust society where, "I love you" is measured in shades of green in exchange for blind negligence of the child's development. Further still, perhaps his origins began somewhere in middle America where "I love you" is enshrouded in a hard-hat who after ten hours of back breaking labor has only enough time at home to eat dinner and drift silently into a catatonic state in his easy chair while watching the local news. In all cases stated and in between, "there" are words and deeds that send subtle MESSAGES to the child that say "you do matter, and I love you," regardless of socio-economic status and time restraints.

After spending several months in my office, a well educated and upwardly mobile young male, aged twenty-six, the product of divorced parents, an alcoholic father, and struggling himself with alcohol addiction, shared the following story. Once as a young boy my father, whose usual expression of love was to burst into the family room rain candy at my feet and give a small grunt as he exited to his liquor bottle, entered our backyard to play baseball with my friends and me. It was a rare moment of bliss that I will remember forever. Although he had in fact been drinking, he came and showed us ten year olds how to "choke-up on the bat" and how to pitch. The experience lasted all of twenty minutes, but for that time in space, I felt as if I mattered enough for "dad" to share his time and experience with me. And for moments like that I would have traded every candy bar in the world. That was one of the few times I can remember not caring that Dad had been drinking.

The client continued…another time I recall being sent home early from my middle school for some behavioral problem only to be greeted by Dad who promptly gave me one of his rare whippings. Afterward, with tears streaming down my face, he took me with his arm around my shoulder to the corner diner for lunch. Again, oddly enough, this was one of the most treasured experiences I had with my father. The MESSAGE; You matter enough for me to take time to discipline you. The client, still experiencing much pain as the memories surfaced, brought to mind the words in the song "You don't have to say you love me, just be close at hand." This now full grown man, a father himself was moved to tears as he continued to visualize and experience the pain of an absent father that he thought he had emotionally buried years ago. It was further evident that he had struggled with this issue for many years and in his search for truth, he shared his desperate need to investigate the feelings and attitudes of his now adult male friends and family members.

To this young man the experiences and stories shared by other males prompted him to include this topic in discussions he had with men attending a GED class that he weekly volunteered to facilitate. During the many class periods he conducted informal polls currently released from a large penal system ranging in age from eighteen to fifty. He further reported that the common thread that united these men, whether African-American, Hispanic or Caucasian from a single-parent or two parent household, poor or middle class was the devastation in their lives caused by an unhealthy or non-existent paternal relationship. He reported that an eighteen year old student stated, 'I wish my father would have been there to teach me right from wrong." Another student, a twenty-four year old student raised in an upper middle class family expressed feelings of abandonment as he shared the following; although my father resided in the home with my mother and two siblings the condescending, almost pious attitude of my father contributed greatly to the sale and use of drugs and subsequent incarceration. "If my father would have only spoken to me as a friend, who understood my problems instead of demeaning my accomplishments and my dream to teach school, I think I would have turned out different." This young man also disclosed his need and desire for male companionship, needy of openly sharing life experiences, compassion, yet a "man's man."

The pervasive MESSAGE from these men is that a father's financial success or social status does not matter. In concert they affirm that it just would have been nice for dad to be "there" and occasionally talk, listen and understand issues that entailed matters of the heart.

How many of our disenfranchised youth such as those in the many gangs of South Central, Los Angeles, Detroit, Chicago, Houston and other major cities have subliminally substituted the 'ratta-tat-tat' of assault rifles and automatic weapons for dad's voice? Further, instead of dad's voice offering affirmation, safety and unconditional love and acceptance, what is frequently heard by both son and daughter implies the following;

Serve me without reciprocal love, and as a matter of course, and I will feed and clothe you but I will not bother to know who you are.

This statement speaks to the painful and paradoxical disconnection between father and child. Translation; we have a relationship that exists without the presence of intimacy or involvement. The following are a few of the responses frequently heard when dad is asked to spend quality time with his offspring:

"I have provided food and shelter."
"I have put shoes on feet that grew every 2 months.
"I made sure that I worked extra to provide those extra things like, little league, piano lessons, guitar, summer camp, what else do you want from me?"

In many homes regardless of race or ethnicity, socio-economic status, these responses are heard on a regular basis. The framework that these fathers have built is thought to also be a framework of love, safety, trust and security. In many ways it is. The basic survival needs are important to us all and are of concern to most parents.

I noted earlier that Abraham Maslow, American psychologist and leading proponent of humanistic psychology, concured. He developed a theory of motivation describing the process by which an individual progresses from basic needs such as food and shelter to self-actualization or the fulfillment of one's greatest human potential. However, of late, his theory has been challenged suggesting that his "Hierarchy of Needs" requires closer examination. The importance of these provisions must never be discounted. But while the basic tenets of survival are met how and during what stage should the child experience self-actualization? Without words of affirmation that say "I'm proud of you, I believe in you, I love you" and further still, a father striving to live a responsible, honest and transparent life, it is unlikely that the child will attain this final yet critical stage.

Less I am accused of relying on old assumptions about the relationship between father and son I again turn to author Donald E. Sloat. Mindful of the differences between sons and daughters, the father must be aware that "sons develop their own attitudes about women by watching their fathers relate to their mothers." Without exposure to other positive male models clients may repeat the behaviors of their abusive fathers through word and deed. They are often surprised, humiliated and filled with shame when they reflect on the behaviors of their fathers that they consciously or unconsciously mirror. On the other hand some admit that physical abuse is both part and parcel of his role in "getting his mate to submit."

> The foundation for adolescent and adult behavior begins in early childhood, and boys as well as girls need positive, caring input from both parents...Fathers as well as mothers need to read to little boys, to play with them, to hold them, to tell them they love them and that they are important.

The essential role of the father necessitated the establishment of numerous organizations. They include The National Center for Fathering and former Vice President Al Gore's private sector "Father-to-Father" project, Promise Keepers and the Million Man March. According to the 1996 Gallup Poll on Fathering, "the most significant family or social problem facing America is the physical absence of the father from the home." Another researcher notes;

> Fathers today spend less time with their children than their fathers did with them...Bringing home the paycheck is no longer seen as sufficient to fulfill the fathering role. Dads are expected to be more involved and nurturing, both physically and verbally.

We may be able to visualize the father with his son at a baseball game or other sport event. But it was a hard lesson to be learned when a young woman related the following scenario. She and her two small children spent several hours visiting with a close friend and her husband. As they shared varying ideologies regarding child rearing the husband spent considerable time with the young woman's son, conversing, encouraging, and roughly tossing him about. But it was later that evening when defenses were lowered that the young woman pointed out the necessity for fathers to play, converse and even challenge the physical limitations of their daughters. The husband, a rather muscular built but compassionate

MESSAGES…AND HOW THEY HAVE FAILED US

man, was surprised. His response was that girls were gentle and so they should be cared for and handled delicately. But as they discussed the situation into the wee hours of the evening their conclusions brought to mind painful remembrances often made by female friends, family members and peers. Although their words expressed, understanding and genuine forgiveness, each confessed feelings of rejection by their fathers, who from their perspective, were more inclined to spend quality time, what little there was, with the boys in the family. Their disclosures created a need to explore the validity of their cognitive and emotional experiences.

Even as I listened to numerous encounters told by both male and female clients, I was forced to reflect upon my own father/daughter relationship. It was then that a pressing theme emerged. Despite my resentment I realized I carried a pervasive need for interaction and permission to exhibit inner as well as outer strengths with my father, who had long since died. But it was Dr. Estes who brought further insights to my dilemma. In her book *Women Who Run with the Wolves*, she espouses that "the father is the primitive spirit of the woman, the woman his daughter. It is the father persona that she needs when there is a battle to fight or an injustice to right. It is also the father who determines the limits of the little girl and later the free spirit of this woman who will take risks, embrace her true self as well as the new and embark upon the unknown".

For many we have assumed that the mother carries the responsibility for molding and shaping the child particularly during the developmental years. However, there are countless MESSAGES that the father imparts. The most obvious MESSAGE is his availability or unavailability. His excuses range from absorption in the role of provider to scape-goating the gender roles i.e. "that's what your mom should be doing." The tragedy is that the excuses for his absence are given without remorse. Although he may physically be present in the home, which he feels is enough, the MESSAGE is that his presence is as serviceable as a coat resting on a rack positioned at the front door. For you see when you look at the coat, you cannot tell by its position whether it has just arrived or is simply in a preparatory mode to exit. The coat changes in response to the seasons and feels proud to do so but it does no more than clothe the superficial being. The coat as an inanimate object is unknowingly part of the collaboration of deceit. However the key here is that the coat doesn't have a choice.

Here again the reader may recoil at the seemingly lack of compassion and or understanding of the father's role or purpose. But it is only after taking an accurate assessment of how dad's MESSAGE, relative to his unavailability, damages so many who need father intimacy and involvement, that the presumption that I lack compassion should be viewed objectively.

At this point in time, there is the need to remind those of you, particularly female, who have experienced incest and/or sexual molestation from the father or father figure that was **too available**. He always seemed available for those special treats, favors and a divergent relationship. His availability is merely to entice the innocent into also being available, but the primary goal is for service and the fulfillment of his own sexual gratification. With the advent of talk shows and support groups, issues of incest and sexual molestation have been exposed. Countless individuals are telling their story of secrecy, fear and shame. But merely admitting the injustice is just the beginning of the emotional journey, the mere tip of the iceberg. The necessity for a grieving process can be long and tedious. As noted in the section on "why mom why", we stated that many wives and girlfriends purposely ignored the unnatural relationship between father and daughter rather than face the painful truth. But what responsibility does the father have? The act is done under the auspices of "this is the right thing to do for me." Simply put, even though you may feel awkward about this act don't trust yourself. And more disconcerting are his sexual drives such that he is willing to place the sacrificial lamb on the altar, that of his own flesh?

What MESSAGE does a child receive when the caretaker and provider commits such a heinous crime? The MESSAGES reinforced although they may not be acted upon until later in life suggest that men cannot be trusted, my body is to be used to gain favors and the most damaging MESSAGE, I cannot trust my own feelings and inner voice.

Another often subtle MESSAGE can be heard when the father pressures his mate into bringing forth that "man child," one who will bring him joy, reproduce his seed and he can be intimately involved in his rearing. After all "only a man can teach a boy to be a man." I too on several levels embrace this arrogant but guileless statement. But when the toy room is filled with assorted baseball gloves, bikes, model planes and boats, it appears that the hard job of fathering, which entails affirming, validating, challenging, disciplining and modeling love, often falls short.

One noteworthy case revealed a client struggling with exhibitionism. He related the following story that was the catalyst for his demise. He was born the fourth son of seven children. There were three older boys and two younger sisters. During his journey to wholeness, an exploration of his family of origin issues was a mandate to determine the source of his malady. His often meager attempts to maintain the dignity of his parents produced more pain as he recalled his father's seemingly harmless words. He had been told by his dad, throughout the majority of his life that his idea of the perfect family included three girls and three boys. The painful reality that he was not a girl created an individual who initially tried to hide his sexual identity and orientation. But by his early teens became involved in pornography, masturbation and exposing himself on a regular basis. Although his father was physically in the home it was now apparent to him that this same father had chosen to ignore all the signals of a troubled young male.

Where do these patterns of absenteeism originate? Dad has been known to blame burnt food, an unkempt house, a lack of sex, job pressures and the like on his unavailability. But it is clear that these excuses serve to shelter him from his primary responsibilities. The issue here is one of choice and at the very core is his need to escape because there are expectations that he feels that he cannot adequately fulfill. The results often stem from their creation of a fairy tale character, at least in the eyes of the children. Every excuse convincingly rendered that traditionally encourages his children to create a dad who is doing "the best he can," until adolescence and then adulthood proved otherwise.

Our society suggests that children seek out and search for their mother's approval, desirous of unconditional and/or maternal love. However, current data indicates that the void left by an absent father is a profound MESSAGE embraced and related by past and contemporary

81

society. It is the father who not only affirms his daughter's primitive nature but he also initiates the first acknowledgement that she is physically beautiful. Conversely, without his affirmation, acknowledgment and actions denoting recognition of her beauty, she indeed will often seek those things through unhealthy relationships and promiscuity, constantly in search of the evasive "prince charming." Donald E. Sloat Ph.D. further adds;

> The father-daughter relationship in the early years is one of the underlying contributors to whether or not an adolescent girl becomes sexually active. It is usually from her father that a daughter develops feelings about herself as a girl, a female, a woman.

Further, her inability to feel powerful may result in a kind of numbing herself through the use of drugs and alcohol addiction, food, spending sprees, etc. Rarely will she learn to tune into or acknowledge her inner voice that tells her she is capable, competent, beautiful and worthy of a responsible yet sensitive mate. Sadly it is the external voices producing powerful MESSAGES that will determine her self-worth and level of self esteem. Other examples reveal an emotionally manipulative tool, generally thought to be used exclusively by mothers, that is also used by fathers. The tool labeled as guilt may be carried through out our lives and used by parents, siblings and later on peers, friends, companions and ultimately our mate or significant other.

A high school sophomore received a prize for the best 1995 essay written in New York public high schools. The essay titled "He Said She Said," surveyed the use of guilt by both father and mother.

God the Father

The son of a highly respected and renown religious leader shared the following statement; "If I had understood the MESSAGES people were sending me on the day I was born, I might just have crawled right back in where I'd come from and taken a rain check." His story, printed by Time Magazine, revealed a son who was expected to grow up fast without self examination, and to ultimately follow his dad's footsteps. His future was predicted to the point that he once overheard one well wisher, "I'll bet your new boy will be a Catholic some day, maybe priest, bishop, or cardinal, possibly Pope." But as his life story unfolded the pressures became so great that as soon as he was able he began denying his legacy, turning primogeniture into prodigality. In his own words he readily admitted whatever was expected of the student body, I wanted to do the opposite. Additionally, I revealed in staying one step ahead of the law. In his case like many other teens, guilt, supposedly a parent's most powerful tool produced the opposite effect. I dare not say with certainty what antecedents were in place that produced a lifestyle of rebellion. But I can surmise that his father, always off on a crusade, left only a distant if benevolent presence. It is here that I go a step further in terms of heralding the impact that our relationship with our father has on our affinity, or lack of, toward God.

In our Bibles God is referred to as "Our Heavenly Father." So sacred was his name that according to Hebrew tradition writers could not fully spell out the name God. Vowels were omitted so that the reader could not readily pronounce His name. Painfully, this title "Heavenly Father" often renders daughters and sons angry at yet another father who has failed them. The following are glimpses at some of the behaviors, thoughts and feelings projected on God the Father because of the covert and overt MESSAGES received from our earthly fathers.

In numerous sessions clients have unknowingly revealed their authentic feelings regarding this supposed Supreme Being. Although the following statements are not verbatim, careful probing regarding ones father/child relationship provided insights into clients' feelings of distrust, fear and quite often disdain towards this sacred yet invisible being.

- I refuse to look to God to get my needs met, after all he is just like any other man who holds a position of authority.

- Hump! why bother praying? God has little regard for my feelings.
- When things are going too well I simply wait for God to either pull the rug out from under me or disappear from my life.
- Where was this God when my drunken father beat me…my mother slept with my friend…
- I feel we are pretty much left to fend for ourselves.
- I'm tired of being punished over and over again for petty failings.
- I view God just as I do my biological father, an observer or judge; keeping track of the things I do wrong.

In summary, our image of God is uniquely personal yet based on MESSAGES from earthly fathers, the church, and personal experiences.

In "Seeing God More Clearly, Juanita R. Ryan notes that some people imagine God as a person with impossible demands, unsympathetic, emotionally distant, cold, abusive, a bully and interested only in our performance and unquestionable obedience. He carries the proverbial hammer just waiting for us to mess up. One client thought of himself as God's court jester, to be called upon for entertainment and then dismissed at will.

Clients repeatedly rail against both biological fathers and males in positions of authority. But their desire for retribution is generally suppressed resulting in anger, bitterness, rage, abuse of self and others, lack of trust and depression. One client was so fearful of being punished by God that she attempted to read every book on subjects that dealt with religion, sin and forgiveness, the church, faith, God, and constantly felt pressured to attend every church service, faithfully take communion, and literally live in isolation for fear of committing a sin. When she was not attending church, she spent time surfing the television channel for evangelist, preachers, pastors and anyone who might possibly provide comfort and even forgiveness for her past and present sins. Regardless of her penitent actions, she continued to struggle with thoughts of inadequacy, incompetence, sinfulness, and low self esteem. Following numerous sessions coupled with increased feelings of worthlessness revealed a father-daughter relationship laden with expectations of perfectionism.

During my years as a Pastoral Counselor I often use an intervention entitled Overcoming Fear through Confrontation. The intervention is as follows; after a number of counseling sessions, certain that I had established trust and rapport, I would position an empty chair facing the client. The client was then encouraged to visualize the person with whom he had unresolved issues. The empty chair could represent a mother, father, sibling, boss, and even the "Great I Am" that he deemed responsible for his depression or other emotional maladies that ultimately led to a visit to my office.

In most cases clients were unwilling to make eye contact or look at this inanimate object fearing rejection or further abuse. With much compassion and verbal reminders that "he/she can not hurt you any more," the client would often confront the empty chair with tears, profane language, or outbursts of words that implied a need for vengeance. So powerful was this intervention that additional sessions were required to address the rage, fear, or physical maladies that ranged from severe headaches to heart palpitations.

It was during one of these sessions that I learned of the disdain and fear of rejection that many Christians had for God the Father. Many were unwilling to communicate or face this father figure whose mere presence evoked panic, rage, shame, and a myriad of other emotions. What MESSAGES had this person received from his earthly father that produced the range of emotions toward the Father of all fathers?

Dessert is Optional

The young man identified earlier no longer cries out in fear, "Mommy there's that man again." It is too late for his imploring at this time. Now in his mid to late thirties he has made a profound statement as to the timing and placement of a father's involvement. Showering candy at one's feet can not begin to say "I love you." Attendance at parent conferences, nightly homework reviews, bedtime stories, responsiveness to the myriad of questions, laughter and tears, and nonverbal cues and communication are essentials for parenting for both mom and dad. This is not optional or subject to intermittent input. What are **options** are the desserts of life. The front row seat at graduation, acknowledgement of your contributions during times of uncertainty and stress, the escort down the aisle on her wedding day, or the midnight dash to the hospital to see the new grandchild are the precious payoffs for providing the diapers and walking the floor with the child who was colicky or dealing with the question "what should I do if…"

The Native American tradition provides a pure yet succinct definition of a man…Author Paula Gunn notes;

> A man, if he's a mature adult, nurtures life. He does rituals that will help things grow, he helps raise the kids, and he protects the people. His entire life is toward balance and cooperativeness. The ideal of manhood is the same as the ideal of womanhood. You are autonomous, self-directing, and responsible for the spiritual, social and material life of all those with whom you live.

One may assume that the primary influences in terms of parenting now end. There's mom, there's dad and frequently granny. However, there is one dynamic seldom explored but no less important. I choose to call it the sibling/surrogate parent.

The Sibling/Surrogate Parent

"I did not ask for another mother, I just wanted a sister." In author Kevin Lehman's book *Birth Order* he asserts that first born children are given the responsibility MESSAGE their entire lives. The first-borns' initial playmates are their parents who speak to them in a language that does not resembles child talk but in fact can be compared to adult-to-adult dialogue. This first born generally achieves his developmental milestones and other advanced expectations. Then possibly one, maybe two or three years later, a sibling is born. As the first born he may be excited about the prospect of a playmate. You know someone small like him. It wouldn't be so obvious then who spilled the chocolate milk. However, things do not go exactly as planned. This new person is too small. They can't walk. They can't talk. They just cry and drink and wet and get changed and sleep. They also need holding just when I want to be held. Things start to improve; she can smile, but still can't walk. He is starting to get loud. Sometimes I have to hold her. I want to go out and play. I wonder if he likes mud pies. Mom is mad because she thinks that I will give her some mud…Mom and dad must go to work. That leaves me, the eldest and more responsible to baby sit. Over and over, "change the diaper, feed the baby, make sure he doesn't hurt himself". I want to go out. I have to take *it* with me!!!. Yuck. If you are 'gonna" leave *it* here with me, then *it* has to do what I say. *It* had better be quiet about the party we had over here when **they** (the old people) went out of town for the weekend.

At this juncture have you considered the child noted earlier who became an "it?" Perhaps **you** are the "it" child with multiple siblings. My experiences have left me wondering why certain sibling relationships are so rich and rewarding. We compare sibling relationships to our own only to become aggrieved when the relationship between siblings has been so fractious that no life event is strong enough to resurrect or create sibling loyalty.

Parenting is a challenging endeavor and carries a heavy price for the novice as well as the veteran parent. Most will relate that as parents a trip to the movies requires more planning than the Gulf War. Sexual spontaneity is out of the question and time management is at best a struggle. For some it is a life-changing event. Most would agree that they were ill prepared for the monumental task but somehow summoned resources from deep inside to meet the challenge. If you disagree consider the dynamics of the child who is thrust into the role of the surrogate parent. Forced upon him are responsibilities out of proportion and inappropriate for his age and level of maturity resulting in far-reaching negative consequences. The role of surrogate parent proves to initiate the loss of the surrogate's childhood. Additionally, this role may leave the child/adolescent "stuck" developmentally and can lead to feelings of resentment, powerlessness or a need for control. Finally, this environment can create the potential for sibling bonds to be non-existent or broken that may leave individuals at-risk for a dysfunctional adult to adult relationship.

Members of a family can be compared to a mobile suspended from the ceiling. There is never a time when one family member is affected that does not affect all. At or about age eleven or twelve, children generally begin to separate from their parents and establish themselves as individuals, despite the fact that this separation may create some discomfort between parent and child. This time period also necessitates actions that assist the child to separate from his sibling/surrogate parent. There is discomfort here as well, however, the pain, as with all pain, is intensified because of a lack of understanding and maturity. Forgiveness does not come as easily as it does with ones biological parents and may I add that this unhealthy relationship between siblings may carry years of unresolved issues from MESSAGES, implied or overstated that are carried over into future generations (remember the first brothers Cain and Abel?).

There is one final MESSAGE here. As baby boomers age, those of us born between 1940 and 1955, we may find ourselves caring for our elderly parent(s). If the sibling/sibling relationship is fractious then this effort may be more taxing than need be. Instead of galvanizing the sister to sister, brother to brother or brother to sister relationship, it may become more contentious and actually intensify sibling rivalry leaving the parent alone, without his/her peers, needy and literally forced to choose sides with his own offspring.

Messages from the Marriage

There is an old proverb that argues, "as a rule a man is a fool, when it's hot he wants it cool, when it's cool he wants it hot, what it is he wants it not." Despite the rising divorce rate, fear of being alone later in life, we continue to engage in the dance and ceremony of marriage. Later I will address the MESSAGES from society that label us as unlovable or unattractive if we are not married or at best committed to another by a particular age. In the interim allow me to address various issues that are not considered when we find ourselves married to our supposed soul mate. How often have wives, fearful of losing their sexuality through the dreaded disease of breast cancer refused to have a yearly mammogram? And how often have husbands, shamed by the societal stigma to regarding sexual performance, failed to have their prostate examined? Not out of obligation but from the necessity to tell the whole story has prompted me to share the sexual MESSAGES that confront men and women. Impotence, or the inability for the male to achieve ejaculatory orgasm as the end of penile/vaginal sex, has been thought to be an occurrence which ultimately comes with age. However, recent findings and stories shared in the privacy of my office have been told regarding a mother/son relationship that encouraged total dependence on mom alone. In doing so she achieves her ultimate goal, and that is to discourage her son from exploring his male to female connectedness as part of adolescence and eventually manhood. Does the mythical story of Oedipus then ring true?

It is within the pages of this work through both client stories and research that I discovered a son's willingness to figuratively kill his own father to remain the only male connection in his mother's life. With this knowledge fictional or otherwise, research suggests that for some, orgasm can only be achieved by the male child through masturbation. Permanent female sexual intercourse is not desirous forcing the adult son to respond to earlier MESSAGES. One of which is; only I (mother) can provide sexual gratification and outside of that you are free to explore unnatural sexual encounters. This may ultimately prohibit him from establishing a sexual relationship with a female. If you question this premise then take note of the number one selling prescription drug on the market…Viagra.

As I continue with MESSAGES from the marriage, be apprised that it is within this scope that I speak of educated men and women who have lowered their fat intake, made exercise a part of their daily routine and spent thousands of dollars on cosmetic products or surgery. What is it that they are trying to conceal, from whom and for what reason?

According to Weeks and Treat, in their book *Couples in Treatment*,

> Marital therapies have devoted little attention to the role of feelings therapy…Proponents of these approaches often speak of the need to avoid dealing with feelings because they are seen as a distraction. Of all the major approaches to systems/marital therapy, not one gives serious attention to the role of feelings, despite the fact that marriage is fundamentally an emotional attachment.

As thinking, feeling individuals we have learned to emulate what has been modeled for us. I now ask you to play the game of suppose and what if. This in no way is an attempt to malign the light-hearted sitcom of Leave it to Beaver but this portrayal of the typical American family has given us its own MESSAGES. Just suppose June Cleaver didn't really love her husband Ward? Or suppose Ward didn't share any commonality with his wife June (other than the two boys)? What if the Cleaver's humorous yet superficial conversations were all they shared? What if Ward Cleaver returned home everyday and read the paper so he would not really have to hear about June's day? What if June Cleaver, like so many mothers and wives continued in this unfulfilled relationship for the sake of Wally and the Beave? Suppose each family on the block was like the Cleavers and kept things together if nothing but for appearances sake? What MESSAGES might June and Ward be giving to Wally and the "Beave" or a daughter if they had one?

Now instead of June and Ward Cleaver challenge yourself to play the suppose game relative to your mother and father, grandparents, neighbors down the street, a prominent church family, or just maybe your own marriage.

The Swallow Returns to Capistrano… Spring Is in the Air

As an introduction to societies measurable period of life known as "springtime," or "when a man's fancy turns toward…," the following brief history lesson will provide you with an overview of nature's way of regulating and predictably timing the life events of the Swallows at Capistrano.

It happens every spring. Every year around the 19th of March, the world pauses momentarily and focuses on that compelling phenomenon of nature—the return of the Swallows to Capistrano. Immortalized in Leon Rene's famous song "When the Swallows Come Back to Capistrano," the return of the little birds to Capistrano every spring has captured the imaginations of millions and served as an annual major media event. The Old Spanish Mission has become world famous as the haven of the swallows and one of many romantic symbols for nature's migration with the seasons. How did it all come about? How long have the swallows been coming back to Capistrano? Why they come here is a secret between the swallows and their Creator. History records that these small birds have been coming to the Mission area long before there was a mission. It is likely the birds were around as the Mission and the town was being built and before anyone paid much attention to them. The padres and townspeople just took them for granted.

However, there is evidence that they were first brought to the attention of people outside Capistrano when bird lovers started to come to study the nesting habits of the swallows in the early 1900's. By 1915, a writer for the Overland Monthly magazine called attention to how the little birds liked to nest at the Mission. Later, in 1930, Father St. John O'Sullivan published the "Legend of the Swallows Return" with Charles Saunders in a collection of stores called "Capistrano Nights." The story is told that after the town grew up around the Mission, one of the padres noticed a storekeeper in town angrily sweeping down the conical shaped swallows' nests and chasing away the 'dirty birds'. The kindly padre invited the frustrated little birds to the Mission where there was "room for all". And they've been returning there every year knowing their young can be safe within Mission walls. It was an event marked by the kindly Franciscan Padres as occurring on March 19, the Feast of St. Joseph.

The swallows have been observed leaving Goya at daylight from the 18th of February, in successive flight, arriving in Capistrano about the 19th of March— an incredible journey of 7,500 miles in 30 days! Most of the way they reportedly fly at altitudes above 2,000 feet to take advantage of fast and favorable air currents and tailwinds and to stay above predatory birds along the way.

One writer noted that this fantastic flight is difficult to understand adding that it raises two questions, how they do it? And or why they go there? **The fact is, they have been doing it for centuries in fulfillment of some inner biologic destiny.** It appears that their destiny was also to become trendsetters because ever since they gain prominence thousands of people have too flocked to San Juan for the biggest event of the year— the return of the swallows to Capistrano.

Does the historical data above resemble any aspects of your life? Are there periods in your life that you too regularly return to old haunts be it mentally or physically? Have you too mindlessly found yourself in search of **fulfillment of some inner biologic destiny?** In many instances our search is prompted by early MESSAGES that hint that by age twenty plus you should be married with children, or at least be involved in a serious relationship. Similar to the journey of the swallows, our journey toward a union with another began centuries ago. However unlike the tiny birds, we are motivated by MESSAGES that are varied, conflicting, self-serving motivated by the needs and expectations of others, or simply to comply with societal standards.

The song *When I Fall in Love* provides us with lyrics that suggest that we are in search of that one perfect person who will be the first and last to bring fulfillment and eternal happiness. The lyrics written by Heyman and Young are as follows;

> Maybe I'm old fashioned feeling as I do.
> Maybe I'm just living in the past,
> But when I meet the right one, I know I'll be true.
> My first love will be my last.

When I fall in love
It will be forever.
For I'll never fall in love
In a restless world like this is

Love is ended before it's begun
And too many moonlight kisses
Seem to cool in the warmth of the sun.

When I give my heart
It will be completely.
For I'll never give my heart.
And the moment I can feel that you feel that way too
Is when I fall in love with you.

Prior to this writing, I would frequently hum along with the performer stuck on the words "when I fall in love." The MESSAGE espoused with certainty that one day I would fall in love. The song's title is not "**If** I Fall in Love," but "**When** I Fall in Love." The assumption is that falling in love is inevitable. However, as time and relationships proved different I began to consciously reflect on the lyrics of this and many other songs that affirmed my familial and societal MESSAGES that love was forever and eternal. However, if you closely examine the lyrics above the writers repeat "for I'll never give my heart…fall in love because love ends before it begins. And upon closer examination, I was struck by one word in particular, FALL. We use this word as a matter of course when speaking about a new found relationship that will hopefully lead to eternal bliss. But the word fall, denotes that we have no control over our emotions and behaviors. Simply put we encounter a situation that propels us mindlessly without knowledge, wisdom, boundaries or good old common sense. For purposes of clarity please examine the many definitions of fall;

To *drop or come down freely* under the influence of gravity.
To drop oneself to *a lower or less* erect position:
To *lose* an upright or erect position suddenly.

To *drop wounded or dead*, especially in battle.
To be cast down.
To *undergo conquest or capture*, especially as the result of an armed attack.
To experience defeat or ruin.
To lessen in amount or degree.
To *decline* in financial value.
To *diminish* in pitch or volume.
To *give in* to temptation; sin.
To occur at a specified time.
To occur at a specified place.
To come, as by chance.

I seriously doubt if the song writers' intent was based on any of the definitions above and perhaps the verb definitions of the word fall are extreme in terms of matters of the heart. However, the MESSAGES given us suggest that to fall, whether it occur in love or down a flight of stairs, in many ways render us hurt, deprived or to some degree wounded.

A mate selection intervention that I integrate into my practice has as its origin one of the many Twelve Step Programs. It entails identifying the positive and negative traits and/characteristics of ones father and mother. The purpose of the intervention is to have the client list those same traits in his mate (or prospective mate) and to determine if they were or are in search of the same. In summary, the results often suggests that the client has and continues to make numerous attempts to coerce his mate into being more like/less mom or dad, or to bring resolution to his parents' marital discord that he had neither the tools or skills-sets to rectify.

Child's Play

Listen to the one who had questions about her role in her family. "I am not a member of this family"? Sure I was born into it but there is no relationship of them and me. There exists a relationship of him and her and yet I am a faceless, invisible rejected entity produced out of expectation. The child concludes if I were never born then my parents would be happier. Further, he may surmise that since my birth I am the only reason they remain in marital discord...adding isn't that what adults do?

What happens to the child born into this union that was at one time alive and filled with energy though misdirected? What happens is the child gets the MESSAGE. If the MESSAGE is "you were a mistake" then it doesn't matter what behaviors you choose, where you go, what goals you establish, who you date and so on. Can you see the seeds of antisocial behavior being planted? Drug and alcohol abuse, unwanted pregnancy and disease as a result of promiscuity? If the MESSAGE is..."You are invisible or you should be," then this may be the impetus for children acting as if they are indeed invisible. It is therefore easy to enumerate seeds that were planted that produced low self-esteem, depression, anxiety, rage that is directed toward self, and other mental and physical maladies.

Bulimia and anorexia are means of becoming smaller and more invisible (smaller in size yet more in control). Compulsive over-eating is also an attempt to run and hide inside a body insuring that the person will not be seen even if sought. Suicide is the answer to becoming invisible and the ultimate form of self-hatred. There are instances of parents walking into a hospital room only to see an emaciated young woman in the bed barely alive. The anorexic child has had to pay a very terrible price to gain some measure of attention and control. Her efforts to wrest some identification as a family member may even cost her her life.

Once it is clear that children may be coaxed into a power play where the most powerful member wins then we can easily understand how initiating and continuing certain behaviors can direct the power away from the dominant players. What happens when the marriage is in danger? If the children were the mortar, the rubber bands and even the bubble gum that kept the marriage together, then when they fail it is logical that the parents would blame the children for falling down on the job.

It's My Fault!

"Mom and dad can't get along. They fight, they argue about money, extramarital affairs, religious preference, me and my siblings, unfulfilled needs and the shortcomings of each other. They never appear to be very happy together. They are never satisfied with the way things are. It's my fault isn't it?" These statements made by a close friend, an adult woman in her early twenties summarizes the analysis at which children arrive when they have been parentified or triangulated and eventually blamed for bad relationships.

To parentify a child is the act of placing the child in the role of husband, wife, or confidant, disclosing the most intimate details of a couples' life. In mathematical terms triangulation is defined as: "The location of an **unknown** point [the child], as in navigation, by the formation of a triangle having the unknown point and two **known** points [mom and dad] as the vertices." Similarly, in the study of mental health, triangulation is the tendency for the third party to be co-opted into any two person system. The two people form strong pressure for the third person to act out a role that will perpetuate and stabilize the two-person system. The person I speak of received MESSAGES from both parents. And their MESSAGES communicate general dissatisfaction.

An environment of pretend was the operating system for many of us during our formative years, and still persists. If asked, both parents would say that their relationship has endured financial calamities, in-laws, infidelity and the like. At one time dad was without employment when the automotive factory closed. Mother worked two jobs during this time to help support the family. During this time both felt unsupported by each other. However, as children or pawns powerless and egocentric in this emotionally charged marital game we may respond as most children do in times of discord or trauma. We may inquire "what will happen to me?" "It's my fault isn't it?" What will happen to my family? If these questions are asked repeatedly and no answer provided, or the answer is interpreted by the child as a blow from which there is no recovery then feelings of trust and security will evade us.

It is my fault, isn't it? Many times it is easier to blame the innocent because they have no voice and no choice. It was easier for dad to blame his infidelity on the pressures of fatherhood and husbandry than to acknowledge MESSAGES of inadequacy and mistrust firmly planted in his family of origin. When a child or adolescent begins to act upon the imprinted MESSAGE of worthlessness by choosing to use and abuse substances and destructive relationships, dad may find excuses to further disconnect from the family. In an effort to do the motherly thing, mom may choose to provide support and make attempts to save the confused child.

I now pose the following; is it possible for a mother to have a pure agenda of motherhood? Or for some is motherhood a means to acquire esteem, acceptance, a love that will never leave, or a guaranteed connection to the child's father? Do we create the illusion of the perfect homemaker and wife and mother in hopes of feeling appreciated? As mothers are our motives attempts to be seen in a positive light because of the things we do and therefore meet with someone else's approval? In many instances, yes, is the resounding answer.

In marriage it is the wife who uses non-verbal cues to have her needs met rather than ask another to intervene. For example one question often raised by expectant mothers "Could you please explain this to my husband?" has been heard throughout encounters with physicians, counselors, car salesmen, plumbers and the like. In the therapeutic setting this may suggest fear, dependence/inadequacy and is often asked when for the first time a client experiences understanding, empathy, solidarity or stands on common ground with another. This question is often asked under the guise of humor though the request is sincere. The following questions have been asked as a means to have the concerns of a female affirmed by another to explain "things" her male counterpart;

"I have not been able to speak directly"
"My issues with my husband can not be addressed for fear of
upsetting the delicate balance or the tenuous peace."
"I have not been taught that risk-taking is a part of life."
"I don't want to be rejected."

"I am afraid."

"I do not want to be alone."

"I have not been given permission to place myself first."

"You should learn to move beyond past things that hurt."

"It will be your fault if things don't work out."

In a real sense the statements above were shared because she has learned from her mate...

"I don't want to hear what's wrong with this relationship"

Where do these statements originate and what do they mean? To state the obvious most of us have witnessed this phenomenon in their own homes. Still many have noted the silence and attempted to break it in their own marriages, but without "permission" the spouse may be relegated to respond to learned behaviors and MESSAGES of self-deprecation. How often do we hear that the marital union gives the individual permission to cast aside all logical thinking, all power of discernment of right and wrong and worse still that this state is one where it is acceptable to sublimate or deny your own personal feelings or aspirations?

It is a state of being where we are permitted to openly disapprove of our mate's parents, dissolve affirming relationships, sacrifice all that we have or ever will have, or remain silent continue to justify unhealthy behaviors. These are all examples of the permissive nature of ill-health that is often seen among individuals who are needy; possess unstable boundaries, confusing right and wrong, and involved in improper and inappropriate behaviors all activated by earlier MESSAGES.

This is our little secret...

Singularly and collectively women, and to a lesser degree men, are exposing the terrible crime of incest that has been perpetrated upon them in their own homes. Their stories reveal much about this phenomenon. Incest is an act of power and the victimizer has an accomplice in the home. These data are well known to those who research the patterns of sexual abuse. It is the second point that I wish to explore. Why does this practice go on for years through generations and sadly with several children in the family? I propose the following reasons; Children are not the protected precious progeny of the family that they were designed to be. There exists another agenda that supersedes the welfare of children.

The need of the mother to have a husband, a mate, or a companion is so prevailing that she may deny that this heinous crime is occurring within the walls of her own home. What is more disheartening she may in some instances offer her daughter as a sacrificial lamb if it will please her companion, oblivious that to the victim this is the ultimate MESSAGE that you don't matter. This conspiracy of silence is the crux for maintaining the status quo or homeostasis. Balance must be maintained. If no one talks, then no one has to listen. If no one objects or sounds the alarm then it is easier to deny later that this act of betrayal happened. Silence preserves the illusions. But, silence is the illusion. Somewhere deep inside of every family member there is knowledge that something is wrong and cancerous and desperately in need of change. Once this knowledge is acquired and appropriately responded to the individual can withdraw his participation in the conspiracy, give voice to the anguish and anger inside, and begin his or her journey as a survivor rather than a victim.

Unlike the painful situation mentioned above, I invite you to consider less repulsive scenarios that are made manifest in the midst of marital discord. Where or when is dad allowed to exhibit his vulnerability without fear of being castrated? What happens when dad is denied sexual intimacy because his wife perceives that he has failed in some area and uses sex as a tool to be negotiated for, bid on, marketed or used as monetary compensation? This diminishes the expression of intimacy through sex, making it a saleable commodity.

Conversely, how does mom display anger and or hurt without fear of being labeled a "b---h." Why does she often feel intimidation and disdain for wanting more, be it improved social status, economic security, and most important her own thoughts, dreams and aspirations?

Clearly, the MESSAGES received in the scenarios noted above produce resentment, hostility and a lack of communication. Additionally, non-verbal cues can render ones mate feeling isolated and inadequate. Hopefully when we envision healthy MESSAGES from the marriage we will predict a celebration rather than a sublimation of the husband or wife's person hood. It is our desire, both male and female, that we will be engaged in a marriage that energizes (like the bunny) and propels us to be better and safer and stronger and more tolerant and grateful. A relationship that started in the intimate places between man and woman and emanates outward to others.

We may clearly embrace the notion of "and they lived happily ever after." But when this fairy tale existence does not come to fruition how and when are the children affected by these various and often subtle MESSAGES from the marriage? Daniel Goleman author of *"Childhood Depression"* suggests;

> Contrary to popular belief, even mild episodes of depression in childhood are often harbingers of repeated, more serious bouts of depression later in life...The finding challenges the assumption that a period of depression in a child is an isolated effect—that children 'grow out of it.

Invariably, children emulate their parents' reactions to stress, anger, conflict, and use of manipulation. Based on a number of studies, not only does the child feel at fault for marital discord but may display symptoms of depression. Unrecognized for years, the problem of depression among children was not officially diagnosed until 1980. The following, taken from the DSM IV, list the symptoms of depression;

> A depressed or irritable mood for most of the day, more days than not, for at least one year (and never being without these feelings for more than two months), plus two of the following:

- poor appetite or overeating
- insomnia or oversleeping
- low energy or fatigue
- low self-esteem
- poor concentration or difficulty making decisions
- feelings of hopelessness

Up to this point my focus has been directed toward families with both biological parents and siblings. However, with the advent of the skyrocketing divorce rate step or blended families are common occurrences that are growing on a daily basis. Since 1980 there has been a fifty percent increase in marriages involving single women and divorced men; and single men and divorced women have increased by over sixty percent. Concurrently, marriage involving two previously divorced people has almost doubled. As we now find ourselves in the twenty-first century it is unlikely that there will be any significant changes in the patterns of the past two decades. What MESSAGES are given and received in these families.

One study was conducted entitled *Parent-Child Interaction and Gender Differences in Early Adolescent's Adaptation to Stepfamilies.* The authors listed four behavioral hypotheses relevant to gender differences in a child's response to remarriage. The first suggested that daughters in stepfamilies are more withdrawn from family interaction and more oppositional toward residential or step parents than daughters in intact families. Second, differences in a child's behavior toward parents in intact families and what we now call blended families is greater for daughters than for sons. Third, stepfathers are less oppositional, less directive, and more positive toward their stepchildren, yet less able to gain compliance from them than are fathers in intact families. And finally, mothers in stepfamilies are more oppositional and less directive toward their children and less able to gain compliance from them than are mothers in intact families. Although the study was conducted through the use of videotape equipment in the home, which obviously affected the validity and reliability of family interaction, my experience does indicate that girls in stepfamilies have more difficulty interacting with stepfathers than do sons. I propose that their avoidance may be related to girls' uncertainty about sex roles. Overall, the results did reveal that important differences in parent-child interaction do occur between stepfamilies and intact families.

One additional study theorized that contrary to what some might expect remarriage families are not more stable than first-marriage families. Author William H Walsh listed twenty major issues in remarriage families and placed them in one of the following four categories; Initial family issues; Developing family issues; Feelings about self and others; and Adult issues. The author proposed that in practice the issues are interdependent and do not fit neatly into categories. However, he includes issues that are said to be "primary precipitators" of a crisis in families. Walsh notes such concerns as loss of the natural parent, name for the new parent, confusion over family roles, discipline by the stepparent and sexual conflict. In light of this increasing phenomenon what additional MESSAGES will all concerned family members encounter?

Finally, I hear imploring of those who gave what they considered was unconditional love but over time realized that there were so many conditions and strings attached that the mate or spouse or boyfriend or girlfriend could not possibly be or meet the expectations of the other. The MESSAGE that should be relayed is that gambling with great treasure is folly and that if an individual is never mated to someone then there is fulfillment in this state as well.

*Relate...**shun**...ships*

Isn't it ironic that the MESSAGES I offered to you throughout this book by adding this section as an afterthought says much about the MESSAGES I too have received relative to relationships. That is to say that there are parent-parent MESSAGES, parent-child MESSAGES and then as the young person moves into adulthood, there are husband-wife MESSAGES, or a recapitulation of the first three chapters. But admittedly an equally important body of thought emerged quietly and powerfully as the following images surfaced with clarity. Images that bring to mind that formidable period of time society labels and whispers with sympathy "being alone."

For most, at least prior to the experience of aloneness, we grow and move physically away from mother and father only to substitute connectedness and dependency by placing a high value on relationships with our peers and eventually a mate. During adolescence we claim nonconformity but in truth the highest conformity is with our peers or the group with which we share kindred spirits and things that we view as vitally important, whether it entails dress, hair style, music, choice of career, common goals or ideologies. Relationship is viewed as a street going two ways. During this period the individual expends time relating to the group and the group relating back to the individual. Additionally, we generally share some commonality in our choice of music, dance, and ideologies, unaware that our choices are the weft and warp of the adolescent quilt. Young women commonly make choices regarding the beginning or end of relationships in accordance with the majority opinion. Likewise, young men make choices regarding their fraternity, be it sports, academia or social circle that they chose to affiliate. But here again, be reminded that there is a period in an individual's life that we may encounter at various times without commitment to or with someone.

This cycle occurs continuously or intermittently and is vital to our personal development because it serves as a mirror revealing what we learn about ourselves and perhaps in the future a coveted relationship(s). Once again, I apologize to the detached that I have initially and without forethought ignored. These individuals, who whether by design or circumstance, are not physically or emotionally connected, to a mate, a mother, father, brother, sister, husband, child or peer. I further add that contrary to the MESSAGES received from society, including friends and family, this is indeed a very special time. The time of aloneness (not loneliness) is a time for introspection and personal growth. And I congratulate you as you have emerged in spite of the MESSAGES as all truth does.

Admittedly, the MESSAGES permeating the social substrata have defined relationship as something insidious, dangerous with the capacity to engulf us much like the science fiction creature "the Blob." However, freezing temperatures won't dissuade its progression. This time a relationship which was meant to sustain us through both wonderful times and tragic times has been reduced to an imitation buddy movie or "Friends" television show or Waiting to Exhale" party without the substantive foundation of trust and intimacy. Encounters between people have now become vignettes where soap-operas are played out…relate, relate, relate, followed by the predictable shun episode and the story line continues. Only the names and faces change. What do we in fact learn during this period of disconnection? The cliché that suggests that "no man is an island," does to some degree bear truth. However, life mandates a period of time when we do indeed walk alone. Without question, we may have the physical presence of well wishers, supportive friends and family, but the painful reality of aloneness pervades our thoughts and dreams. Questions that may come to mind include: Will I be alone during old age? What will happen to me when the company downsizes? How do I handle the loss of a spouse through death or divorce? Where can I go to find comfort when my children have full lives and no longer need me? Who will be there when my parents need constant care and perhaps a place to die with dignity? Although these questions entail the necessity of support and understanding from someone, anyone, the harsh reality is that we may indeed find ourselves facing these situations alone.

Several writers and psychologists have suggested that for most, age thirty-five is the approximate age when individuals encounter the dreaded "Midlife Crisis." Gail Sheehy, in her book entitled *Passages,* defines midlife somewhere between adolescence (ages eighteen to thirty-four) and elderescence (age fifty-five plus). She notes that during the stage of adolescence we believe that possibilities are endless. At this young, rather naive' stage of existence, we may maintain the hope or illusion that one day we will marry, become president of our company, bear children and/or experience great wealth. But once age thirty-five no longer looms on the horizon we may express and manifest signs of hopelessness and futility. Sheehy further adds that our assumptions are in truth based on the Biblical standard that promises us seventy years of life, noting that half of seventy is thirty-five. Obviously, the question may surface, whether stated aloud or muttered quietly, that asks "what should I do now that half of my life over?" For women the urgency of attaining a mate and child bearing becomes a major issue. For the male the possibility of acquiring that position of status and financial security may begin to fade.

If one investigates the mindset of both male and female they may hear the subtle parental and societal MESSAGES that mandate marriage for the female and success for the male by a certain age.

The words resonate; "Be connected to someone or something to have worth and value!" Once again if we are not in some way connected, our beliefs, based on the words from numerous MESSENGERS, suggest that we will spend our remaining years in despair. Consequently, support groups abound from singles groups to parents who have lost children. These groups may in some instances provide some measure of circumscribed solace. However, it is during the late or early morning hours when the blanket of isolation, hopelessness, and aloneness cover us to the point of suffocation and we know with certainty that unlike Dorothy on the yellow brick road, we do not have the Tin Man (with a heart), the Lion (full of courage), or the Scarecrow (who possesses intellectual genius) to lessen the fear of the unknown.

Each time that we rise from the position of aloneness, dust covered, eager to brush ourselves off and respond to the MESSAGE "oh don't be so selfish...consider your blessings," we may later experience moments of anger, resentment and rage buried deep inside. But the subtle MESSAGES at play demand that we ignore feelings that we have been indoctrinated with and replace them with the MESSAGE that "it is more blessed to give than to receive." But to give what? Our time, talent, and finances? or To give our essence? To sacrifice the who of us at all cost.

This brings to mind the words made by the character known as Spock in one of the many *Star Trek* sequels. In one episode Spock, the pointy-eared, deeply philosophical Vulcan is enclosed in a glass cage. He is indeed touted to be the most gifted, talented and/or influential contributor to the whole of society, yet he is imprisoned by a glass cage filled with radiation, struggling to breathe but determined to do what is best for all of mankind. Although Captain Kirk entreats him to free himself his life ends (until the next sequel) with this statement; "the one for the many." The viewer's initial response may range from how wonderful to what a tragedy. In truth he like many of us was alone and prepared to make this supreme sacrifice. The key here is that he was first alone and second prepared. In fact he has chosen to sacrifice himself fully informed and prepared for his destiny and responding to the MESSAGE that his life, though valuable, must take second place as he considers what is best for all of mankind.

Although the scenario above has several positive implications we often fail to recall the times when Christ, our Savior was alone. During his aloneness on the cross (the most critical), suffering not for the many but for all, he cries aloud "Why has thou forsaken me?" This verse recited in annual Easter plays and in the powerful movie *The Passion of Christ*, has often been recited as a matter of course or for dramatic purposes. But consider the times Christ spent alone and in preparation for His calling. He was alone in the wilderness (Mat. 4:1) "Then was Jesus led up of the spirit into the wilderness to be tempted of the devil." John chapter four speaks of Jesus alone when approached by the woman of Samaria. And how often did Jesus attempt to steal away to be alone to pray to his Father? Our retort may be the scripture in Genesis that states "it is not good for man to be alone." But what of Paul's rendering when he notes the gift of being unmarried? From Paul's perspective aloneness is generally a time to be coveted. A time to replenish. A time to hear our own thoughts. A time to hear from God through the Holy Spirit.

Many great men and women have shared both the excitement and ennui of being alone. We have no clue as to what Thomas Edison experienced alone in his workroom as he felt compelled to light the world. Neither do we know what Ameila Erhart thought as she attempted to navigate around the globe in her single engine plane. We may further believe that she, like so many other intellectually endowed individuals, was alone on several levels. Ms. Erhart was alone in vision, thought, commitment, feelings of disappointment and possibly the fear of failure. Does that explain the possibility of her flying off to regions unknown? We can only speculate. Now reflect upon and then ask yourself how often or in what situations you have willingly given your "essence" for the good of another only to be mocked, demeaned or taken for granted.

Many individuals enter my office with what they perceive as obvious issues or maladies readily and easily defined as depression, suicidal ideations, unwanted pregnancy, social phobias, eating disorders and the like. But it is only through keen insight that real issues are exposed. These core issues may have been lying dormant beneath the absence or potential break in one relationship or another. Individuals disclose that each time they experience passion and connectedness, there appears to be a cycle of first relating on a meaningful level followed by a moving away or sense of being shunned, then involvement in another relationship, then moving away and the cycle continues. It is here that I question who in fact initiates this cycle? Is it the individual being shunned by another? or Does the fear of intimacy encourage the person to use various devices, guaranteeing relationship failure? Let us examine this cycle more closely.

We are all too familiar with the word sabotage. According to John Ayto's *Dictionary of Word Origins,* "the etymological idea underlying sabotage is of 'clattering along in noisy shoes.' Sabotage originates from its French ancestor, sabot, a word of unknown origin which means 'clog.'" He adds further;

> From it [sabotage] was derived saboteur 'walk along noisily in clogs,' hence (via the notion of 'clumsiness')...and finally destroy tools, machines, etc. deliberately. This in turn formed the basis of the noun sabotage, which originally denoted the destruction of machinery by factory workers, but gradually broadened out to include any deliberate disruptive destruction.

But now consider its meaning relative to the establishment or disengagement of a relationship. Keep in mind that relationships include parent to child, friend to friend, sibling to sibling, teacher to student, boss to subordinate, man to woman and so on. Further, as mentioned above, the relationship supposedly begins with a sense of connectedness and communion. Words often spoken or implied include; "My purpose in this relationship is to serve," "Everything or person you like I like," "I will always agree with your point of view," "Your friends and family are different, but divine," "My needs will always be second to yours," "I am willing to sacrifice who I am to please you," "I see your shortcomings but they are insignificant." These statements implied or otherwise stated are frequently heard during the so-called "Honeymoon period."

It was through the use and administration of an instrument that I used during my years as a training manager that I embraced the notion of three progressive stages that occur during any and all relationships. The Fundamental Interpersonal Relations Orientation-Behavior (FIRO-B) tool assesses how an individual's personal needs affect a person's behavior towards another. This self-report instrument offers insight into an individual's compatibility with other people, as well as providing insight into that person's basic characteristics. Additionally, the FIRO-B measures a person's needs for:

Expressed Behavior (E)—what a person prefers to do, and how much that person wants to initiate action.

Wanted Behavior (W)—how much a person wants others to initiate action, and how much that person wants to be the recipient

It further measures a person's need for:

Inclusion (I)—recognition, belonging, and participation

Control (C)—influence, leading, and responsibility

Affection (A)—closeness, warmth, and sensitivity

In addition to the above measurements, the FIRO-B identifies three stages that occur in any and all our relationships.

Stage 1. Orientation
Stage 2. Conflict
Stage 3. Cohesion.

At and during stage one or the orientation stage, the two individuals are predictably tentative with each other. They are generally cautious, polite and both parties are likely to be extremely flexible and dependent upon the other. We have all seen or experienced the kind of "goo goo-eyed" looks each give the other, coupled with an aptness to appear somewhat non-assertive. Conversations are directed toward the needs and desires of the other individual. The all too familiar dialogue may begin with; "Where would you like to go?" or "What would you like to do?" "Oh, it's up to you" "No, it's up to you" "I don't care it's really up to you." Obviously, this scenario is generally played out by individuals of the opposite sex, attempting to display a non-threatening or non-controlling position. The outcome, two people naively enter into a relationship believing that the other is genuinely and sincerely there to meet his or her needs. The assumption is then made that we are relating or have established an enviable relationship.

One extremely insightful yet frustrated client envisioned himself as a vessel filled to the brim with cool water and with anticipation that "someone" would appear who was willing to drink. He further shared that during the initial stags of his relationship with a supposed thirsty individual he offered his entire vessel, patiently waiting and expecting some degree of reciprocation. After several months into the relationship he discovered that his vessel was now half full and the reciprocity he expected never came to fruition. He endeavored to encourage his partner to open up and "share her experiences and expectations" only to be shunned and ultimately left with excuses for little or no dialogue.

Perhaps the above level of intimacy does not subsist with teacher, boss or peer however the same general principles apply. During this stage, the pervasive themes are caution, polite conversation, attentiveness and a tendency to appear other person focused. Both parties have consciously chosen to present "their good side," for the sake of the relationship. In an earlier chapter we listed Erikson's eight stages of development. The fifth stage (ages 12-18) emphasizes an integrated image of oneself as a unique person. How and when do we lose this unique person so willing to sacrifice ourselves and ignore the promptings from what I define as our soul sentinel? The answer is obvious, if we are not taught to value ourselves, our uniqueness, candor, and apprehensions we may indeed begin a journey that starts with relating only to end with an experience of rejection. One comedian likened this stage to role playing. He stated that during the initial stage of dating we are not involved with the other person it is their "representative" that we are engaged.

The following quote personifies the second stage of relationship— CONFLICT

"I have lost friends, some by death...others by sheer inability to cross the street." Virginia Woolfe In her statement I find a greater and more in depth understanding of a loss relationship. The person who is unwilling to be vulnerable, to take risk, to reach out, to make sacrifice or to put ego aside to pursue may be taken aback when for seemingly unknown reasons the waiting individual withdraws from the relationship.

Cohesion is the final stage. It is during this stage that we experience a period of coming together due to our acceptance of the other individual (warts and all). Although cohesion is stated to be the third and final stage please note that we continue to cycle through the various stages as each person experiences change.

Hopefully, you have identified the origin of the numerous MESSAGES that you received from parents and other family members that ultimately failed. This knowledge, the most difficult to embrace, will start you on your journey toward awareness and fulfillment. However, in the following chapters I offer additional insights into MESSAGES sent and received from academia, religious institutions and society that continue to impair our journey to a life replete with optimism and hope.

CHAPTER FIVE

It's More than the 3 Rs

Education makes people easy to lead,
But difficult to drive.
Easy to govern, but impossible to enslave
—Henry Peter Brougham

In his work, *No Exit*, Jean-Paul Satre states that we are formed into the very beings that others external to ourselves perceive us to be. Another writer suggests that it is not who we think we are, or even who others think we are, **but** who we think other people think we are. In this chapter I review other noteworthy statements that are in concert with our views relative to our educational systems.

Based on the MESSAGES that we receive, we regularly review our list of titles, labels, and roles that have been assigned to us. Despite our efforts to ignore or dismiss the MESSAGES that attempt to mold who we are, paradoxically we find ourselves embracing these same labels, identities, classifications and or personalities that others have given us. What thoughts regarding the who of you do you regularly visit or repeat?

It was during the writing of this book that one of my editors disclosed that my style of writing would positively influence people from all walks of life. His words gave me the impetus to continue to reveal the authentic me. In essence throughout my years of writing I had learned to ignore the numerous accolades, writer's awards, statements of excellence and so on.

The positive MESSAGE above was negated by earlier MESSAGES that suggested that my writing was "too emotional." In essence I was programmed to believe words that discouraged because they simply were more powerful and continued to take precedence. I was guilty of one of David Burn's ten distortions "Disqualifying the Positive." Have you moved forward or remained stagnant because of negative MESSAGES received from another? You may recall the MESSAGES from a parent, family member or caregiver who thought of you as an average or below average student or perhaps an exceptional scholar. You may have affirmed their perceptions regarding your academic abilities and despite your own inner voice responded accordingly.

Parents or caregivers are not the sole contributors to our emotional and social development. In an earlier chapter, I noted that our educational experiences influence our thoughts, behaviors and unquestionably mold our basic nature. Most if not all of us can recall our first day of school. As you reflect on that first day you may recall feelings of either fear of the unknown, parent-child separation, or feelings of ecstasy about the opportunity to be a big girl or boy. Regardless of our early remembrances the experience introduced and prepared us for the required skills for appropriate socialization and academic success or failure.

Within our Bibles or the sacred text there are verses that remind us of the fragility yet forthrightness of children. Jesus frequently referred to children as examples of individuals in God's kingdom. One story notes that when groups of children approached Christ his disciples made efforts to send them away. This event brought to mind times in our home when the adults were engrossed in conversation and if I or my siblings entered the room we were plainly told that "this is grown folk conversation." The MESSAGE was clear, disappear, become invisible or find another way to get your conversational needs met. Conversely, Jesus' retort to his disciples was "suffer the little children to come unto me and forbid them not for such is the kingdom of heaven." Matthew Henry notes in his commentary:

It is well when we come to Christ ourselves, and bring our children. Little children may be brought to Christ as needing, and being capable of receiving blessings from him, and having an interest in his intercession. We can but beg a blessing for them: Christ only can command the blessing. It is well for us, that Christ has more love and tenderness in him than the best of his disciples had. And let us learn of him not to discountenance any willing, well-meaning souls, in their seeking after Christ, though they are but weak. Those who are given to Christ, as part of his purchase, he will in no wise cast out. Therefore he takes it ill of all who forbid, and try to shut out those whom he has received. And all Christians should bring their children to the Saviour that he may bless them with spiritual blessings. Mat 19:13-15

Further research on this scripture revealed that in this case the word children, does not necessarily imply chronological age. The children that Christ spoke of included the newly saved or weaker Christian.

In academia the student is first taught to know his place. No interruptions please despite the teacher's failure to recognize that a real need may exist. Sadly to date this MESSAGE is an unspoken part of the curricula offered in the majority of our schools or institutions of higher learning. What is communicated by many teachers is for the student to; "Be good!" "Be smart!" "Be quiet!" "Fit in!" "Use the color green for grass, blue for the sky and yellow for the sun," and most import "Color inside the lines!" It is because of these very MESSAGES that later in life we endeavor to dispel the hold that these restrictive MESSAGES may foster.

I Pledge Allegiance

From our early years in the formal institutions of learning we embark upon a quest of learning intended to teach the basic tenets of math, reading and writing and to shape our fundamental social skills. At home we are taught everything from "potty training" to saying "please" and "thank you." At pre-school and elementary, we are taught to share our toys at recess and how to play "team" ball or "wait our turn." The value of such education is certainly immeasurable else we would become a society of narcissi. According to the Diagnostic and Statistical Manual of Mental Disorders (DSM-IV), Narcissism is defined as "a pervasive pattern of grandiosity (in fantasy or behavior), need for admiration, and lack of empathy, beginning by early adulthood and present in a variety of contexts..." But first allow me to identify the MESSAGES that were fostered during our years in academia.

So what if little Johnny never learns to "color inside of the lines?" What if little Susie does not want to "share" her new Barbie doll at recess today? Remember knowledge empowers and provides choices. And empowerment is the ability and act of taking the knowledge, assessing it and applying it creatively and instinctively to differing situations.

Does Johnny truly understand that according to the standards set forth by our institutions of learning, that it is better to color within the lines? If so, what penalties will he face when his own intuitive and cognitive assessments rail against this MESSAGE? In his home he was taught to question, explore, examine and use the gifts that he had been given. In this regard, why then is Johnny potentially labeled, antisocial or learning disabled when he chooses to apply more creative skills when coloring? At this point, the knowledge of coloring inside the lines has actually worked to Johnny's possible demise.

Johnny, for his flare to view life in the abstract which is the truest expression of freedom, becomes destined to be treated as weird or non compliant until he receives a MESSAGE that encourages and acknowledges his inalienable right to self expression.

In defense of academia I pause here to insert the following, the examples above and following speak against the **"educational system"** and not education.

Educators and teachers are esteemed positions yet their salaries suggest otherwise. These individuals are responsible for helping to shape the minds foremost of our young children, and ultimately the adolescents and young adults who will one day determine the issues that concern generations to come. Throughout scripture Jesus is called Rabbi and Master translated Teacher. Consider the various tools that he used to "educate" both disciple and follower. It was through his use of parables in the Synoptic Gospels (Matthew, Mark, Luke, John) that he clarified, informed, challenged and simply taught life's truths. He felt no need to impress others by speaking in words that his followers would not understand. Even the Apostle Paul only spoke of his credentials when speaking to the church at Philippi and possibly when challenged by a sect known as the Pharisees that presented themselves as superior intellectually and spiritually. It is here Paul lists, as we may, his education, family tree, certificates, degrees, awards. He writes;

> For we are the circumcision, who worship by the Spirit of God, and glory in Christ Jesus, and have no confidence in the flesh: though I myself might have confidence even in the flesh: if any other man thinketh to have confidence in the flesh, I yet more:

> Circumcised the eighth day, of the stock of Israel, of the tribe of Benjamin, a Hebrew of Hebrews; as touching the law, a Pharisee; as touching zeal, persecuting the church; as touching the righteousness which is in the law, found blameless.

> Howbeit what things were gain to me, these have I counted loss for Christ.

> Yea verily, and I count all things to be loss for the excellency of the knowledge of Christ Jesus my Lord: for whom I suffered the loss of all things, and do count them but refuse, that I may gain Christ, and be found in him, not having a righteousness of mine own, even that which is of the law, but that which is through faith in Christ, the righteousness which is from God by faith.

In verses five and six Paul informs his audience and now we as readers that he was not just an "average Joe." As we might say today he comes from "good stock." However, Paul does not end his statement here instead he adds that his education and background mean nothing as he compares this to knowing Christ. Perhaps as teachers and/or educators we may best serve others by reminding them that an education is important, and a necessity today, but it is our total dependence on Christ through the aid of the Holy Spirit that will touch the hearts and lives of our students.

Consider such esteemed great minds as Thomas Edison who was labeled addled by his teachers, or Pablo Picasso, who was considered a hopeless pupil because he refused to learn mathematics. Were these men exceptions to the rule or just lucky to have achieved success despite their inability to grasp and apply the curriculum based education set before them? Suppose for a moment that the answer to this question is yes. How many Einsteins, Edisons or Picassos lurk behind the walls of the "special education" wards of their grade, middle or high schools? Is this a question that we as society and even more importantly, we as parents can afford to leave unanswered?

Education should be edifying and perpetuating. If we as teachers, parents and the whole of society intend to establish an educational foundation we have a mandate to first conduct an assessment of Johnny's learning style.

Through my many years of teaching adolescents, adults and graduate students I quickly learned that each person approaches learning from different perspectives. In hopes of determining how students and clients learn, I began to administer the Learning Style Inventory (LSI). It was through the use of one of many invaluable tools that I became privy to the "ah hah" that follows when individuals are told that their particular approach to learning is acceptable.

Further, this assessment, in concert with the client's knowledge of failed MESSAGES, has brought liberty, freedom and self acceptance to those who have been labeled weird, slow or dumb and produced confident, creative and positive individuals.

The prescribed rigid style of teaching that was designed to produce cookie cutter learners, has in fact contributed to increased drop-out rates, poor academic results and in the end may be responsible for stifling the creativity of the next Einstein, Colin Powell, Bill Gates, Dr. Maya Angelou, Hillary Clinton, a dedicated working husband and father, committed foster parents rearing six learning disabled children, that single parent, or YOU!.

Reading, Writing and Restrictiveness

Voila! Middle school. Adolescence. The beginning of puberty. Development of independent/peer relating tendencies.To the average pre-teen the importance of education decreases as he becomes more susceptible to influences outside the home, namely his peers. Paradoxically, educators place more credence on our ability to grasp concepts that lie at the root of academia and form our cognitive skills— mathematics, literature, grammar and science. In summary, the student's score on the MEAP test and later the MCAT (medical entrance exam), LCAT (law entrance exam) and other college entrance exams are assumed to determine our potential for success. After all, we need to start preparing for college and consider what we want to be when we grow up.

In sum, this is a critical stage of development for young learners. It can also be a time of volatility or excellence. To gain further insight, relative to our academic prowess, it is necessary to explore the MESSAGES we receive during this stage and revisit the unanswered questions that we asked about social structure, creativity and choice of career path. Further, we must list the things that we witnessed or were partakers of in our home or outside of the classroom that were not in compliance with the "please" and "thank you" or "sharing time" that we were taught.

As noted earlier, Erikson refers to this time period as the fifth stage of his eight life stages. It is a time when the adolescent attains identity or role confusion and hopefully "an integrated image of oneself as a unique person." Erikson purports that during the second, third and fourth stages of development our educational system may have done irreparable damage to some by labeling them educationally and emotionally disabled because they refused to color inside the lines. And just maybe we have labeled others educationally astute because they were more compliant and willing to color inside the lines. In either case, the innocent child has started his/her journey down the path of contradictions as we now communicate to him that he can be or do anything he wants when he grows up. Well…that is as long as it is a doctor, lawyer, engineer, teacher or someone who makes lots of money.

As a parent, it is certainly my intent to encourage other parents to provide their little Johnny or Susie with every opportunity (never afforded me) to fully express themselves via the knowledge and education they acquire. Consequently, as little Johnny (who could never color inside the lines anyway) approaches me and says, "I want to be an abstract artist," how should I respond? Through a subtle form of manipulation I carefully explain to little Johnny just how beneficial college would be to his abstract artist career. When you really think about it this advice is absurd, at least in Johnny's eyes, for two obvious reasons. The first belies the importance of sending a child to a structured and regimented faction of academia to formally teach him how to artistically express what lies at his essence. It is as absurd as teaching him to breathe or blink his eyes. This contradictory MESSAGE is one that has been promoted by our contemporary educational system. Secondly, I am now willing to subject little Johnny to the very same system that labeled him less than average.

Again, I pause here and add that it is not my objective to imply that college is not necessary for Johnny. As an educator I am keenly aware of the benefits of a formal education in the fine arts. However, rather than minimizing Johnny's gift, the better MESSAGE is to regularly expose him to the "masters" and encourage him to use every tool available to **enhance** his existing skills. Certainly, this example may be construed as extreme, but on some level it is applicable to a larger population than one might imagine.

Consider now the opposite scenario. Little Susie always colored within the lines and said "please" and "thank you." Now through positive affirmations, Susie scores extremely high on all standardized I.Q. tests, hence she is consistently told what a great "doctor" she will make. Susie, who has now been ostracized by her peers who can not or will not color inside the lines, is placed into a group of sixth graders labeled by the system as exceptional and perhaps the ultimate success story. Susie is now committed to comply so that she may continue to receive accolades that make her feel good and affirm her reason for being. Painfully, Susie may be placed on a path that she may not be ready to take. The MESSAGE is no longer we want you to succeed; instead the MESSAGE is we expect you to succeed...so you must!!

I recognize that there are students who seemingly never adhere to any social mandates or authority figures and simply lack the desire to learn. Succinctly put there are a number of students who fall into this category. The position I take here is that far too often I am witness to students who upon investigation were recipients of MESSAGES from our educational system that miserably failed them. Consequently, by middle or high school any behaviors conveyed academically or otherwise by students are simply responses to the MESSAGES received from our schools of learning. In light of these facts, the student's educational ineptness or astuteness is not necessarily indicative of the quality of the education he received but of the quality of the educational system from which he received it.

Attention Deficient Disordered children or ADD, as a viable diagnosis was at one time thought to be a reason (or excuse) for failure. In the classroom children are medicated which in of itself sends a MESSAGE that something is wrong with me. What of alternative vehicles for learning? The systems subtle MESSAGE is that it is more cost effective to surrender the unduly labeled student into the hands of the school counselor, psychiatrist, therapist, priest or social worker.

But the fate of our children mandates a reassessment of our current educational system and its distinction from the education it is suppose to foster and carefully discern those MESSAGES that have failed.

It is generally known within our colleges and on university campuses that some of our best teachers (you know, people who can paint a picture so clearly that learning is effortless along with those who extract the best from you) for whatever reason never make it through the tenure gauntlet. It is a required practice that full professors bowing to the pressure of publish or perish summon graduate assistants to teach lowly underclassmen. This expresses the focus of academia as an either or phenomenon. Either I am a good researcher or I am a good instructor. The ideal would be to add validation to those who are purely teachers and also to discontinue requiring non-teachers to teach. Those who do both well should be acknowledged for their diverse talents.

Education is a function of faith and love. We are asked to learn tables, facts and formulas often with no indication as to where this knowledge will be applied. We learn them because we trust the teacher, or we have an inherent love for the subject matter. Very little is retained and applied in a vacuum. But in truth real education and learning starts, continues and ends in the home and with people whom you love and who love you.

It is also evident that our schools are a microcosm of our society at large. Therefore, it has become a place where students are prejudged and predestined to succeed or fail because of their ability to fit into the caricatures of the societal cartoon. It is obvious that I consider academia critical to the survival of our society. However, the realization is that schools are made and managed by people and that people will bring with them certain preferences into the academic environment. But there are no excuses for MESSAGES that stifle and restrict creativity. It is important to acknowledge that school is a place that we are legally required to attend. This so named institution of learning has as its charge the young and those who are not permitted a voice.

Without question schools are made and managed by people and that people will bring with them certain preferences into the academic environment. But we can not excuse the transference of responsibility from teacher to parent or parent to teacher/society because of the harm it does.

A Higher Yearning

Education can not simply be assessed by what is taught behind hallowed ivy-covered walls. It must be viewed as awareness that transcends the mere learning of reading, writing and arithmetic; it is holistic in nature and pervades every aspect of our lives. Further, true education is that which reaches beyond our DNA. Therefore, a child who receives MESSAGES that teach him to judge people based on differing cultures, religious preference, socioeconomic status, or skin color is in the purest sense, uneducated. However, if this same child has a positive encounter with someone differing in ethnicity, financial status AND his misconceptions are dispelled, then it can inarguably be said that this child has indeed been well educated.

Once we complete the required twelve years of education many of us look forward to an advanced degree that guarantees success if not esteem and admiration. But there is another MESSAGE on the horizon. Consider the accreditation process of our colleges and universities (which set the overall educational mood of a nation, society, or culture.) These schools of higher learning are seeking accreditation in their respective curriculum. Accreditation however is based on the number of research grants given in a particular time period, for certain areas of concentration, the number of students enrolled, the number of doctorate of philosophy professors on staff etc. Unfortunately these are all designations that are meaningless to the true pursuer of an education. What MESSAGE does academia send to those of us in search of an education versus a degree (there is a difference)? After all, had little Johnny been made to understand that education is not in "coloring inside the lines" but in knowing what crayons are, that they come in a rainbow of colors and that they are available to him, perhaps he would not have given up so easily on life.

Relative to our educational system, I offer one essential MESSAGE and that is to discontinue teaching our children what to think and start teaching them how to think. How would our society advance if we prepared its members at the earliest possible moment to gather information in mega doses, analyze, and draw logical and insightful conclusions that avail them the opportunity to actively and passionately proceed and finally to implement a plan based on the information that they have gathered?

Further what benefits would our society gain as a whole if we were empowered, enlightened and encouraged to learn for learning sake? It is almost inconceivable to think of where our nation would be if the energies and talents of people were maximized first for individual edification and improvement then for the betterment of society as a whole.

Simply stated, education serves as a vehicle that can drive an individual to the bounds of self-definition. A good education can only be measured by its ability to take us where we choose to go but would not be able to go on our own natural gifts and talents. In light of this, the measurement of one's successful allocation of the education he has received should only be measured by how close he came to his own stated goals and objectives.

Finally, what would be the outcome if our institutions were evaluated like last years wardrobe? The serviceable garments with the appropriate fit would be kept, augmented and preserved for future use. The antiquated and ill-fitting would be discarded or recycled in an appropriate manner. Wouldn't it be immensely rewarding if we, as part of our society, were astute enough to recognize value in the truly valuable and discern inefficiency in waste?

He who opens a school door
Closes a prison
—Victor Hugo

CHAPTER SIX

Society, What Is Your Agenda?

Society; associate, sociable
Latin; socius, meant companion or partner.

In our daily conversations we generally refer to society, of which we are a part, as they, them or those and in doing so make attempts to remove ourselves from accepting responsibility for the demise of our children, governmental and educational systems and the whole of society. But we are part of and do have responsibility for others regardless of the MESSAGES that infer them, their, or those people.

In this chapter hopefully you will claim your inclusive rights and acknowledge the **WE** of the societal MESSAGE.

How have societies come to be? We may observe the animal kingdom as well as our own species for some basic answers. For example, sea creatures or organisms that are swept by ocean currents onto a beach form a loose type of society. Such groups, however, have limited *survival value.* Conversely, animals that tend to locate in an environment that satisfy the needs of the entire group ultimately increase their chances of survival. An environment that is conducive for the acquisition of food, water, shelter, protection and raising ones young have high priority and are deemed essential to the survival of the species. Animal groups, as with mankind, are highly organized in a cooperative manner and become specialized to perform specific jobs. The survival of the group or society depends on the close regulation of these specialists.

I am reminded of the "reality" show entitled "Survival." Although I have not followed the series the implication or premise is that the successful group or winners work collectively to accomplish specific tasks. Individuals that are not contributors are viewed negatively as he or she impacts the group as a whole and in effect determines the success or failure of the group. But how do we define societies whether from the animal kingdom or mankind?

One writer reports;

> Social behavior enables a species to transcend the limits of individual capabilities. The members of societies can specialize to perform different functions, then form groups and integrate their skills. The complexity and efficiency of the group can exceed that of the individual. These two basic qualities, specialization of individuals and integration of groups, are the yardsticks for measuring animal [and human] societies. When integration is sufficiently elaborated and tightened, and combined with high levels of individual intelligence, it can lead to the next great step in the evolution of behavior: the invention of culture-the transmission of learned information from one generation to another.

Forming groups produces a number of positive results. First, grouping brings the sexes together for reproduction. Second, it permits specialization such as leaders, pathfinders, sentinels and protectors. Other members can specialize in such functions as food gathering, feeding, and rearing the young. Work of the society may be distributed along gender lines. Males are more likely to function as hunters/bread winners, protectors and leaders. Female members of the society are generally relegated to function as nurturers/ caregivers, and homemakers. This gender assignment of tasks was and is linked to the member's physical makeup. Third and finally, grouping results in outstanding accomplishments (the Pyramids, NASA, the Great Wall of China) born of orderly, highly functioning societies.

There are however, negative consequences brought about by the formation of groups. When we form groups, we inevitably create a new set of conditions that in turn create new problems. The new problems arise from closer contact among the other members of the group or society. In due time, this increased interaction will influence the behavior of each individual. How the members behave under these circumstances depend on their ability to adapt. A number of researchers investigated the behaviors and impact of individuals living in a large housing complex. Their studies reveal that crime, assault and other heinous crimes were the consequences of living in close proximity of another. Other researchers have even suggested that racial riots and other tensions are due in part to neighborhoods built too close together. Still others espouse competition for mates, food, jobs, and space increases exponentially when organisms are overcrowded. Additionally, competition increases conflict and fighting within the group. The result is that some of the energy that might have been used for the group's survival is exhausted.

Are the MESSAGES above accurate that suggest that shared space among too many family members with too few bedrooms or neighbors with insufficient yard space (rarely if ever used) prone to produce maladaptive behaviors?

Reflect now on each character identified in your Bible and then consider the efforts of each individual whose contribution influenced others either positively or negatively. The first society was comprised of just two individuals, a male and a female. And as God ordained the birth of children was mandated to populate and replenish the earth. Now we have the first formal institution that each of us are part. In just a few chapters things change radically and one brother takes the life of another.

As the scriptures also note, fighting for recognition and position occurred between several of the twelve disciples that followed Christ. Events are recorded that reveal a mother who asked for her sons to be and or receive a position of high esteem. And then there was a disciple who questioned the relationship of another disciple to Christ. These and other situations are not foreign to us despite the passage of two thousand years.

It has been said that to productively channel the social energies of each member, there is a need for social order or some hierarchy so that its members are able to coexist peacefully and harmoniously (the operative word is coexist). However, it is my belief that the MESSAGE of mine, my own, my space, my room, my lawn, has contributed to a general feeling of dissatisfaction, discontent and covetousness. Further, these MESSAGES have encouraged us to initiate dialogues that begin with; them, they, and those that ultimately establishes a foundation that is built on prejudice and racism.

Who's in Charge?

Within the past few decades, the MESSAGE that a dominant individual, invariably male, that led other members from place to place, watched over their activities, occasionally intruded to settle disputes, and vigilantly guarded against enemies, has lost its bite. Is it because the male (as noted in chapter four) must be "there" to defend those that follow him and followers no longer base leadership qualifications on gender? The true leader employs diplomatic routes or strong aggression in order to determine the best defense or method of protection.

Consider traveling from downtown Los Angeles to San Francisco minus clearly posted signs, lines in the highway, speed limits, and appropriately labeled exit signs. If you were to drive without these guidelines how would you determine the side of the road that you should drive? Without policemen to enforce traffic to ensure the safety of both driver and passenger an orderly progression through busy intersections would be non-existent. This would impede your progress such that you would probably never arrive at your final destination. Frustration would likely be your companion and in an effort to vent this anger you may fail to adhere to the posted signs or scream profanities at the driver who has little concern for your needs. This scenario is intended to illustrate the high level of organization in our society that is required to perform simple tasks in highly populated areas. There is and will always be mandates whether implicitly or explicitly communicated for a social system whose basic tenet is order. In Clarke's Commentary the idea of order is addressed relative to First Corinthians 14:40:

> Every thing in its place, every thing in its time, and every thing suitably. Let all things be done decently and in order, is a direction of infinite moment in all the concerns of religion, and of no small consequence in all the concerns of life. How much pain, confusion, and loss would be prevented, were this rule followed! There is scarcely an embarrassment in civil or domestic life that does not originate in a neglect of this precept. No business, trade, art, or science, can be carried on to any advantage or comfort, unless peculiar attention be paid to it. And as to religion, there can be absolutely none without it. Where decency and order are not observed in every part of the worship of God, no spiritual worship can be performed. The manner of doing a thing is always of as much consequence as the act itself. And often the act derives all its consequence and utility from the manner in which it is performed.

The face of the Washington monument bears witness to this fact. It is a majestic symbol standing five hundred fifty five feet, five and one-eight inches above the western end of the Mall in Washington D. C. It is seen from nearly every vantage point in our nation's capitol. Yet when we closely observe the monument there is a difference in the color and size of the initial stone. Construction began in 1848. However, political chaos and the Civil War (1861-1865) halted the construction effort. After the war and when the politicians could agree that this project should be continued the monument was completed. Today we can easily observe the effects of social disorder and disarray on the monument erected to great presidents.

The information above has been included here to illustrate the need for social order and MESSAGES to define the parameters of social interaction. There are, however, social MESSAGES that when applied are contrary and obstructive to achieving a purpose. The statement "the majority rules" intended to tout the benefits of a democratic society decries the fact that in many cases it is the single individual, the small group or the "two or three gathered in my name," that initiate the most significant change. Susan B. Anthony says it best in the following;

> Cautious, careful people, always casting about to preserve their reputation and social standing, never can bring about reform. Those who are really in earnest must be willing to be anything or nothing in the world's estimation, and publicly and privately in season and out, avow their sympathies with despised and persecuted ideas and their advocates, and bear the consequences.

More MESSAGES

In the animal kingdom, the "fit" do survive. Among the fittest is the struggle for dominance and a position closest to the top of the chain of command. This dominance hierarchy is a set of aggressive relationships that develop within a group of animals living together. During my research of the animal kingdom's hierarchical system, I discovered similarities in the thoughts and behaviors of middle to upper management and executives in Fortune 500 companies.

Is it not the goal of entry level management to rise to the top of the corporate ladder? My unscientific study suggests that many managers are prepared to assert themselves, experience verbal abuse, and use various methods of manipulation in order to excel. I further observed that employees, management and otherwise, acknowledge that they must work longer, harder and appropriate the corporate image to secure promotions and gain the coveted higher echelon positions synonymous with power, prestige and wealth. The rewards are tremendous and include; enviable financial compensation in the form of bonuses, profit sharing packages, and stock options. This proverbial "carrot" sends the MESSAGE to win, at all costs even if it means sacrificing valuable time with family and ethical mores.

In light of societies worship of sport icons a common example of the winning MESSAGE is given the high school football, swimming, basketball or track star. The personal exhilaration, the prestige among peers, admiration of adults and dominance in the social pecking order (popularity with members of the opposite sex, invitations to all the really cool parties and guarantees that you will never be labeled a geek) reinforces the win-at-all-costs MESSAGE. This is not a judgment; who among us has not wondered what it would be like to hear the approving roar of a crowd. Perhaps you have even rehearsed an acceptance speech at the Oscar's or stood to receive a standing ovation. Has your hairbrush ever doubled as a microphone? The MESSAGE…this is the stuff of which dreams are made and dreams, as we know, do come true.

Winning is a great motivator for a person or people to strive toward excellence. Winning as the ultimate goal of those who choose to play a game is certainly appropriate. What is inappropriate and what ultimately fails us is the MESSAGE that those who don't aspire to bring home a trophy are losers, less valuable as human beings, or deserve little, if any, consideration. The individual that willingly compromises himself in all areas of his life for the sake of fame, trophies, and money, has the win-at-all-cost MESSAGE to blame. This MESSAGE may be subtle or overt.

The athlete who graduates from high school but can not read or spends four years in college without hope of graduation pays a very high price. This is the price athletic departments, alumni and even the athlete believes he or she has to pay to be a winner or even participate on a winning team. To have an edge or to gain the advantage many athletes with the sanction of their coaches, have sought performance-enhancing drugs. As a result some have long-lasting negative physical consequences such as jaundice, cardiac abnormalities, hepatic cancer or orthopedic maladies. Some have died. Yet, this knowledge has done little to curtail the dangerous methods used to insure that life will be lived behind the so-named sacred velvet rope rather than in front of it.

Society has paid a terrible price in justifying or rationalizing the deficits of the athlete who did not learn to read or who did not acquire the degree to move on to other productive levels Individuals who can not read are easily victimized. In fact, diminished self worth, carte-blanche nullification by a society that has exploited them may lead to anti-social behavior, physical and sexual assaults, or substance abuse.

Advertising agents also exploit the dominance MESSAGE as well. A recent commercial screamed "gain the advantage", "take control", "leave them in the dust". The choice was not to invade Eastern Europe, meet consumer demands of lower gas prices, but to buy a particular expensive brand of automobile.

Another symptom of our ever increasing social sickness is the growing prevalence of gambling among teenagers. A most astute psychologist offered the following analysis of the etiology of teen gambling. "We can all recite the don't MESSAGES; don't drink, don't smoke, don't take drugs, don't have premarital sex. However, you are given the 'win' MESSAGE every day of your life." In this instance the translation is, use, take or involve yourself in and with any vehicle to numb the pain of the past so that you may become faster, stronger and better. Sadly, no one informed the individual about the eventual cost of the MESSAGE. Further, what is more unsettling is the negative regard or even justification for the exclusion of or aggressive tactics toward those who do not conform to the societal image of a winner.

"I-Robot"

Aside from the sports icon-hero, there are other images of a winner. In the corporate world height, weight, hair, grooming, and attire are prescriptions for success. The ideal top level executive is male, at least six feet tall, at or about one hundred and seventy five pounds, married, the father of 2.5 children, with hair length never past the ear. Even the dress of a winner is easily identifiable. John T. Malloy, in his book, *Dress for Success*, suggests that "custom-made suits are unacceptable, white shirts are favored, and light blue is the only acceptable option." Additionally, upper management must never wear loafers. Shoes must lace. Fingernails must be manicured but never with glossy polish. Jewelry should consist of a simple wedding ring without a diamond.

Women in the corporate environment also have a uniform. Just as there exist recommendations for the color of a man's suit, women's suits should be in the navy, gray, or brown family. At one time wearing black was considered taboo, particularly for women because the color was too powerful suggesting the apparel of a mortician (what a visual MESSAGE). Further, women should never wear colored hose, only natural skin tones. It is also suggested that blouses have long sleeves, not too revealing yet feminine enough to be considered female. Purses are thought to look silly with a brief case therefore toss the purse. MESSAGE; remove any article of clothing that may be a reminder to yourself and others that you are a woman. Succinctly put if you want to play the game—be a man.

Contrary to the prior goal of outstanding customer service, creativity, commitment and excellence, in the global markets of today the proclamation of the **conformity** MESSAGE is the company's top priority. It has been predicted that individuals in this current generation will have had 5.2 jobs during their lifetime. In times past the goal of the average employee was to attain a prescribed number of years with the same company and hopefully retire with a moderate yet satisfying pension. In most companies the visible suggestion box was esteemed and individuals with innovative ideas received monetary rewards. We now move from company to company with hopes of more money, better benefits and maybe a substantial relocation package.

There is a need for creative expression not only in the art world but also in other disciplines. From the technical field to the exact sciences there comes a time of serenity. After the rules have been learned and the prescribed methods applied, the mind invariably ponders the "What ifs". This I feel is the first step of all creative processes. With this mindset our energy can now be used to move the company and ultimately our society towards its intended purposes, partnering, camaraderie and survival.

You Must Be...Beautiful

In concert with the win-at-all-costs MESSAGE and the biological tension between the sexes comes the selection of individuals mated to produce the perfect offspring. This insures the prolongation of the species and a higher place on the biological and social pecking order. The beautiful plumage of the bird, the pheromones secreted by the white whale and the shameless seductive movements of the lioness in estrus, all under genetic control, attract and awaken the members of the opposite sex. Much like the MESSAGE in the DNA of the lioness we too are recipients of pervasive societal MESSAGES that tout beauty-at-all-cost regardless of possible long term health risks.

We are bombarded with images of those who have attained super-model status. The clothes they influence us to buy and the fabulous financial compensation for their jobs provide compelling evidence that we should do whatever is necessary to be beautiful. Opportunity, attention from the opposite sex, privilege and wealth all excuse, even mandate our obsession to be beautiful. The pay-off, we are told, is sex. Somehow, in the dominance-leader-attraction chain of events, sex becomes the reward. However, when given the opportunity to choose the big pay-off defined as relationship, men and women agree that intangibles such as affection, understanding, caring, character, and intimacy would make for the better choice.

Barbie and Ken presented an image not only of physical beauty and perfection but also of life-style. Barbie has the largest wardrobe in the world, her hair is perfect, and she drives great cars (convertible of course). She has a house on the beach, another very large elegant house at an undisclosed location and a camper. She has Ken, the perfect man, and until recently no need for a job or profession. Barbie recently celebrated her fiftieth birthday but her appearance is that of a woman half her age.

No wonder there is always a smile on Barbie's face. Of course, Barbie is a doll. The MESSAGE is more palatable, seemingly benign, and even embraceable when viewed in the form of a child's toy. After all, "Who can argue with an image?"

Magazine covers, print advertisements and even our toys exploit our need to be beautiful, young, and with perfect bodies. Most of us fall short of the body ideals exemplified by the popular Barbie and Ken dolls. According to Yale University psychologist Kelly Brownell, to look like Barbie, the average American woman would have to grow two feet taller, add five inches to her chest and lose six inches from her waist. To measure up to Ken, the average man would have to grow twenty inches, add eleven inches to his chest and ten inches to his waist. "If healthy, normal-weight individuals use such models as standards," concludes Dr. Brownell, "discontent is the logical outcome." Discontent is not only the logical outcome, but mental health disorders such as Body Dysmorphic Disorder (BDD) are in part the outcome when every man has to look like the G.I. Joe and every woman a picture on the cover of Playboy magazine.

Where and when did the MESSAGE of perfection originate? Upon examination of past generations perhaps we may gain some insights to the current craze that society holds regarding ones physique. As individuals, women have been participants in essentially all of the activities performed in human societies. However, have women been identified with particular roles ascribed to them by their societies? These roles have commonly been presented as naturally linked to women's physiology, including childbearing and infant care. Even in societies where women have been given broader responsibilities and power, men have generally dominated our political life. The emergence of classes, financial status, and major religions written about in *Religion in America*, *Megatrends* and *America 2000* have universally strengthened male dominance. In *Black Labor: White Wealth,* author C. Anderson notes that the rise of capitalism has furthered this tendency. Within our society there is a capitalistic justification to place women's issues aside or to acknowledge them only in passing. Our society affirms that women's issues become important only when they represent more dollars to the bottom line. You have only to take a walk through a large book store to see the literary works by women and for women. The needs have always been present but when publishers discovered that concerns expressed by the female became relevant investing in this endeavor would be a profitable venture. How many billions are spent on advertising to entice us to buy one product over another only after the need for a certain product has been created? This follows the earlier MESSAGE that mandate "we must be beautiful" "we must be thin" "we must appear enticing at all times."

What do you want now?

The concerns of women are more easily tolerated by her husband when they do not upset the breadwinner. But what if women were equally responsible for winning the bread? Would her perceived elevation of status also allow her to relay the MESSAGE that her basic intent is to dominate? These MESSAGES are communicated again and again from the women who run, own or manage our offices and businesses and yes our homes. Their attempt to play by the rules coupled with hard work, and ascend the ladder in corporate America has them confused. This sense of confusion occurs when they try to confront, as men do, maneuver, as men do, even chastise or tease, as men do, only to find that they are again labeled the "b" word or a "ball breaker." Conflicting MESSAGES from society and yes even in their own homes make certain behaviors positive for one gender and negative for another.

The need to have basic transportation to get to and from work, allow us to attend to daily tasks, spend an occasional weekend at the park, has been extended to a need to have an expensive, eye-catching, sleek, high-powered road machine if it will facilitate greater success with the opposite sex. How many advertisements for automobiles or toothpaste include the image of a "pretty" woman or a "great-looking" guy? But in reality the model-perfect physique only exists in a small percentage of the population. The rest of us assume our natural position on the bell-shaped curve.

What MESSAGES will we receive after we have failed to achieve the sleek svelte perfect body? What punishment will society render after liquid and grapefruit diets have caused our weight to yo-yo leaving our metabolism a police outline on the pavement? How can we respond to the glaring eyes of society when it is obvious that anorexia, bulimia, gastric stapling and lipo-suction have left us financially compromised, surgically scared and emotionally barren? How angry will we become when we realize the price we have paid because of a societal MESSAGE has failed us.

Obese individuals say almost in unison that obesity is the one condition where discrimination is socially acceptable. Exclusion from certain jobs is a standard business practice. Accommodation at certain restaurants and even on public transportation is a problem for many although it is economically good business to include everyone. The disturbing epitaph is that this negative MESSAGE is perpetuated whole-heartedly by the majority. We have only to listen to the taunts of very young children of an overweight classmate on the playground to realize how deeply these MESSAGES go and how early they start. It is not the responsibility of young children to protect and bolster the self-esteem of another child, but this does point to the parental MESSAGE that has been passed on. It is disheartening to read the statistics of elementary school children who describe themselves as ugly. Further, it is painful to see children adopt the diet, starve, binge, starve, restrict, binge method of weight control like their parents. Not surprising, there are increasingly more adolescent hospital admissions for eating disorders.

When discussing strategies to improve the health status of an obese child, I include weight loss as one of many objectives. The mother's response, conditioned by the societal MESSAGE, defends her position adding that she can not afford tuition at the eating disorders clinic or kid aerobics. The better MESSAGE is to reject programmed activities (a note of caution, it is not the programmed activities that I reject but the MESSAGE that only this type of exercise regiment will work). Instead, I suggest that she make bike riding, roller skating, jump rope, pick up games of basketball, football and other fun activities part of her daily routine. I further encourage group and team activities where fun makes time fly, friendships are forged and valuable social skills such as communication and conflict resolution are learned through active participation and interaction.

Message of Mediocrity/ Buyer Beware

Does life imitate art or is life and art shaped by the MESSAGES received? I contend that the image of life or reality is dictated by MESSAGES. As the 1998 Nagano Winter Olympics approached, America was set to crown our ice queen heir apparent, Michelle Kwan. There was, however, a belligerent lady-in-waiting, Tara Lipinsky who refused to help write a story that had already been written. Tara, with poise and athleticism beyond her 15 years, earned a gold medal. When asked about a flawless program that included countless triples, Tara flashed a huge grin and replied, "I just went out to have fun". Is that all Tara? Is that all it takes to win a gold medal? Eating cheeseburgers and fries after a movie with friends can be classified as fun. What other ingredients contributed to your gold medal effort? People your age go out and have fun all the time. Teenagers have fun when going to the movies, playing computer games "just for fun." Eating with friends at a fast food chain certainly belongs on the list of things that people do when they go out to have fun. Surely you have experienced and received a number of MESSAGES between going out to McDonalds and going out to win a gold medal in Nagano. What about the very early mornings that found you on the ice while others your age were asleep. What about the thousands of miles that you have traveled to competitions? Tell us of the struggle to remain focused in the off-season. Doesn't the possibility of physical injury arrive at every practice session and competition just as you do? It is evident that your parents have chosen to live apart so that you could be near your coach. What expenses have your parents incurred to give you the best chance at success? We can not congratulate you alone for the wisdom that you display at such a young age because we all know that Mattel does not make dolls in the image of people that work hard, conversely, they make dolls that encourage people to think of beauty fun and fantasy.

Arguably, there is danger in the MESSAGE that does not communicate the true price of accomplishment. Somehow, traits such as tenacity, dedication, passion for the sport or art, talent, and heart are not celebrated. We never speak of the big pay-off or work ethic. Acquisition and fine-tuning of skill are never mentioned. If we do not know the price of accomplishment, how can we ever appreciate the achievement? How then can we sincerely applaud the spirited efforts of a champion? Why then should we aspire to become a champion? The answers to these questions lie in the MESSAGES of truth. Truth that is depicted in the Nike advertisement that featured an athlete vomiting on his shoes! The caption explained that the young man captured in such an unflattering posture had just finished qualifying for a marathon. The race, the weather and the stakes of winning had obviously greatly challenged this individual.

Nike reminded us that the process of winning was not only the trip to the awards platform but also involved sweat, exhaustion, and even nausea and vomiting. Yes, the whole enchilada! I and hopefully you will salute the Nike Corporation for capturing and celebrating a true and realistic championship moment. It is this commercial that allows us in our minds eye to go behind the scenes of Wimbledon and follow Serena and Venus as they endure their rigorous routines.

Escape the Pain

Why was Nike's commercial so innovative? Is reality a new concept? Is truth so ugly that we dare not look? Nike dared to distance itself from an old MESSAGE that says it is ok to escape all unpleasant situations. The ad appeared in black and white and on plain not glossy paper. In so doing we see and hear a resounding refusal to participate in the status quo that would salve and powder our realities into something a little more palatable. If any of the creators of the advertisement were to read this analysis they might offer a quick rebuttal. They might say that I have gone overboard in suggesting such an empowering meaning to their commercial. To this I reply that there is a reason that I found the advertisement so appealing and worthy of memory.

Contrast commercials for headache medication, indigestion preparations, and medications for every ailment from arthritis to male sexual dysfunction. The MESSAGES espouse that these maladies warrant speedy recovery. However, the MESSAGE of the quick fix and quick-escape extend beyond headaches, heartburn and sinuses and are applied to everything that ails us. He's a cocaine addict: Put him in jail. The kids are hungry: Put Mom in jail! He's drunk: Fix a cup of coffee! She is hysterical because her marriage is over: Fix her up with Bill. We have become so adept at the automatic solution and speedy analysis that bumper stickers, photo ops and sound bites have become societal snapshots of who we are. One has only to turn on the television to hear that minor irritations should not be tolerated. After all, you do not have to suffer.

This same MESSAGE spoken in the seventies communicated to us that a little Valium would calm the waters and help us cope with the stresses of life. The same was said of Xanax in the 80's. Although the 90's were a depressing time, we did not have to feel the pressure of the hour, day or week as long as we had Prozac. As a licensed practitioner I do recognize the value of these prescription drugs in our medicine cabinets, however, no pharmacological agent can substitute for the difficult mental work of exposing the failed MESSAGES central to our deepest concerns. The fast food, drive-through, immediate gratification approach only serves to numb the pain that we feel and temporarily postpones the inevitable.

We expend vast amounts of energy to strategically place pacifiers in the mouths of our children and pain numbing medicine along our path so that we will never have to feel...anything. Our remedies are thought to distract us from our issues. Tell me, what is the farthest point from an unhappy marriage? Answer: the mink coat store. How far is graduate school from your house? Answer: It depends if you go by way of Jamaica. I am angry that I could never do enough to please my mother. Answer: I volunteer at the Mission on the weekend.

The societal MESSAGE says it is okay to escape, exclude, numb out and withdraw. The results...we soon discover that the MESSAGE of the quick fix has also failed us.

"Things Like This Don't Happen to Us Here..."

This statement was made with the sincerest of convictions after the shocking news that the body of a beaten and raped twelve year old girl had been found. The setting was a very quiet middle class neighborhood that was shaken to its isolationist foundation after two intensive weeks which produced five hundred volunteers, fifty thousand dollars in reward money, endless yellow ribbons, flyers, and prayer vigils. As the search ended volunteers packed their bags with heavy hearts, emotionally, mentally, and physically drained. The National Guard marched away into memory and tearfully family members gave poignant statements to the press. The common theme which ran through the community and the tie that bound the sixteen nights of television coverage left each person in a state of shock. The event presented compelling evidence that the best efforts and the micromanaged lives of this otherwise stable, secure and prosperous community could fail in its exclusion of crime and evil.

Things like this...

Oh you mean the murder of children, home invasions, rape, carjacking, and the like? Consider the global selective annihilation of entire countries, and cultures. Consider the fact that each day sixty thousand children die in a world from disease, starvation and the casualties of war.

Oh you mean, there is no need to acknowledge that intruders are about? Or does the MESSAGE communicate that evil could not possibly look like me. If this is true then think of the hundreds of children killed in anonymous drive-by shootings by people who could have lived down the street or worse that probably grew up down the street from their homes. Think of the date rapes. Why is there a need for stalker laws and why is it that serial killers can kill enough individuals to earn the title of serial? The MESSAGES transmitted to the American public and the majority of the world is most certainly....you are to blame because you do not look like me.

Not to Us...

Who is Us? Actually, the anger expressed is more the anger of a breach of contract. If I work hard and go to school and get a good job that pays me a lot of money, then I will be able to escape the social ills that naturally follow those who don't make the same choices. I demand immunity because of who I am and what I have accomplished.

Not us, is a MESSAGE of non-community. Not the community nestled serenely behind sentries and iron gates but the community of man. The indisputable truth of the matter is that no child or human being should live in fear for his life. No individual should enlist their bathtub as an armored cocoon against stray bullets to assure that they will not be killed in their sleep. No one has the right to take, violate, trespass or transgress what belongs to another person anywhere, period.

One has to resist the urge to retort; if not us, then them. How sad to know that no matter who you are, you will never be more than "a them" which of course is not as good as us.

Bumper Stickers

My child is an honor student at...
Have you hugged your kid today?
Honk if you love Jesus
I love my dog, cat, home, boat...

We are compelled to ask this question after parents are slain and playgrounds become hunting grounds. Children kneeling in prayer are easy prey for angry juvenile gunmen. We thought that the Menendez Brothers were an aberration. We thought that they were just spoiled rich-kids who were greedy and angry because they could not have their way. Actually, they and their act of violence were the first names of the present day "who's who" of dysfunction, disillusionment, and MESSAGES that failed.

More Blessed to Give Than to Receive

The MESSAGE of giving for the good of another brings to mind the story told by Dr. Johnetta B. Coles, president-emeritus of Spellman College who related the following:

> There was a young girl on the beach after a storm. The beach is littered with starfish as far as she can see. Walking along, the girl stops and picks up a starfish, one after another, and throws them back into the sea. A man stops the girl and asks what she is doing. 'The starfish will die in the hot sun unless I throw them back,' she explains. 'But there are millions of starfish,' the man counters. 'How can you make a difference?' The little girl picks up another starfish, throws it back, and says 'It makes a difference to this one.'

How the young girl came to walk upon the beach after a storm is easily imagined. After a storm things are usually clean and peaceful. Walking on the beach undisturbed is one of those things to which we look forward. The storyteller does not inform us if the rescue of the starfish was her purpose for walking on the beach. We only know that this circumstance presented her with a choice. She could have counted the number of starfish displaced and stranded without a way back home which ultimately would have simply been counted as a mere consequence of the storm. She could have complained that the starfish carcasses marred the beauty of the beach and hampered the peaceful feeling one seeks when walking barefoot in the sand. She could have walked away from the beach fearing that her feet would hurt if they contacted the starfish. She instead decided to do what she could at that moment. Can you envision the pervasive societal MESSAGE at work? Why does the man who starts out with an innocent question persist in reminding the little girl of the enormity of her task? Would her decision to help the starfish have met with greater approval if the News-at-Eleven crew had been there to record the event? Is it significant that the MESSAGE comes from a male?

Is it significant that the female is the caretaker and is young in age? And what of the starfish? At the beginning of this chapter, I pointed out that some groups or societies have no survival value. They have no disaster contingency plan. They have no organization and therefore exist at the mercy of nature.

Some of us identify with the starfish. Some of us have found ourselves displaced and disoriented after a hurricane, flood or storm (Katrina and Rita), or an illness, a devastating loss of someone or something, a failed business endeavor, a stock market crash, or a national or world event may have shaken us briefly or permanently to our foundation. It is at this time that we require someone, anyone to consider our situation with compassion. This negates the MESSAGE that all those in need are responsible for their tragic circumstance. Could it be that the man felt the starfish undeserving of life because they did not have the ability to correct a problem that they did not cause? It is important to note that the young person made the decision to help. She operated with a different definition of success than our society-at-large. Her actions were based on principles that humane societies should adopt when responding to individuals we deem as deserving of esteem. The response to the needs of one starfish was important enough to continue the exercise. Was it a difficult task to be undertaken in an atmosphere where the expectation of failure resided in someone lacking compassion?

Brillcream, a little dab will do ya!

Let's further examine the sex/gender MESSAGE for this is truly what it is. Today the vast majority of television programs offer comedic and dramatic relief often included in our favorite talk show. Print and mass media find it challenging at best to sell toothpaste without some big sexual payoff. Coincidentally, because we no longer raise objections, the toothpaste MESSAGE has been touted as the model for positive long-lasting relationships, the ideal for which we strive. We choose our car because it will attract someone of the opposite sex. We buy deodorant because our relationships can not afford body odor even when we are working out or taking part in strenuous activity. How ridiculous it is to expect that we would want to suspend natural consequences of work and play because a member of the opposite sex will be offended. But we do because we accept media's standard of propriety and decorum. The sex MESSAGE is dangerous in that it reduces us to mere participants in an act. Our worth and unique qualities get lost and unrecognized making recognition of our individuality impossible.

Communication between the sexes becomes generic and merely a game to land the other in bed only to feel more used and empty than ever before. Sex is now viewed as a tool of control and dominance. Additionally, sex has become a commodity that can be shopped around to the highest bidder or used as currency for the purpose of acquisition. So, is it any wonder that unwanted pregnancies are at epidemic proportions? Is it any wonder that women are not considered valuable resources at home or in the workplace? The incidence of rape as a mechanism of dominance and power is increasing? There is little wonder that these are mere symptoms of the illnesses and diseases within our society.

Many years ago a professional athlete authored a book chronicling his sexual conquests that numbered over twenty thousand women, or so he reported. How does one foster love, caring or intimacy (in-to-me-see) with so many partners? The answer is simple. You don't. Obviously the sexual conquests were not requirements for satisfaction. What the athlete got was sex but probably more important, feelings of power and self-importance along with the bragging rights of a conquistador. The women did not get love, intimacy or commitment. What they got was admission behind the sacred "Velvet Rope" that previously separated them from the famous, the esteemed, the popular...

The societal MESSAGES have failed because they have precluded the cheerleader from being the star athlete. The White House intern is rewarded because her energies are directed toward being in the closest of proximity to the president rather than being properly mentored and prepared so that an astute politician will emerge. It has a lot to do with the worth we place on a thing or position or place of employment. If we feel that the job or career or we ourselves are priceless then there is no investment that is too great and no price too high for the amount of time that we will invest to ensure a successful outcome.

One More for the Road

I now address the societal MESSAGE of addiction and the addicted. As stated throughout this writing and in the writings of others, this quick-fix phenomenon pervades our society. How many clients present symptoms with an expectation for a prescription for something; anything that will make them feel better fast. As noted earlier, Valium was heralded as the anti-anxiety drug of the seventies, Xanax the drug of the eighties and Prozac the drug of the nineties. Truly these are all very effective drugs and as a clinician I am grateful that they are available as **adjunctive** therapy. But medication alone without the hard work that one is willing to do, to examine the cause or the problem, is incomplete and simply places them in a position to need greater quantities and larger doses.

Society has sanctioned the fast food, fast fix, immediate gratification phenomenon as a necessity. Answers to problems like the development of problems take considerable time. In an environment of deadlines and ten to twelve hour work days there is little time for unraveling the convoluted thread of discontent. Therefore, pacification of uneasiness, numbing of pain and masking of problems is thought to best meet the societal agenda. What would happen if all those ten milligram a day Valium users worked at getting to the core of their issues and once there dealt with them in some way? Author Larry Crabb asserts that our issues today can be likened to an iceberg. The old adage this is just the tip of the iceberg has credence specifically as it relates to our emotional health.

Going beneath the surface for purposes of listing and describing the MESSAGES that failed us is at the core of our need to gain some semblance of the abundant life. Consider the Titanic, the second sea going vessel of its kind (the first was the Olympia) has been reported to have been 882 feet and 9 inches, approximately the length of nine football fields and having a gross registered tonnage or internal volume of the 46,328 tons. However, despite its enormous size it sank after hitting an object that later revealed enormous depth beneath the surface of the ocean.

What would happen to our society if all substance abusers (illegal an otherwise) could experience permanent recovery from their drug of choice and the persistent pain initiated by MESSAGES from their past? What would the gross national product of this country look like if all the shop-a-holics came away from the sale racks and focused on the things that forced them back to the scene of the crime? How would food addicts and compulsive gamblers spend their time and money if their hunger was satisfied in healthy ways? How many marriages could be saved if the couple chose to examine their soul hunger and need for real intimacy that escaped them during their formative years? It is too late to ask the voyagers of the Titanic if they might have survived if only the person in charge had explored what lay beneath the sea. But we can learn from this tragedy if we express a willingness to examine the size and depth of our hidden MESSAGES and go beyond the tip of the iceberg.

"If You Argue for Your Weaknesses...They're Yours"
—Stephen Covey

Somewhat a novice in the complexities of computer science I often found myself frequenting a number of computer stores, appearing starry eyed and confused. But amid the quandary of peripherals, hard and floppy disks, laser printers, color monitors, software for entertainment and databases, megabits, kilobits, gigabits and now terabits I was intrigued by a number of books written specifically for the supposed unenlightened entitled "----- for Dummies" (for the specific soft or hardware). Eager to learn the intricacies of the computer so necessary for the twenty first century I asked a salesperson to suggest additional books on the subject matter. I took special note of his response when I pointed to the books written for "dummies." It was an experience not soon forgotten and speaks to the attitude that we have fostered within ourselves. The salesperson in a very polite yet assertive tone made the following statement; "I find it appalling that an author would prepare a technical document denigrating people and even more shocked at the number of individuals who, even in jest, willingly consider and then purchase a book entitled "...for dummies."

Initially, I felt that perhaps the salesperson was a bit radical but after speaking to various computer users, unaware of the purpose of my query, whose responses were both thoughtful and candid I concluded that perhaps his insight may indeed have validity. One young lady in particular who had recently upgraded her computer proudly shared the fact that she had recently purchased one of the dummy books. As a counselor trained to listen to what is not said I shared the thoughts of the sales person. She was initially pensive and then responded that his words were a resounding MESSAGE that she believed about herself from high school to her present status in life. Yes, I am indeed a dummy! But as I now reflect on our brief conversation I am reminded of another more subtle MESSAGE looming about. It is the MESSAGE that states I don't have time to really learn I just want a "Cliff Note" or instrument that will quickly get me from point A to point B.

The MESSAGE is so powerfully relayed that suggests that we have become as automated and robotic as the computers we use to surf the Internet. The adage "Garbage in, Garbage Out" has indeed become a reality to many of us. We take in volumes of information which serve little or no purpose. The results are shallow conversations, one-up-man-ship and a deadened sense of self in search of a perpetual high. This high is not only sought after through drugs, alcohol, sex, shopping and the like, but through socially accepted activities.

A trip to Las Vegas, where the "what happens here stays here" MESSAGE revealed the emptiness and desperate need to fill the void in our lives. Although the city and surrounding sights provided tremendous opportunities to enlighten and entertain, the countless blank stares at slot machines, roulette tables and dice evoked a sense of sadness. From old to young, varying races and cultures covering the globe, the constant search for the illusive lady luck produced in essence "Dead Men Walking."

The headlines of our newspapers reveal a terrible truth that despite the formulas and prescriptions for a perfect life, there is at our very core unrest and pain that will not be soothed and satiated. In truth we eventually learn;

"He who conceals his disease cannot expect to be cured…"
—Ethiopian Proverb

CHAPTER SEVEN

Church, Do You Really Want Me to Be Better?

"Yes mommy I want to go to heaven…will they have grocery stores, toys and cars there?" These words spoken by my cousin's six year old son exemplify the mindset that many of us have regarding our ultimate end and that is to reside comfortably in our mansion, walk down streets paved with gold or more notably experience a promised existence without tears.

Living in a world fraught with constant chaos, uncertainty, disaster, grief and pain affirm a quote made by one of my seminary professors; "despite the pain and suffering that we experience here on earth, for many of us we embrace the notion I want to go to heaven…I just don't want to die." I must admit that for many years my thoughts about heaven were filled with visions of white fluffy clouds with winged angels floating about playing harps…BORING! But it was only following a wise sage who willingly (and emotionally) shared the overwhelming sense of awe and peace while in the presence of God that I gained a renewed vision of this heavenly place. Further, his MESSAGE produced in me a longing that is spoken of in the book of Romans, chapter eight; "For we know that every creature groaneth and travaileth in pain, even till now. And not only it, but ourselves also, who have the first fruits of the Spirit: even we ourselves groan within ourselves, waiting for the adoption of the sons of God, **the redemption of our body.**" Translation, every creature, plant, seedling as well as mankind has a longing to be freed from our earthly existence.

And so I invite you to begin an investigation into the role that religion and the respective institutions have played in your life. Further, it is imperative that we closely examine the corresponding MESSAGES about our final destination and a belief or lack of in eternal life in the heavenly places. This journey must include MESSAGES that have been delivered from pulpits, Sunday school classes, biblical scholars, and family members.

In a biblical counseling class taught by a young compassionate and gifted professor I recall making an attempt to visualize the daily routines and activities that would occur in this supposed utopian state of existence. As an avid shopper and traveler I remember feeling somewhat apathetic relative to the images that came to mind. Consequently, I began to ponder the following; what will I do for pleasure without Marshall Fields, Target, Sears, Neiman Marcus, and Wal-Mart? Will I really have my own mansion and can I decorate it as I please? Can I at best pick the room size and color, number of bedrooms and will it have a pool? Will men and women be allowed to date? What about sex? Will my mother recognize me since I've aged?

Perhaps the questions above may appear a bit juvenile but during discussions with friends and family I listened to and witnessed the laughter of people once they too shared their thoughts about this unknown state of being.

However, for many of us the thought of the afterlife and visions of angels floating about with only select folks as partakers of this state of existence are simple reminders of the failed MESSAGES that have kept of fearful, angry, distrustful and filled with guilt. Note the following; "I'm so afraid that if I don't do what God (translation the Church) wants me to do I will be severely punished. And you do know that He watches every step I take. Sometimes I feel like raising my fist to him and cursing but I'm just too afraid of the consequences."

These words frequently stated aloud but more often silently uttered to ourselves have kept many of us frustrated, fearful, angry and yet experiencing a sense of shame as we entertain the thoughts and feelings that we have towards the so named "man upstairs." These feelings become manifest when religious MESSAGES about the existence of a loving, caring, compassionate God begin to fade with each contradictory experience whose end produced more pain and disillusionment. Our experiences include disappointments of varying degrees.

As clients begin to share varying physical and emotional maladies I concluded that there exist a common denominator or core issue that could easily be traced to the beginnings of depression, compulsions, addictive disorders and the like. That common denominator is frequently an experience of loss, rejection, abandonment, or abuse by a loved one. The data were astounding as client after client reflected on the loss of a grandmother, aunt, uncle, neighbor or best friend and the profound impact the loss had on their behavior and their corresponding view of God. I further noted that the loss need not be a loss through death but could include the loss of a friend when the person moved away, the loss of a parent through divorce or who began to work during the child's formative years, the loss of innocence when they experienced sexual and physical abuses and more often the loss of a loved one who for whatever reason was emotionally detached or unavailable.

Father...God the Father

Very little research has been done on the relationship one has with his/ her father and the corresponding relationship one has with God. Abandonment or the absence of a father in the home may set the stage for inappropriate behaviors, signal that God is and will eventually follow suit and that He too is unavailable. Punitive or abusive relationships between father and child further suggest that like our earthly father, God's role is to beat us into submission through the execution of some form of corporal punishment. In essence the statement above regarding "the man upstairs" is in reality a composite of many allegations made secretly and in desperation in the only place individuals feel safe, the counseling office of, for all intents and purposes, a stranger.

Contrary to the MESSAGES we have received, our Father is not taken aback when we question Him or express anger toward Him. Conversely, it is during these times that our true feelings pervade and we become aware of our finite existence and His infinite power. Further, one client shared that it is during times of fear, failure, uncertainty and pain that he visualizes himself literally "jumping into the arms of God the Father."

Their "stories" generally begin with the realization that moral and ethical injustices persist. Under the guise of the general decay of humanity many of us share the depressing details that include the loss of lives through worldwide disasters such as earthquakes, floods, famine, unexplained shifts in weather patterns and the actions of sadistic mass murderers, who with their trigger finger take the lives of adults and innocent children. But if you listen closely you will hear the ache of a soul questioning his or her plight and destiny.

But what of the lessons taught in Sunday school, morning mass and other religious services where MESSAGES espouse if you do good deeds, say your prayers each night, honor your parents, contribute your time, talent and finances (I will address later in this chapter) to the church your life will be fulfilling if not palatable. Are these edicts with their corresponding promises untrue? Generally, it is only through feelings of hopelessness, fear and rage that clients, in the "safety" of my office, "confess" that regular church attendance, weekly mass, and the celebration of Yom Kippur have failed to alleviate feelings of depression, compulsions, isolation and suicidal ideations. However, the fear of questioning, communicating these feelings and yes, even challenging the tenets of this "Higher Power" leaves them with one of two choices. The first suggests that we simply leave our place of worship and dismiss the rhetoric heard in every service. The second alternative is to continue to attend church, pray, recite on cue, read and listen to the MESSAGES that condemn, misinform or placate hoping that one day things will improve.

Allow me to clarify that my words are not merely directed at the church, temple or synagogue but at all religious institutions that under of the guise of spiritual healing and connectedness provide mere band-aids when major surgery is the minimum requirement. But where can we go when according to our religious upbringing the need to be heard and understood without judgment can only be found via this omnipotent (all powerful), omnipresent (everywhere simultaneously), omniscient (all knowing) being. Herein lies the paradox, we are encouraged to seek out the very Being for help whom we feel has harmed. Additionally, that Being seems preoccupied or as one minister relayed in his Sunday morning MESSAGE "God has better things to do...sister, brother, just keep praying." It is during these times that the compulsion to not only raise ones' fist but to shake it in the face of God becomes overwhelming.

In the Oscar winning movie "Forest Gump" (also the name of the main character), there is a scene that perfectly describes the position that many of us have found ourselves. Forest has joined the military but upon his return home encounters his old army sergeant. Forest's sergeant has also returned from Vietnam but is now a double amputee unable to find employment and obviously disenchanted with the response of his own country's involvement in the war. Forest invites him to join him in a business venture that entails the purchase of a shrimp boat. Initially, the sergeant, filled with anger, disillusionment and hurt, refuses Forest's offer. But later succumbs to the offer and joins Forest in his project. The storyline continues and reveals their many failures, however, one late evening without warning a storm arises and the small shrimp boat bows to the wind and the waves of the sea. Mindful of the possibility of losing the boat as well as their lives, the legless sergeant climbs to the top of the mast and with fists raised literally dares God to go for it, screaming out "is this the best you can do?"

How often have we too had the desire to challenge God "right in his face" when feelings of abandonment are our constant companion? Only this time our words are no longer muffled sounds but words loudly spoken that scream the true longings of our soul. However, it is during these times when we literally cry "Abba Father," or daddy, that in essence our heavenly Father hears our plea for help and a long awaited surrender of self.

Larry Crabb, a renowned author, psychologist and speaker, defines this action as humanities "demanded-ness." That is to say that we, as finite human beings have neither the right nor are in a position to demand that God meet our needs or desires. That same MESSAGE is relayed in our religious institutions leaving us fearful of this invisible Being who paradoxically bears the name alone that suggests an understanding of our "demandedness, "Our Father!"

I must concur that certain emotions best be expressed with dignity and respect. However, if we are indeed God's children and he Our Father, then like our own children are there not times when a good ole' tantrum serves as a catharsis providing the parent with insight as to exactly what the child really wants? Granted, as parents we must decide what is best for the child but the essential lesson is to listen to what is being asked for. And listen carefully because the request may not be the thing that is asked for. With the child's limited vocabulary he may simply be using words and exhibiting behaviors that communicate a need that is uncommunicative. **Warning!!** Statements and/or questions to individuals, parents and especially to God left unspoken, foster resentment, distrust, resulting in shallow if not superficial relationships.

In reference to the earlier statement regarding recent disasters and unexplained changes in weather patterns I noted a common response among survivors. The newscaster is seen with microphone in hand interviewing someone who has just lost his home and all his belongings. The typical response is "Thank God, we are just so glad to be alive!" But several days later when the realization that precious memories have been lost the survivor is seen digging through piles of debris in search of some memento. What MESSAGE had the survivor been given in lieu of his tremendous loss? The answer is obvious...just be glad you are alive, God spared your life and after all you can always replace things. But what are friends, family members, well-wishers, and obviously the church really saying? Don't feel the pain of the loss of your grandmother's picture, your child's favorite toy or even a place to live. For many church attendees the MESSAGE suggests that in times of grief, calamity or loss the expression of sadness, disappointment, ingratitude, diminished or loss of faith is inappropriate. But what of the times of mourning and the Bibles rendering of a common occurrence when individuals literally tore their clothes apart?

In ancient funeral processions wailing relatives, often accompanied by professional mourners and musicians, preceded the body to the grave.

Nelson further notes;

> The experience or expression of grief, as at time of death or national disaster was common. In biblical times, the customs of most cultures encouraged a vivid expression of grief. The people of that time would be puzzled by our more sedate forms of mourning...The Old Testament has many Hebrew words for mourning. These words range in meaning from anger and indignation to the more common idea of grief over a calamity or death. In addition to wailing and weeping, outward forms of mourning including tearing the clothes.

Here again in our culture intense expressions of feelings even if justified are discouraged. The more dignified the mourner the more respected. (Mrs. King, Jackie Kennedy) Reflect on your own experience at the funeral of a friend or family member. Regardless of religious affiliation there is a staff of trained personnel whose primary task during times of grief is to keep everyone calm and maintain control. Outbursts of any kind prompted by painful remembrances or the sense of loss are quickly handled or the individual is quietly escorted out of the service. It appears that the church or better still the MESSENGER has mandated specific protocol to adhere to during our most fragile and vulnerable times. In the midst of our loss, the priest, pastor, minister or rabbi may even make attempts to soothe and even minimize our pain by asking a rhetorical question...why is it that people can't see a God who despite our situation knows what's best, loves and cares for us unconditionally and has placed our loved ones in a better place (remember your picture of heaven)? And the one response that is most disturbing "they are no longer suffering." It is during these times I am tempted to say "but I am."

"Jesus Wept"

Responses of this nature often force us to choose the first alternative mentioned earlier and that is to walk away from the church disillusioned and more often filled with guilt for questioning God about the loss of a loved one or even our material possessions. If it is not appropriate or acceptable to grieve during calamity, loss or even feelings of abandonment what feelings are acceptable? What of the wayward child? The discovery of infidelity in a twenty plus year marriage? The struggle with one addiction or another? An incurable disease?

Although I believe in one true God, his son Jesus Christ and the Holy Spirit on some level I understand the rationale of the atheist. During my search for answers I began to question whether the atheist simply does not believe in God based on a lack of knowledge or is unwilling to accept the fact that this supposed loving, merciful, compassionate supreme being exist who has allowed humanity to experience such pain and inner turmoil both past and present.

You have seen, felt and heard the historical MESSAGES. What of the Crusaders who left oceans of blood in the name of God as they publicly and with pride announced their right to force their religious beliefs upon another? The Doctrine of Manifest Destiny is a phrase that expressed the belief that we the people of the United States have a mission to expand and to spread our form of democracy and religious freedom. Advocates of this doctrine believed that expansion was not only good, but that it was obvious ("manifest") and inevitable ("destiny"). Originally a political catch phrase of the nineteeth century, "Manifest Destiny" eventually became a standard historical term often used as a synonym for the territorial expansion of the United States across North America towards the Pacific Ocean without regard to the indigenous people whose lives and livelihood were connected to their land.

Manifest Destiny was always a general notion rather than a specific policy. The term combined a belief in expansionism with other popular ideas of the era that included a belief in the natural superiority of what was then called the Anglo-Saxon race (referring to white Americans and the

British). While many writers focus primarily upon American expansionism when discussing Manifest Destiny, others view the term as a broad expression of a belief in America's mission in the world, which has meant different things to different people over the years. This variety of possible meanings was summed up by Ernest Lee Tuveson, who wrote: "A vast complex of ideas, policies, and actions is comprehended under the phrase 'Manifest Destiny'. They are not, as we should expect, all compatible, nor do they come from any one source."

The phrase "Manifest Destiny" was first used primarily in the mid nineteenth century to promote the annexation of much of what is now the Western United States, the Oregon Territory, the annexation of Texas and Mexico. But how indeed was this movement incorporated into our religious beliefs? The answer can be found in the historically misguided missionary zeal that espoused that this directive came from God. We did and continue to use God as the lightening rod to justify our actions. However, our actions supposedly given by the direct commands of God, have left people, who once resided in prosperous and pure societies, diseased, spoiled, corrupted and destitute.

In the minds of the individuals noted above and even ourselves perhaps this God is, just as philosopher Aristotle spoke of, "the unmoved mover who has positioned man in the path of war, destruction suffering and death" untouched and apathetic toward our plight despite our many pleas and railings. However, in our attempt to justify our actions another theory known as Deism, suggests that this supposed God of the universe has simply wound the proverbial clock of life and left man-kind to his own devices. Devices that will ultimately lead to his own destruction.

This concept or theory known as Deism is not new. It was introduced in the eighteenth century and grew in popularity among the very elect. At the very least it does seemingly provide answers to the following questions. Where is this supposed loving God while wars continue, racial hate and prejudice mount, babies die, drug and teenage pregnancy are on the rise and individuals become desensitized to rape, pornography, and murder? To the Deist no complex answer need be sought. God simply does not choose to intervene. He sits on his throne and as the minute and second hands move quickly toward that the end of all time, God folds his arms, clears his throat and awaits humanity's last act...total annihilation. As we examine the state of our world today and more precisely our own painful existence it seems logical to embrace this doctrine.

I bear witness to the pain and suffering of others as they grieve the loss of what little faith they once had. A faith that began with a belief in Santa Claus, the Tooth Fairy and the Easter Bunny, only to be told by an older sibling or friend that neither exist. Sunday after Sunday our churches are filled with people who have grown chronologically, however, upon close examination of the longings of their soul, these "adult children" admittedly covet that time of innocence and unwavering faith in the invisible. We simply want answers to questions like; why is my son smoking crack? Why is my fifteen year old daughter pregnant...again? When will my husband stop drinking and physically abusing me...he is a good man when he is sober? Why can't I find someone to just love me? And the most pervasive yet unspoken question, where is God in all this?

Perhaps we eventually conclude, just like the magical beliefs that we once held, that God, like the tooth fairy, the Easter bunny and Santa Claus is just a myth.

It is interesting to note that for those of us who do believe in a God of love regularly experience very negative images of God. In Juanita R. Ryan's article "Seeing God More Clearly...Recovering From Distorted Images of God," she notes;

> But the private images of God were in direct-and painful conflict with their intellectual convictions about God. I have observed in myself and in others that this kind of internal conflict about God is fairly common. It seems that people who believe in a God of love and compassion sometimes experience private images of God which are disturbing.

But exactly where do these images, thoughts, feelings, and/or MESSAGES originate? Aside from the stories shared by others in my private office I too have concluded that our personal images of God may have originated during our formative years and from the MESSAGES of varied religious institutions or lack thereof. Ryan continues;

Unfortunately, some distortions of God grow out of teaching and preaching in [our churches] that inadvertently perpetuates disturbing, sub-Christian images of God…Distorted teaching from Christian leaders can have a significant impact on our images of God.

Where's the beef?

It has been throughout my many years of searching for truth and the reasons behind my personal failures that I began to raise the question of the meaning of surrender. If like myself you too have felt self-sufficient, fairly decisive, educated in the ways of the world and biblical truths a request for total surrender may seem absurd. What else could God possibly want from me? I pray regularly, pay my tithes as the preacher screamed during that predictable period in church known as the time to give God His due. He recites the verses from the book of Malachi chapter three, "Will a man rob God?" However, what the preacher failed to explain was that this verse spoke to the need for an annual tithe for the maintenance of the Levites (Lev. 27:30). The tithes were for the Levitical priesthood whose only job was to offer sacrifice, serve as intercessors for God's people, pray and keep the children of Israel mindful of God's ultimate power. Here Wesley defined the store—house—as one or more large rooms, built on purpose for this use. He further notes "that there may be meat—For the priests and Levites to live upon."

Following my research on these verses I immediately envisioned my local Costco or Sam's Club. A place without price, only sonship with God is required to have access to ones daily needs. "The second tithe was brought to Jerusalem for the Lord's feast (Deut. 14:22). Every third year, however, the second tithe was kept at home and used for the POOR." In verse ten of Malachi chapter three, the prophet writes; "Bring the whole tithe into the storehouse, so that there may be food in My house…" How many individuals have **reluctantly** and under the threat of negative consequences from God given their bill money, grocery money and/or rent money to keep God from being angry with them? I have spoken to numerous individuals who openly expressed that tithing was a mandate from God. But in the privacy of their homes felt the bondage of giving ten percent fully aware that their sacrifice meant a shortage of food for their family. And what of that income tax return? Should I pay tithes on that as well? I posed this question to one pastor only to be told that I had cheated God most of my life so I "owed" him at minimum ten percent of my refund. Talk about a blatant guilt ridden MESSAGE.

Again the prophet Malachi uses the word storehouse. According to the Hebrew language storehouse is defined as a house, a depository or in the "greatest variation of applications especially family."

I recall experiencing a feeling of pride as I viewed my name and amount of money given in the church bulletin. But I also felt awkward when during the offering the pastor announced from the pulpit "will all tithers come first." What of the scripture that espouses "Each of you must give what you have decided in your heart, not with regret or under compulsion, since God loves a cheerful giver." (2Cor. 9:7).

Father God is that you?

Our religious institutions are but one place where we receive MESSAGES about God and righteous living. There is yet another place that has a profound affect on our view of God and our belief system...It occurs within the supposed sanctity of our own homes. Although parenting is an honorable profession, it is by far one of the most underrated of all positions one can hold. The influence that parents have on a child's concept of God has been underestimated.

Until the advent of the recent "feminist movement," the job of home-maker was thought to be a burdensome chore, reserved only for the uninitiated, the woman who could not make it in the real world. However, sometime later movies were produced that began to present a different perspective on parenting. Several that come to mind include, "Three Men and a Baby" and "Mom," where a role reversal was clearly evident.

Shortly thereafter, a generation of Baby Boomers, began to demand paid maternity leaves, for both mother and father and what is now known as the Family and Medical Leave Act (FMLA). Day care became a major issue. And then there was the fight over child adoption laws that brought tears to the eyes of both "Baby Jessica" and her adoptive parents. And sadly enough, child abuse became the hot topic of the day and was presented and debated in the highest courts. An honorable profession? Indeed!

In light of this renewed view of the profession of parenting, have we considered or even investigated just how important the role of parenting is in modeling who and what God is? What a real loving father is like? What skills, maladies and behaviors, through our DNA, are inherited from our Heavenly Father? At play here is the highly debated issue of "Nature versus Nurture." These questions need be asked and answered, and yet have been debated for centuries, from the great philosophers to scientist in DNA research. But for purposes of this chapter the important question is what MESSAGES do parents relay to a child that influences his view of God, the church and religion in general.

During my tenure as a Pastoral Counselor I have been privy to MESSAGES that clients reluctantly shared regarding their relationship to religious institutions (the church), that were passed on to them by their parents. A few include; "I don't care how sick or tired you are, you will be in church Sunday/Saturday morning…" "If you can go to school you can go to church." "I know Sister Mary humiliated you during catechism but she is only trying to teach you a lesson about discipline…" Translation: what you feel physically and emotionally doesn't matter. "What would Jesus say if he saw you…" "Every time you do wrong it is like hammering the nails into the hands of Jesus." and one of my all time favorites, "What would Jesus do…" Numerous clients shared the belief or MESSAGE from their parents that going to church would keep them from being punished or going to hell. Simply put, blessings, gifts and rewards from God came with a price.

In addition we have received "gratitude MESSAGES" that infer that we must be thankful regardless of our present circumstances. When we complained or felt that our basic needs were not met we were reminded of the following platitude; "I cried because I had no shoes, until I met a man that had no feet." The purpose of this MESSAGE was to remind us that others were worst off and to encourage us to maintain perspective. The issue is not one of ingratitude but a point generally overlooked...*I still have no shoes!!!.*

Regrettably, as we grow older we may begin to view this God of our parents as nothing more than the ultimate task master. And over time the picture of Jesus seated surrounded by playful children, now becomes a picture of an angry God (an archetype of our father or mother) who demands perfection in every aspect of their life.

Clients speak of the litany of sermons given by the various priest and pastors filled with emotion almost theatrical in their nature. The MESSAGES were spoken with conviction about the wages of sin, that include spilling one's seed to a failure to say the proper rosary. All of course would inevitability lead to one "burning in hell" or being sent to purgatory. The results, clients learned early to walk in constant fear and obedience but paradoxically, waiting for that moment in time when they could escape the cruel demands of this taskmaster. The consensus of many of my clients was that God was just as demanding and abusive and an even greater task master than their parents. The use of the following Biblical text was regularly used to force children to adhere to the "rules" established by God.

Note the following from Matthew Henry's Commentary;

> Honor thy father and thy mother, that thy days may be long in the land which Jehovah thy God giveth thee, (Exodus 20:12) was given and then later repeated to the generations that were not alive when the initial commandments were given to the children of Israel. In the book of Deuteronomy, the author writes that same commandment as; Honor thy father and thy mother, as Jehovah thy God commanded thee; that thy days may be long, and that it may go well with thee, in the land which Jehovah thy God giveth thee. (ASV). The commandments were given a second time or repeated to remind the Israelites of the importance of honor.

However, in Strong's Concordance the Hebrew translation
of the word **honor** is defined as;

A primitive root; to *be heavy*, that is, in a bad sense (*burdensome, severe, dull*) or in a good sense (*numerous, rich, honorable*); causatively to *make weighty* (in the same two senses):—abounding with, more grievously afflict. As I pause here, be reminded that I believe that honoring our parents is a commandment that aids us later in life as we see the relevance of obedience to our Heavenly Father. The reason annexed to this commandment is a promise: *"That thy days may be long in the land which the Lord thy God giveth thee."* And may I further add that this is the first commandment with promise. But I do espouse the law of reciprocity that is to say when two entities are involved there is a give and receive dynamic. The verse, "Fathers provoke not your children to wrath" (Eph. 6:4) is frequently overlooked in our places of worship. Accordingly Matthew Henry continues;

The duty of parents: *And you fathers,* Or, you parents, 1. *"Do not provoke your children to wrath.* Though God has given you power, you must not abuse that power, remembering that your children are, in a particular manner, pieces of yourselves, and therefore ought to be governed with great tenderness and love. Be not impatient with them, use no unreasonable severities and lay no rigid injunctions upon them. When you caution them, when you counsel them, when you reprove them, do it in such a manner as not to *provoke them to wrath.* In all such cases deal prudently and wisely with them, endeavouring to convince their judgments and to work upon their reason." 2. *"Bring them up* well, *in the nurture and admonition of the Lord,* in the discipline of proper and of compassionate correction, and in the knowledge of that duty which God requires of them and by which they may become better acquainted with him. Give them a good education." It is the great duty of parents to be careful in the education of their children: "Not only bring them up, as the brutes do, taking care to provide for them; but bring them up in nurture and admonition, in such a manner as is suitable to their reasonable natures. Nay, not only bring them up as men, in nurture and admonition, but as Christians, in the admonition of the Lord. Let them have a religious education. Instruct them to fear sinning; and inform them of, and excite them to, the whole of their duty towards God.

One client after struggling with sexual abuse that he endured from age three to fourteen stated, "I still believe that we have been created as nothing more than puppets, set on a stage, with the puppeteer [God] pulling our strings for the sole purposes of his entertainment."

The similarities between ones earthly parents and a heavenly parent are not coincidental. However, the difference is that our earthly parents, through their own unfulfilled longings, rarely provide the positive role model that ultimately encourages us to establish relationship with a being that has no flesh to touch. In the mind of the child the face of God is the same face that he or she sees in his parents.

We lack concise or comprehensive manuals that will provide us with parenting procedures to aid us during times of uncertainty. And so the age old question remains what steps should I now use that will guide me through this awesome task. Author Virginia Satir explains that when one person in a family experiences pain, which appears symptomatically, every family member is in some way affected. She further notes, "The family system is the primary learning context for individual behavior, thoughts and feelings." Based on her theories it seems reasonable to conclude that as children our reactions, feelings and thoughts regarding God are directly influenced by our parents. The absence of an involved, contributing, loving father (noted earlier) greatly influences our view of an unseen Heavenly Father. Further, these interactions, or lack of, greatly influence our view and relationship toward God.

In summary, is God seen as compassionate, honest (keeps his Word), approachable and understanding or as a punisher, withholder of love and constantly looking for any mistake we make? It is only as children, and later as adults with the aid of real parental modeling can we honestly answer these questions. In Susan Forwards' New York Times Bestseller entitled *Toxic Parents,* she begins with the necessity for the reader to take his psychological pulse. She states, "it's not always easy to figure out whether your parents are, or were, toxic…When we're very young, our godlike parents are everything to us. Without them, we would be unloved, unprotected, homeless, and unfed, living in a constant state of terror." But as we age and mature we may discover that our perfect parents may fall into one of six categories:

> *The Inadequate Parent:* Constantly focusing on their own problems, they turn their children into "mini-adults" who take care of them.

> *The Controllers:* They use guilt, manipulation, and even over-helpfulness to direct their children's lives.

> *The Alcoholics:* Mired in denial and chaotic mood swings, their addiction leaves little time or energy for the demands of parenthood.

> *The Verbal Abusers:* Whether overtly abusive or subtly sarcastic, they demoralize their children with constant put-downs and rob them of their self-confidence.

> *The Physical Abusers:* Incapable of controlling their own deep-seated rage, they often blame their children for their own uncontrollable behavior.

> *The Sexual Abusers:* Whether flagrantly sexual or covertly seductive, they are the ultimate betrayers, destroying the very heart of childhood—its innocence.

Is it possible that the MESSAGES we received from our parents are the mirrored images and thoughts we have regarding the ultimate "Parent." More precisely, have we begun to view Father God as a controller, inadequate, or verbal abuser? Have we questioned His seemingly nonchalant attitude as we feel abandoned, left to our own devises or raped of our innocence and belief in the abundant life?

Now ask yourself what MESSAGES you received about God, via your place of worship and religious teachings during your developmental years. Many of my clients come to my office angered to the point of suicidal and/or homicidal ideations about the early MESSAGES they received. Some were told via the many religious institutions that God only loves you when you performed or were good. So singing in the choir, preparing holiday baskets for the homeless and serving at the minister's table became the ticket to eternal life. Yet some of us were told that we will never be good enough so we must continually present ourselves contrite before him. Consequently, acts of false piety, specified dress, and preset greetings became rehearsed and adopted without introspection.

Some of us are convinced that God wants us to suffer here on earth and that the more you suffer the more convincing your testimony of godliness. Still others remain in dangerous and unhealthy relationships only to sit in the church with a pretend smile to demonstrate how the Lord was sustaining them. Like a losing player in a poker game standing pat attempting to bluff his way, we do not consider biblically based options and spiritual connectedness as the impetus to change. I have also observed clients who received MESSAGES that unfulfilling relationships and poverty were to be accepted and more than this celebrated because after all God **IS** pleased with ones willingness to suffer.

Despite the daily establishment of churches it is evident that the man made ranks of the liturgical hierarchy to condemn others for their apparent acts have begun to fade as the very elect of God falter. Excommunication and open confessions, (practices where individuals are asked to leave the church for certain sins or choose to step down from their position of leadership), and the denial of communion have no theological basis but yet they exist and on some level push man further and further from the greatest source of help, solace, and comfort that he was always to have.

Women fill the pews and coffers. They dust the furniture and prepare meals. They contribute money and rally for benevolent auxiliaries. But do not, in large numbers, sit in the pulpit or serve the wine though it may have just left their hands. Sadly, it is within our places of worship that a young girl may first encounter sexism.

In concert with feelings of anger, clients also present a horrendous amount of shame perpetrated by our religious institutions. Author Ronald Potter, in his book *Letting Go of Shame*, begins his book by first offering a definition of shame. Potter defines shame as "a failure of the whole of self." He does however add that shame can be a great teacher and can motivate personal change, conversely excessive or chronic shame creates devastation, feelings of inadequacy and hopelessness. The person who is shame-based has become "stuck in his shame…This shame-based person sees himself as deeply and permanently flawed." And might I also add, shame generally creates a need for us to distance ourselves from God. Shaming MESSAGES can trigger a strong sense of emptiness and nothingness. Shaming MESSAGES received from our parents and in conjunction with our religious institutions obviously affect our relationship with or view of God. As a child we may conclude, if I am not good enough or loveable to my own parents then most certainly I am not loveable enough for God. Further, rejection or abandonment adds fuel to the fire. "The betrayed child may become distrustful…believing that someone else will eventually reject him," And that someone else may indeed be God the Father.

Potter continues noting that shame begins with the infant, develops in the family of origin and is encouraged by an overly shame-focused society. And once we live in one shaming relationship, it becomes easier to seek out and involve ourselves in other shame based relationships. Potter does add that we may simply perceive the relationship as shaming. Our relationship with God, although the highest and most accepting, can also be perceived as shaming, particularly when we do not meet the rules and demands established by the church.

Through the many MESSAGES presented from the pulpit, religion classes, Sunday school, and various spiritual leaders, we have learned that perfection is the order of the day if we are to receive unconditional love. The consequences of these skewed religious MESSAGES prohibit us from trusting others, prevent us from speaking up and questioning others, and may force us to live in a constant state of anxiety characterized by a need to follow a list of rules. Additionally, we may be taught to feel guilty about who and what we are, and more painfully, that we will continually experience feelings of fear more than love from God. In summary the MESSAGES from the church are, don't talk, don't trust, and don't feel.

Author Donald E. Sloat, in his book entitled *Growing Up Holy & Wholly*, provides further insights as he purports;

> The conflict between the Pharisees and Jesus was over this identical issue.
> The Pharisees had developed an extensive system of rules for spiritual living, meticulously following them gave them a sense of self-righteousness and holiness...Too often our evangelical churches apply a similar system of rules for Christian living.

He further notes in his book *The Dangers of Growing up in a Christian Homes*, that many churches have adopted a master-list of sins. This list includes; Christians are not supposed to have sinful thoughts, you must dress appropriately for Sunday service, never display anger or resentment toward your child, mate, Christian brother or sister. The MESSAGES clearly state if you want to see God, live by the rules. If you fool around with your own thoughts and feelings you are going to incur God's wrath because those feelings are wrong. Obviously, many of us have been exposed to this master-list of do's and don'ts that were presented by the church and established a motivational system that emphasized the fear of God. However, Sloat adds that this motivational system, designed by the liturgical staff, resort to scripture (often taken out of context) to reinforce their personal efforts at control.

Later in life, for those of us who continue our search for this elusive being called God, we may encounter historical data regarding the church and her participation in several religious based wars and may become more confused and even skeptical about the need for continuing these various rites. However, our search may encourage us to reflect upon the following; when we look at the church, what do I really hear? We may hear historic messages. "Go ye therefore into all the world," only to be reminded of the Crusades that left oceans of blood in the name of God. We may see untainted societies and pure races of people left corrupted, spoiled and diseased by those who came to introduce a better, translation less primitive way to worship God the Father. I have read the stories of women, with different theologies, who were burned at the stake as heretics. I hear the voices of church leaders telling me to be quiet which is another way of telling me to be blind, deaf and mute. I see judgment administered by two different yard sticks; one for males and one for females. I see many churches, like their corporate counterparts, with glass ceilings for women. I hear the holy word of God used to demean and discount those who it was intended to reach, heal, and comfort. I see a king whose lust and lies provided the rationale for the beheading of several wives whose need for ultimate control orchestrated the cessation from the church in Roman. I see scrutiny and pronouncement of wrong met with and an order of excommunication (Martin Luther). These are the MESSAGES of oppression

So often we vacillate between behavior that defines God as the cosmic bell-hop and one who is a sadistic wrathful being. We may bear an image of God as the overindulgent patron that has no other goals than to make us happy. Translation, to give us everything that we think we ever needed. To suspend the laws of physics, time and space so that we will never be late or responsible for…

Conversely, we may travel through life expectant of impending doom. Afraid to be too happy because our God enjoys knocking us down a peg, or in the case of Job, gambling with the lives of our children, not to mention the material possession as well as our own life. Coincidently, why are we so angered by Job's wife who after loosing all ten of her children said to her husband "Do you still hold fast your integrity? Curse God and die!" (NASB Job 2:9) For just one moment put yourself in her shoes as a mother who despite the waywardness of her children, she alone experienced the painful process of delivering each child, only to be told that each one was dead.

We say repeatedly that we want to experience true freedom,

emotionally, spiritually and otherwise, yet we rebel and separate ourselves from God on all levels, but who among us does not back peddle when the consequences are disastrous? So is it any wonder that we may rail and rage at God when we perceive that his supposed gift of free will leads us down the path(s) of depression, isolation, fear, anger, disappointment, illness, wayward children, various addictions, poverty, and ultimately the greatest sin—disbelief.

CHAPTER EIGHT

So Is It Any Wonder?

Based on previous chapters now imagine yourself covered with an assortment of colored post-it notes, each containing a different MESSAGE. Face, arms, legs, literally your entire body covered with MESSAGES from parents, academia, society and religious institutions that have misinformed, misled, demeaned, constrained and ultimately failed you. So is it any wonder that because of these MESSAGES we regularly struggle with feelings of anxiety, depression and experience other emotional, spiritual and physical maladies.

Post-its or sticky notes were initially designed to serve as simple reminders so that we had ready access to information, to avoid missed appointments, a place to record our passwords to access various sites on our computer, or prompt us to remember items to be purchased at the grocery store. Other purposes offered assistance so that telephone numbers, appointments, names and instructions were readily available yet portable. They also served to remind us as employees, parents, students, or business owners when a needed task should be accomplished if not in its entirety that minimally some action should be taken in the near or immediate future.

Relative to the MESSAGES identified in the preceding chapters, our post-its were attached to us by others not only to remind but also supposedly to motivate and/or encourage change for the better. Conversely, at other times they were attached with intent to demean, discourage, promote self hatred, control or influence our sense of self.

Figuratively speaking, the majority of my clients enter my office covered with post-its, making it difficult to see the real person less known allow me to begin the assessment process, offer an accurate diagnosis or at best begin the necessary steps toward effective and meaningful interventions. But what are the reasons behind our need to continue to hide our true feelings and real identity? Further, is the need to hide done on a conscious level? Authors Harvey and Katz respond to these questions in their book entitled *If I'm So Successful Why Do I Feel Like a Fake?* The authors introduce what they describe as the "Impostor Phenomenon." This phenomenon suggests that there are three basic signs of the impostor phenomenon;

> The sense of having fooled other people into overestimating your ability.
> The attribution of your success to some factor other than intelligence or ability in your role.
> The fear of being exposed as a fraud.

In my counseling practice I observed that Harvey and Katz's third indicator of the imposter phenomenon, the fear of being exposed as a fraud, was the most prevalent among my clients. From the initial session well into completing the required *treatment plan*, clients would use any and all means they deemed necessary to protect them from being seen or exposed. When attempts were made to connect the dots between events that occurred during their formative years and the feelings and behaviors they currently exhibited, changing the subject, silence and even tears were produced to end the direct yet gentle probing.

Generally speaking, we all share an innate need to protect ourselves and our loved ones from being exposed, particularly our parents. And like Adam and Eve in the Garden of Eden we strongly believe that our act of disobedience (translation sins) force us to hide only to discover that our nakedness is in need of some physical covering. This need to excuse and protect ourselves and our love ones makes us complicit in the abuses inflicted upon us by our parents and others.

In our attempt to maintain equilibrium which is driven by the instinct to survive, we skillfully yet unknowingly suppress the MESSAGES that propose I am not acceptable or to a greater degree my parents' teachings and disciplinary actions failed me. The results are individuals fighting to hide their perceived inadequacies, issues of low self esteem, feelings of self-hatred and fear of establishing healthy relationships.

And so is it any wonder that these same clients enter my office covered with post-its that imbibe MESSAGES that have harmed, misled, resulted in feelings of self-doubt, influenced their choice of occupation, place of residence, mate selection and in many cases led them down the path of isolation.

So is it any wonder that we convey the same MESSAGES to our family members, friends and unsuspectingly to our offspring. Further these MESSAGES perpetuate the cycle of powerlessness leaving the next generation vulnerable and fertile soil for MESSAGES that will predictably fail them as well.

Now imagine two individuals covered with sticky notes each representing hundreds of MESSAGES that they too have gathered throughout their life. However, their desperate attempt to establish and maintain a long lasting, for better or for worse, relationship evades them both. At the onset or initial stage of the relationship both are committed to maintaining the illusion of having it together. But slowly and imperceptibly the notes begin to fall off revealing a needy, frustrated, and frequently insecure or prideful individual. Both unaware that they are in search of that perfect parent to "re-parent" them and provide them with unconditional love and validation.

After we have been bombarded with MESSAGES that state; you are…, you can't…, you should…then I can say with certainty that it is relatively easy for us to continue their propagation to others (remember the ham story).

Parents...so is it any wonder?

Parents are given a blank check to say and do things to and for us despite the fact that it may not be in our best interest. In the book of Matthews, chapter seven, the writer states "If ye then, being evil, know how to give good gifts unto your children, how much more shall your Father which is in heaven give good things to them that ask him?" Barnes Commentary adds;

> Christ encourages us to do this by the conduct of parents. No parent turns away his child with that which would be injurious. He would not give him a stone instead of bread, or a serpent instead of a fish. God is better and kinder than the most tender earthly parents; and with what confidence, therefore, may we come as his children, and ask what we need! Parents, he says, are evil; that is, are imperfect, often partial, and not unfrequently passionate; but God is free from all this, and therefore is ready and willing to aid us.

Unaware of the consequences we allow our parents to purchase, blackmail, and extort from us affection and control. Consequently, our behaviors fluctuate between the dependent four year old who wants and should be nurtured and the now independent thirty year old who should have moved from child-parent interactions to adult-adult dialogue.

I add a footnote here to address the susceptibility of young girls lacking adult-with-parents skills that often become prey to the ever present predator. Dr. Estes puts it best;

> As in the animal world, a young girl learns to see the predator via her mother's and father's teachings. Without parents' loving guidance she will certainly be prey early on. In hindsight, almost all of us have, at least once, experienced a compelling idea or semi-dazzling person crawling through our windows at night and catching us off guard. Even

though they're wearing a ski mask, have a knife between their teeth, and a sack of money slung over their shoulder, we believe them when they tell us they're in the banking business.

During a recent workshop, I presented an exercise that asked the female participants to write a letter to the damaged child within. This letter was intended to speak to the child who had experienced physical, emotional, verbal or sexual abuse. They were encouraged to express their true feelings, not on an intellectual level but to write from the heart. The writings were informative and indeed touching, even heartbreaking. But after the exercise I posed the following question; "Was this letter written solely by you or did you integrate dialogue that occurred between you and your parents?" Many were emotionally and physically moved and sickened as they realized that they had not written words created from within, instead they remained entombed inside of their mother's womb and that they had emerged ill-equipped to separate, make choices, fail, succeed, grow, or even to honestly express themselves in this exercise. In her book *Toxic Parents* Dr. Susan Forward shares the following;

> In many ways the letter to the damaged child within you may be the most difficult letter for you to write, but it may also be the most important. This letter begins with the process of 'reparenting' yourself. Reparenting means to dig deep within yourself to find a loving, validating parent for the hurting child you still carry inside. This is the parent who, through this letter, comforts, reassures, and protects that part of you that is still vulnerable and frightened.

The constant fear of reprisal or punishment from the person whose MESSAGES implore us; to be polite, don't offend, be a lady/gentleman at all times, may suppress our authentic feelings and according to Dr. Estes ignore the fact that;

Further, intuition provides options. When you are connected to the instinctual self, you always have at least four choices...the two opposites and then the middle ground, and 'taken under further contemplation.' If you're not vested in the intuitive, you may think you only have one choice, and often that it is an undesirable one. And you feel that you should suffer [underlining mine] about it. And submit. And force yourself to do it. No, there's a better way. Listen to the inner hearing, the inner seeing, the inner being. Follow it. It knows what to do next.

Church...so is it any wonder?

I must fall in line because that is what God wants me to do. Well, in reality that is what **you** (Pastor, Evangelist, Deacon, Father, Sister, Bishop, Reverend, Priest) said God wants me to do. I lack the ability to hear what God has to say to me directly (yes He does speak to us directly). For you see others hear from God more readily than I.

Prior to the birth of the incarnate Christ, only a select few were privy to direct communication with our heavenly Father. However, in the Synoptic Gospels (Matthew, Mark, Luke and John) Christ encouraged open dialogue even with children. Consider the woman at the well, the blind man named Bartimaeus, the rich man seeking eternal life, his disciples, the woman with the issue of blood, Lazarus' sisters, and the list continues.

So is it any wonder that we abandon the religious institutions and churches sensing that our prayers will not be heard because we lack a personal relationship with "the man upstairs." Even this colloquialism suggests distance between me and Him. The moving away from any formal religious institutions is distressing but predictable. Many have chosen to spend the day once reserved for worship and family gatherings for time on the golf course, in the backyard or in front of the television mindlessly surfing the channels for the right MESSENGER with a word from God. They have concluded that their questions will never be answered regarding child rearing, marriage, sexuality, salvation, death and the hereafter, or other pressing issues.

Weekly attendance at our chosen place of worship has evolved from a parental mandate into a habit and now a decision has been made to break free. Our decision to break the habit is in part based on the numerous disappointments that come with an invitation to choose a certain path toward a fulfilling life only to be denied any interaction and certainly no dialogue regarding the hard questions we need to have answered.

Relationships…so is it any wonder?

The newspaper headlines read;

> **"1 out of 2 Marriages End in Divorce"**
> **"Domestic Violence is on the Rise,"**
> **"Living Together Before Marriage Proves…"**

Long term relationships require more than love, more than same or similar goals, more than financial security. Most marriage vows include the statement "what God has joined together…" Let me pause here and pose the following question; how many marriages were ordained or joined together by God? Did we consult with Him or ask for His guidance when choosing a mate? Before the ink is dry on the marriage certificate many of us have consciously listed our expectations and sense of ownership of our mate. In so doing what do we communicate to our mates regarding our own needs? Do we dare ask for and expect honesty and openness? If our mate is unkind, inconsiderate or ignorant of where and who we are do we take time to educate and inform him/her regarding the hurtful MESSAGES s/he may relay? Do we dare risk losing this relationship because the thought of the unknown or aloneness is more frightening? (A familiar hell…).

In counseling numerous couples I have observed and noted a common thread that existed despite the couple's age, race or anniversary date. First, the ability to read the others mind is considered a requirement for a successful relationship. In summary, I know what you need and want before you say it. Second, if you as my spouse fail to do what I expect then I will investigate outside activities that satisfy. These extracurricular activities often lead to distrust, physical and emotional abuse and the ultimate betrayal known as infidelity. The other alternative that ones mate may choose is to suffer in silence. This silence is often a signal to the other to ignore the need for inquiry, understanding or empathy. If I say nothing eventually my spouse will get the MESSAGE. Silence on some levels may avert heated arguments and hurtful words, however it may also send the pervasive MESSAGE that things need not change.

Self…so is it any wonder?

After we receive and respond to the labels and titles assigned to us we may act accordingly. If we embrace the MESSAGE that we are unlovable we are more inclined to internalize the MESSAGE and act accordingly. We may spend time aggressively pushing people away to affirm the fact that we are not only unlovable but also unworthy of their time.

Be apprised that we do indeed have a choice to follow or ignore a prescribed path that began with a single MESSAGE. Here I offer a word of caution that suggests the need to use discernment in selecting your path. Scripture says it best; "I call heaven and earth to witness against you this day, that I have set before thee life and death, the blessing and the curse: therefore choose life, that thou mayest live, thou and thy seed;" (Deu 30:19) Matthew Henry provides us with further insights on the issue of choice. He notes; "Those that come short of life and happiness must thank themselves." However, I must add that choices can only be made when one has had the opportunity to view alternatives.

The often misquoted scripture in the book of Proverbs, "Train up a child in the way he should go, and even when he is old he will not depart from it," has been shared as a guarantee that if children are reared in a sound Christian based or religious home if they depart from their moral teachings, ultimately they will return to them. Upon investigation of the Hebrew words "in the way," are correctly translated "as a course of life or mode of action."

As far back as I can remember my passion has been to teach others regardless of venue. My desire carried over into my place of employment, as a babysitter for cousins and other family members as well as my weekly place of worship. Through the years I examined this passion and found that I had a overwhelming need to be on stage. Despite my resistance to this passion, and a withdrawal from all teaching/speaking opportunities, to date, some 50 years later, I find comfort as an educator in formal religious and academic settings. It was my mother who recognized my "theatrical bent," that guided me (really forced me) into situations that would allow me to utilize my gifts and talents. I firmly believe without this exposure I would not have returned to school or accepted opportunities to serve as a workshop leader or speaker.

The "Self" does indeed require support outside of us. Just as in many cases marriage does indeed enhance and in many instances prolong life, committees accomplish things beyond the scope of the individual by coordination and an amalgamation of efforts, resources, and energies of its members. Businesses make tremendous profits because they have perfected the fine art of maximizing the quality of their products and services. However, in our efforts to minimize the importance of self we must avoid what has been so named "the processional caterpillar persona." For most this insect is thought to be harmless creature. It lives all of its life communally and moves in a genetically determined posture which is; the head of the follower is always affixed to the hind-parts of the one in front. And so it has existed for longer than we know. Therefore there are benefits in being part of a cooperative life effort.

Conversely, an experiment was conducted to determine the depth of their genetic MESSAGE. The caterpillars were enticed into a circle. They proceeded as predicted, around and around. Food and water were introduced to determine at what point hunger would prevail and when the ranks would be broken to preserve life. Preservation of life is widely accepted as the strongest drive in nature but the response of the caterpillars proved to be astonishing. To the experimenters surprise the ranks were unbroken except when one became unable to continue in formation, the circle was then closed and they marched until they were all dead.

The MESSAGE above suggests that despite the need for conglomeration and support individuals often need to withdraw from the crowd and choose his own path in order to survive.

So is it any wonder...Baby on Board

I do not know how or when it happens, but it is said that along the path from childhood to adulthood we learn how to hide our true feelings from others and ourselves. I in part agree. The conspiracy to conceal begins with the MESSAGE we receive;

I need not verbalize what I need...just take care of me!!

And so on many fronts the following serves to define our desperate need to be cared for.

My car is out of control. I am careening down the road without brakes and at a high speed. I am approaching a busy intersection at rush hour. There is a driver in another vehicle attempting to cross the intersection ignoring the red light. In the back window of the vehicle is a diamond shaped note suctioned securely that reads "Baby on Board." It is the expectation that certainly I would not choose to demolish this car because of the sign. The baby on board sign serves as an indication to all that this vehicle deserves special consideration because of its cargo. The needs of those that may impact the immediate environment are insignificant. We live by this assumption because as children OUR needs were not met. This scenario dramatizes the disappointments we have endured and a need to be taken care of. Our expectation of the way we are approached and the relationship part of the interaction is to be considered because of specific needs, past and present circumstances and covert MESSAGES that drive us.

I do think that consideration for and from others is a virtue. Considerate, however, does not mean clairvoyant. To make assumptions is to juxtapose our values, tolerances, boundaries and limits onto another. To determine whether you have either used or witnessed any of these assumptions simply reflect on the last time someone attempted to coerce you into agreement with them adding the mandate that you concur or serve to rescue them from their plight.

Here I am to save the day

The needs of caretakers must be examined. If the attitude of enabling is at the foundation of the caretakers' methods then the mission has already been sabotaged. On the other hand, the mission to help another may have been a ploy in the first place. Some of us enter the helping profession or do benevolent work because it makes us feel better about who we are (guilty as charged). If we feel small and helpless, then somehow our ego is bolstered when we see, hear of, or help those less fortunate. We feel more powerful in relationships that involve a defocusing on our problems as we focus on the problems of others (oh my!!). One mechanism that we use to insure that this power dynamic never changes is to enable those that we help to remain dependent…solely on us.

Children frequently lack the necessary skills to communicate their needs, and in many instances, their wants. Tears, tantrums, pouting, silence are examples of behaviors that suggest I want you to respond to my needs, wants and demands…NOW!! However, as adults we learn that childlike behaviors may alienate others so we choose alternative methods to get our needs met. So common are the conflicting MESSAGES given by word and action that an entire vocabulary was revealed in the book *Body Language-How to Read Others' Thoughts by Their Gestures*. In his work, Allan Pease describes gestures, shoulder position, blinking of eyes and crossed arms etc. that betray the individuals true feelings. The

MESSAGE is still the same "take care of me." The fact that this book was written is a MESSAGE in itself. At times we are interested in another's opinion however there are times when we do not want to be placed in a position where we are forced to respond honestly to the truth.

We demand that everyone around us participate in protecting, loving, and meeting our needs and wants. Yet we are appalled at the mere suggestion that we endure the painful processes of growth and perseverance that lead to a mature adult. Conversely, are we to have no expectations of anyone or anything? Are we to exist in relationships unable to ask for assistance when it is needed or accept acts of kindness when they are extended for fear that we may allow ourselves to be infantilized? Finally, is it to our detriment that our traditional caretakers anticipate our needs?

Relative to the last question the answer is it depends. If our mother did not respond when we cried, then we never learn to trust. If dad does not positively interact with us during and through our formative years, then we never learn security. Conversely, if mom and dad do not allow the baby to crawl for fear he will endanger himself or they pick him up each time he falls the sense of autonomy will not be established.

During the period of infancy through age five, the tender touch, the countless kisses and lullabies develop a foundation of love. You may have been witness to parents in the swimming pool urging their child to jump into loving arms proving that a time will come when it is ok to jump even when there is no one there to catch them. The effort is always followed by praise, accolades, and encouragement as the child thrashes wildly at the water until he learns to feel good when the choice to swim is his alone. These precious gifts anchor the individual to his past and present and set the stage for the future.

Without this love and sense of security, the voyage is perilous and seemingly doomed at the outset. Continued life affirming experiences sink the roots even deeper. As we grow, hopefully fostered by unconditional love, a metamorphosis occurs. The strong roots have fed the tiny wings and they have emerged strong, powerful and wide like their nurturers. They catch and negotiate the wind carrying us far away. Paradoxically, the strongest roots permit the farthest journeys. Journeys that must be taken to satisfy the deepest yearnings of the heart.

CHAPTER NINE

Life Breaks Free...
When I Come to Myself

How dreadful knowledge of the truth can be when there's no help in truth!
—Sophocles' Oedipus Rex

This chapter is a celebration of life. It is a bold pronouncement that the MESSAGES that failed us and the MESSAGES that hurt us and the MESSAGES that would destroy us no matter the intent of the giver can no longer control us. Our inner voice objects, as it must, whenever we gain awareness that we are or have been partakers in the devaluing and depersonalization of ourselves. All bets are off. We stand boldly and fearlessly as we reclaim the person we were intended to be. This awareness is ever-vigilant. This sentinel here is equipped with historical data such that an individual who cuts you off on the expressway is a mere representation of someone in your past who has disregarded your rights or your personhood. However, today we will not respond with obscenities or beep our horn until we have the attention of all drivers on the road. In summary, we can now choose to remind ourselves and acknowledge the similarities in the events and actions of our past and the devastation they caused. Be mindful that this conscious state occurs in nano-seconds. The operative word is choice because we have been liberated from prior reactive responses and the auto play button.

Consider a woman born post WWII who was raised with the expectation of completing high school followed by marriage, children, grandchildren, etc, etc. The MESSAGES were pervasive and rather generic. But just suppose she was partly aware of the individual inside who had needs transcending the needs of her family, transcending the need of society for order, and for conformity to gender expectations. Just suppose she knew on some level that there was a talent and a great resource that could be expressed through anthropology or other sciences. Let's envision she was in reality a little girl who lay in the grass, looked up into the sky but did not just see the big dipper but was learning about the cosmos and the universe inclusive of the make up and origin of the stars. What would happen to her if her expressions of wanting and curiosity were co-opted, sublimated, and indefinitely set aside? The answer is simple. She may become sullen, dissatisfied, angry or depressed. Clarissa Estes notes;

> A healthy woman is much like a wolf, robust, chock-full of a strong life force, life-giving, territorially aware, inventive loyal, roving. Yet separation from the wildish nature causes a woman's personality to become meager, thin ghostly, spectral...When women's lives are in stasis, it is always time for the wildish woman to emerge...Afraid to bite back when there is nothing left to do, afraid to try the new, to speak up, speak against, becoming conciliatory or nice too easily-these are all signs the wild nature is not present. There are times when we experience her, even if only fleetingly, and it makes us mad with wanting.

We celebrate at this juncture because of the possibilities. This dissatisfaction has the potential to force us to change. We decide, for better or worse, that we can speak with our own voice about our dislikes and choices. This is a power that can move an abused woman away from an abusive mate. This is a power that can move a top level executive from the ivory-tower to his own business because he is no longer motivated by yearly bonuses, a six-figure salary and a seven day work week.

I do not propose that we proceed impulsively and whimsically through life, but rather to accept your role as complicit in the eventual outcome. Frightening, yes, but is this any less frightening than existing for someone else or to fulfill another's needs. All the while doing battle with the soul sentinel whose voice grows increasingly louder and struggling to build more and more reinforcements around him so that the dissatisfaction won't manifest itself at the grocery store, at our place of employment or on the interstate.

In summary I add six questions posed by Dr. Charles Stanley that address the issue of change and pose questions that help determine our need for people pleasing;

- Am I willing to suffer the consequences of this act to please others?
- What will I have when I have the approval of others?
- What will I have to do to sustain their approval?
- Am I willing to continue what I'm about to begin to retain their approval?
- Am I able to continue this action to retain their approval?
- What have I really lost when I lose the approval of others?

Seemingly after asking ourselves these questions instinctively we can not estimate the amount of energy needed to meet the expectations of another. We may begin to fully understand that the expectations of another are beyond the scope of human possibility. In short it will never be enough.

To break free requires first faith and then obedience and often without a clear path. Biblically speaking, it requires the steps that Abraham took as noted in the book of Hebrews;

By faith Abraham obeyed when he was called to go out
to a place that he was to receive as an inheritance. And he
went out,
not knowing where he was going. By faith he went to live in
the land
of promise, as in a foreign land, living in tents with Isaac and
Jacob,
heirs with him of the same promise. For he was looking
forward to the
city that has foundations, whose designer and builder is God.
Heb 11:8-10
—English Standard Version (ESV)

It was through Abraham's obedience to journey to an unknown destination that produced and introduced a generation of people and ultimately fulfilled scripture that spoke of the incarnate Christ. Journeying to the unknown can be both challenging and fearful. As I reflect on the promptings of the Holy Spirit to move to Houston, Texas despite unforeseen events I am reminded of the good and bad times, the people with whom I connected, and the completion of this book. In an earlier chapter I defined the word risk as doing something that will allow you to lose. We unknowingly take risks on a daily basis. However, the risks we take are generally calculated. For example what risk do you take when you begin the day with your usual routines of preparing for work or other tasks? Even those of us who have been displaced due to employment or economics generally have some idea of the outcome. But just suppose you were told to gather your belongings, your immediate family and just start walking with no clue as to the reason behind the move or final destination. Today we have electronic gadgets that can literally guide us to a local business or across the country. These state of the art tools are more than maps because they provide more than visuals, they speak to us aloud directing each turn until we reach our final designation.

I pose the question here regarding your decision to gather your belongings but unlike Abraham venture out alone, guided and accompanied by God the Father, God the Son and the Holy Spirit toward the promise of fulfillment, freedom and a new state of being. Until we make this decision breaking free will exist in the distant future or perhaps never.

CHAPTER TEN

Gathering Your Resources...
The Hardware Store

What tools or interventions do we need to journey home or return to ourselves and to God as He so ordained when we were formed in our mother's womb?

The visit to the hardware store is simply a metaphor to identify the myriad of tools that are necessary and available to start the journey...to return home...to return to ourselves. We need much more than the ruby slippers that Dorothy used in the Wizard of Oz. The ruby slippers that she clicked 3 times to initiate the journey did suffice in her world of fantasy, but we are in need of tools that produce the same result, are just as precious, but focused towards the business at hand. Be reminded that more than one tool is needed each one acts as a resource to serve, aid, instruct and direct us.

The first tools needed are the power tools that symbolize family and friends who willingly and without malice, forethought, and judgment embrace us unconditionally. To operate adequately and provide permanent results and relief, each tool must be plugged in or work in concert with our Heavenly Father who alone created us and counts the very hairs on our head. These tools encourage us to first draw on Him as only He can provide the needed electrical power (energy) to make the tools operational. Further, these high powered tools begin the process needed for the first stage of healing. They tackle the most obvious and critical areas of pain, hurt, resentments, betrayals and rage. Also these tools represent the people who answer the call of need with love. They do not need explanations, your need is enough. Through these willing souls we move closer to the first stage of life that may have evaded us…learning to trust. We receive permission and approval to be just who we are and where we are without shame and condemnation.

The next tool or resource entails the small hand tool, labeled support groups, books and manuals that provide self help and instruction. They serve in a variety of ways but principally to provide or suggest a path through the muck and mire of hurt and confusion to take further steps toward home. They provide the hands on and the necessary "how to" through a sometimes complex step by step process. These tools espouse the old adage when in doubt read the instructions.

The third and most often overlooked tool is the precision hand tool. Its purpose is to get at the hard to remove debris that has covered the festering abscesses that developed over the years. Prayer, biblical studies, taught by a fully trained man/woman of God, surrender, and continuous dialogue with God the Father must be combined with individual, and group therapy. These precision tools provide us with the interventions to work through specific problems and provide forums to speak the unspeakable. What we need during this process is a safe place to expose the scars and pain, fears and disappointments of past events despite numerous disappointments. Author Irvin Yaloom reports;

> People need people—for initial and continued survival, for socialization, for the pursuit of satisfaction. No one— neither the dying, nor the outcast nor the mighty— transcends the need for human contact…finding out what we are not is progress toward finding out what we are.

Yalom further divides the therapeutic experience into eleven primary factors. From personal experience as both a group participant and group facilitator I have found at minimum the following as the foundation for successful group intervention and human interaction:

Instillation of hope,
Catharsis,
Imparting of information,
Interpersonal learning,
Corrective recapitulation of the primary family group.

As the last factor implies, clients enter group therapy with a history of a highly unsatisfactory experience(s) in their first and most important group—the family. Negative MESSAGES from our parents can be the most damaging and ultimately produce a lifetime of poor choices, failed relationships, feelings of isolation, depression, and an endless list of emotional, spiritual and physical maladies.

There is a mandate to experience trust and to encounter an environment of safety as we embrace the evolution to life the way it ought and was meant to be. At this juncture I caution the unskilled user of the precision tool as he attempts to probe deeply into the realm of his past. The precision tools are the most expensive and difficult to use. They require formal training, focus, a steady persistent hand, a period of trial and error, and at best internship. However, this tool is necessary following the use of the large power and hand tools.

An example of their usefulness can be seen in the simple maintenance of the floors in our homes. Picture if you will a kitchen or family room surrounded with fine wood cabinetry, matching appliances, expensive art work and the most inviting furniture to sit or lie on. In both rooms the hardwood floors are shined to a high gloss devoid of stains despite their use from high traffic or spills. For just a moment envision mom using her electric buffer at least once a month to maintain the floor's sheen. And then weekly the use of the small hand tool, perhaps a mop or sponge to remove obvious debris. New equipment, manual and electric, have been introduced to maintain that just polished look. Friends and guest frequently compliment her on the mirrored look of her floors.

Some years later, the children are grown and gone, there are fewer family gatherings and constant high traffic has decreased. Mom and dad while sitting quietly in the spacious living room reflecting on days long past notice a bright red color seeping through several small crevices in the mirror-like floors. The use of the electric buffer, mop, sponge and a variety of stain removers and disinfectants are of no avail. Conversely, each time the red color is removed it reappears almost instantly. It now becomes obvious that more than the usual cleaners are required. A decision is made to get at the root of this annoying seepage. The large power tool serves to first strip the top layers of wax and sealant. Second, the hand tool perhaps level is used to remove the tiny specks of glue that secured the wood floor. But the bright red color and now a distinct odor begins to emerge. With sheer determination and will dad locates the tiny precision tool to remove the nails that secure the floor boards. Underneath it all he discovers a dead body bloody from various wounds. Here lies a body that has been buried for many years and now uncovered. The stench is overwhelming but the task must be accomplished.

What does this all mean? Within our daily lives we have presented to the world a picture of perfection. A seemingly healthy life that is maintained weekly through proper exercise, cosmetics and diet but eventually our real selves have been deprived of the essentials necessary to feed both mind and emotion. Ultimately we are starved to death buried beneath the pretense of perfection. How did the body find its resting place beneath such a comely floor? Perhaps it was years of unresolved issues or a MESSAGE that one must keep things looking good for the sake of the children. Maybe perfection was presented so that the illusion would prevent others from asking questions about our past, fulfillment, or emotional state that we could not answer.

I now ask you what part or parts of you have long been buried? How long can you suppress your longings, desires and needs? Or have you perhaps become cold and apathetic about life leaving unexplained feelings to imperceptibly seep from your inner being to the surface? A decision must be made. After all we do have choices. Will you, as the poem noted earlier, sit as the frog in the pond "sunned sated and satisfied" or will you begin to devote the necessary time and effort to the various tools, particularly the precision tools that enable you to get at your core issues and delve into the meaning behind the many MESSAGES that failed? It is the combination of these tools that offer us mental health, freedom, fulfillment and the ability to first identify, grieve and then respond appropriately to those various MESSAGES.

A word of caution here, the use of the large power tools under the guise of "religious words" or simply quoting scriptures often produce more resentment and anger towards our Heavenly Father and may reduce the possibility of emotional and spiritual healing. In seminary we refer to this cure-all as "God talk." William Hulme concurs;

> The power of a relationship is in the confidence and security
> it stimulates, whether it be a relationship within the family or
> with friends or with counselors. The same can be said of our
> relationship with God.

He continues;

> The Apostle Paul has also given us our most familiar
> expression of agonizing impotence in Romans, Chapter 7: I
> do not understand my own actions. For I do not do what I
> want, but I do the very thing I hate…Wretched man that I
> am! Who will deliver me from this body of death.

If indeed we are unaware of our own actions as we struggle daily to respond differently to old yet pervasive MESSAGES, we must experience a time of reflection, grief and loss, anger, and paradoxically, the acceptance of our powerlessness. It is through the writings of Elisabeth Kubler-Ross that I learned the importance of the five stages of physical death and their similarity to the stages of emotional death in order to "be born again."

Our knowledge of the early MESSAGES that continue to wreak havoc in our lives require more than memorizing chapter and verse from scripture. This painful process requires the use of the three tools noted above, but instead of identifying them as physical tools from the hardware store I encourage you to consider their use as spiritual tools, viz a viz, the Father, Son, and Holy Spirit. Ever mindful that our Heavenly Father is our creator whose watchful eye is ever present, providing us with new mercies on a daily basis asking only that we acknowledge Him as supreme. Jesus Christ, the son and savior, our mediator and high priest who through his death has provided us with the freedom to come before the Father and to do so boldly before God's throne of Grace. And the Holy Spirit who serves as our guide our paraclete walking along side and prompting us to wholly surrender to God. Without the amalgamation or the work of the Holy Trinity working for our good our journey at best will render us lacking direction and real joy, peace, and the promise of eternal life will evade us.

CHAPTER ELEVEN

The Paradoxical Journey

In the previous chapter I make reference to the five stages of physical death and briefly noted the similarities to emotional death. Kubler-Ross identifies the stages of death as;

Stage One: Denial and Isolation
Stage Two: Anger
Stage Three: Bargaining
Stage Four: Depression
Stage Five: Acceptance

It is through these stages that I personally discovered what I now term "The Paradoxical Journey." In essence embarking upon the paradoxical journey was an attempt to attain healing from the losses I suffered during most of my childhood, adolescence and yes even the events of today. To do so I was encouraged to revisit the many MESSAGES that failed me. And while on this journey I occasionally found myself literally fighting for every breath as I experienced the five stages noted above.

In this chapter I endeavor to offer relief and may I add spiritual and emotional healing from the MESSAGES that failed me.

To do so first requires awareness, knowledge and understanding of what is mandated to return to our true selves and make the necessary arrangements to return home. The journey is strewn with tiny pebbles, seemingly immoveable rocks, dangerous curves, periods of aloneness and isolation, tears that flow without warning and emotional struggles that prevent us from hearing the quiet steady beat of our own heart. But we must go back so that we can return home, return to our authentic selves and finally experience trust, innocence, playfulness, and faith in the impossible.

In scripture, notably the book of John, Jesus encountered a man who after being told that to inherit eternal life "he must be born again." As I picture this man's quizzical look at the Master Teacher I can only imagine the confusion on his face perhaps even a desire to laugh out loud. The dialogue was as follows;

> And there was a man of the Pharisees named Nicodemus, a ruler of the Jews.
>
> He came to Jesus by night and said to Him, Rabbi, we know that you are a teacher come from God; for no man can do these miracles which you do unless God is with him.
>
> Jesus answered and said to him, Truly, truly, I say to you, Unless a man is born again, he cannot see the kingdom of God.
>
> Nicodemus said to Him, How can a man be born when he is old? Can he enter the second time into his mother's womb and be born?
>
> Jesus answered, Truly, truly, I say to you, Unless a man is born of water and the Spirit, he cannot enter into the kingdom of God.

As a counselor I ask your indulgence as I take liberty with these verses and incorporate this dialogue into the very process of the paradoxical journey. As a mother who experienced fifteen plus hours of delivery to finally deliver my eight pound thirteen ounce son I concur with Nicodemus' question. Is it possible to reenter our mother's womb (I'm grateful for Jesus' response and the laws of nature) and begin the process of emotional growth? (there is a form of therapy that mimics this rebirth in hopes of gaining emotional health). Obviously, the answer is a resounding no!! However, we can revisit those periods in our lives that we have, for whatever reason buried deep inside.

In the film entitled "The Mission," the main character (Robert DeNiro) portrays the role of a mercenary. Although the film is a dramatization of fact, the film chronicles the events that occurred in South America in the eighteen hundreds. A political battle between Portugal and Spain ensues over ownership of a particular area or piece of land and the Catholic Church must decide the outcome of the natives that have resided there for decades (sound familiar?). DeNiro's role as a mercenary involves the capture and enslavement of the Waunana Indians. Early in the film Deniro's love for a woman, who has now turned her romantic and sexual attention to his brother, leads him to murder his own brother. Imprisoned for life, his wish is to die through self imposed starvation. In doing so he chooses to detach himself from all human interaction and basic nourishment.

As the story continues, a priest offers him an opportunity to bring "religion" to the very people he once enslaved. After much imploring he accepts the offer to take the long trek to the uncivilized world. Filled with remorse, shame, and self debasement he chooses to carry a netted bag filled with the same weapons and armor he used to stalk, capture, and murder the Waunana Indians and finally sell them on the auction block. From the viewers perspective he is weighted down with useless equipment that is heavy enough to cause pain and quell his progress through the treacherous mountains and jungle.

Further, to the viewer it becomes obvious that this netted bag of armor serves to feed his overwhelming need to castigate himself and do penance. In one very moving scene, numerous attempts are made to ascend the treacherous mountains but the weight of his bag makes every step painstaking. As he nears the top of the mountain, one member of the Waunana tribe observes his plight and with sword in hand frees him from his useless burden. The observant tribesman sensed that the penitent man had spent sufficient time grieving his past. The appropriate time had come for him to be set free.

We too carry useless baggage collected from the myriad of MESSAGES that accuse, demean, and produce guilt, yet we are unwilling to first forgive ourselves for acts we have committed and additional acts committed against us. How often are we told to "take it to the Lord and leave it there?" However, the daily glimpses and reminders of our insignificance, sinfulness, self-loathing, and interactions with our perpetrators prevent us from moving beyond our yesterdays.

How is it that we eventually deviate from who and what we were created to be? There are numerous species each with their own uniqueness that can not be hurried through the process of change or evolution. To prohibit or aid in any way this process would prevent the necessary period of evolution and may produce some level of deformity. As we view the events in the film we may ask ourselves "what self-inflicted MESSAGE did the character respond to that shaped and lessened his own sense of value to the point that forgiveness was not an option?'

However, much like the reformed mercenary, we may carry useless burdens assuming that we are obliged to do so. However, our meager acts of a penitent heart often create feelings of resentment, hopelessness and periods of regression. Myths that we readily embrace have convinced us that there is a direct correlation between our performance and corresponding rewards or consequences. During our developmental years we wholeheartedly embrace the concept that if I do X then most assuredly Y will follow. For example as children we may assume that tears will bring comfort, throwing a tantrum will gain our parent's attention and rebellion or going against the main stream will enhance the chances of getting in touch with who we really are. Even nature through the knowledge of science, instructs us that for every action there is a corresponding reaction. But there are exceptions to this rule one of which includes timing or ones level of maturity.

Through simple observation it has become apparent that our performance no matter how carefully practiced and orchestrated does not necessarily guarantee the success or approval we so desperately desire; not with parents, not with relationships, and certainly not with God. So what must we do to return home, that is to return to our true selves? The answer lies in exploring our past.

"Sometimes to move forward, you must retreat"

Beneath this quote, taken from a magazine ad, was a lone individual sitting in a row boat gazing off into the distance holding both oars ever so gently. The individual is surrounded by a rippling body of water with the sun wistfully shining and subtly reflecting the greenery of the surrounding trees. The peaceful scene did indeed produce a feeling of calm. The ad encouraged the reader to contact a particular spa resort guaranteeing the same experience of serenity, a relaxed state of mind, and rejuvenation so that "you can move ahead to whatever life has in store."

The words from the advertisement so ideally typifies the final stage involved in the paradoxical journey. That is to say that after collecting and re-examining all of the MESSAGES we received from parents, society, academia and religion we may find ourselves reeling from the events of forgotten or denied memories that necessitate a time to retreat. The process suggests a time for healing and as some say to begin recovery. Biologically speaking cells must be replenished. One client shared the following which further places things in perspective regarding the need to take pause and catch her breath. She began her story;

My husband loves to dance and occasionally we find ourselves dancing in our bedroom. As is his habit he frequently attempts to teach me a new dance step. With my two left feet I generally end up stepping on his feet or losing my balance. This particular evening he was adamant about teaching me a new dance step and so after numerous attempts followed by both verbal and physical directions, he suddenly stopped and said 'before I change directions I will always pause." I do this no matter what dance we're learning. The pause is necessary or I would end up snatching or pulling you in a different direction without giving you the time and opportunity to adjust accordingly. The woman stated that a light went on in her head and obviously the new steps were learned resulting in a flawless dance routine.

As with both scenarios the MESSAGE is indisputable, we must retreat, pause or reflect before changing direction. The reasons are numerous and varied. We have learned to live life in somewhat of a fog or as the helping professional refers to as a constant state of denial. Client after client will frequently relate past and present situations or life events of which they have no clue to their origin or impact. The result is a need to "feel better…" "get over…" "move beyond…" "bring resolution to…" the situation which is creating the distress. The obvious situation known as the precipitating event and defined as the reason to seek the aid of the helping professional is often overlooked.

Melody Beattie, most known most for her work on Co-dependency, wrote the following in her book *The Language of Letting Go*; "why would anyone look back after having a glimpse of something wonderful ahead. If we happened to look back then why would someone choose to go back?"

We often wonder why Sojourner Truth after escaping to the North in search of freedom from slavery made the decision to return time and time again into hell risking her own life or worse her freedom. It has taken me many years to understand what Sojourner Truth so clearly understood and that is her inextricable connection to the whole of her people. She could no more disengage herself than a finger from its hand. And so it is with the long journey back. In order to break the strangle hold of the MESSAGES that fail us we must understand how our past relates to our present and future and in doing so our actions may aid others as they too begin their journey toward wholeness and the abundant life we are promised.

A perilous journey with some potential for hurt and harm but one we must undertake. Potential for harm you say? Yes of course. The time traveler, like Sojourner Truth, could be enslaved by the same circumstances that would have ensnared him in the first instance if proper vigilance is not observed. When we revisit the pain it is expected that one would cry and grieve again, it is even expected that the rage may surface anew. Understand that painful and intense emotions can be liberating forces and that our failure to acknowledge events from our past can only continue to cause damage with our permission. With this in mind, you can now move toward immersion without fear of drowning.

I now invite you to revisit the times, places or environments of the many MESSAGES both positive and negative. Envision your home, your first day of school and smell the fragrances long past but not forgotten. I can recall the excitement that my mother exuded as I agreed to participate in a prestigious speaking contest. Time travel you see is quite possible. Hear the tone and the words again. Look into the eyes of the MESSAGERS and see them not as an isolated entities existing for the sole purpose of surveillance and torment but as unseen stitches that hold together the squares in our life quilt. It is easy to understand why parents born during and immediately after the depression would relay the MESSAGE that waste was tantamount to sin.

As we journey back we may find it easier to understand (not accept) the abuse of an abuser. This does not suggest that you excuse behaviors that damaged you. But with knowledge comes power.

One client shared her feelings of hopelessness. Based on past experiences she had looked in the eyes of the many MESSAGERS, heard their words and tone but failed to understand their intent. Her failure to understand the intent of the perpetrator produced feelings of struggling "in quicksand." As I explored the precise feelings associated with being in a rut the client stated that the more she struggled to be set free the more bondage she felt. Wanting the client to visual herself physically in quicksand I suggested that she first envision herself seated in her car surrounded by 2 to 3 feet of snow. By doing so, she immediately shared feelings of frustration while shifting gears from drive to reverse to no avail just simply stuck in the same spot. Following each session she reported that her level of frustration mounted. After several interventions she was encouraged to verbalize other feelings and thoughts regarding her seemingly hopeless situation. The client stated that her first instinct was to cry, scream, swear and throw what she defined as an adult tantrum.

Further probing, focusing on what she would do next, disclosed the following steps toward resolution. Determined to free herself the client would force the car door open crawl out of her car and eagerly search for someone to provide assistance. As her thoughts raced she pictured someone passing only to stop, back up and come to her rescue. For purposes of the exercise a female of slight stature and build was chosen to assist her. The client immediately exhibited further frustration adding that the suggestion was unfair. After convincing her that this individual was the only resource available the intervention continued. She began to think more about her situation and the possibility of involving herself in this seemingly hopeless dilemma. Her first attempt to free herself entailed pushing the automobile while the "Good Samaritan" sat inside the auto controlling the gears and steering wheel. However, their efforts were met without success. Suggesting that her rescuer just happened to have a bag of sand in her trunk, both went about tossing it around the four tires. Finally, a decision was made to call road service from her cell phone and she bid farewell to a new found friend. The tow truck arrived signaling to the client that her involvement had ended. But she readily discovered that she had yet another role to play. She was instructed by the tow truck driver to get into her car, turn her steering wheel, and place the car in neutral while he added a chain to the front of her vehicle.

Perhaps by this time you might question the purpose of the above scenario. My response is that initially the stranded motorist felt much like our earlier description of a "baby on board." This stage signaled feelings of powerlessness. We each consciously or otherwise chose one of two cycles; the cycle of powerlessness or the cycle of power. If one chooses the first cycle (powerlessness) we become enmeshed in this cycle which can potentially serve as the antecedent to focus on the past and/or the future, neither of which can be amply addressed, at least at this juncture. Our decision to remain encumbered by the past produces resentment and regret and any attempt at predicting the future produces fear. In this situation the client may have perhaps questioned why she parked in this particular spot (past) and now what would be her ultimate fate (future). Conversely, if we choose the power cycle, we first identify the purpose of the event or better still what should I learn from this situation and finally consider revising our response.

Be advised that during times of trauma that it is permissible and even encouraged that one initially experience feelings of powerlessness by taking the paradoxical journey. It is interesting to note that clients often enter the offices of psychologists, psychotherapists, or counselors convinced that there is no need to revisit their past. The question or statement frequently posed is "what purpose will visiting the past serve? I can't change a thing about it." But through open-ended questions and meaningful dialogue accompanied with feelings of compassion, the counselor soon discovers that the client is really saying that the past is too painful to revisit. Further, I have numbed myself to those hurtful times and I see no connection with my present status or behavior. Still others retort, if I conjure up the past my future will be considerably bleak. In their minds they fear the future and the certainty of being "stuck" in an endless cycle of powerlessness. But the opposite is true. In response to both clients my role is to encourage him to secure support from trusted friends, allies or family members. All the while keeping the client mindful that the power cycle will soon follow and is the better choice.

As mentioned earlier our journey home will first entail defining or identifying our purpose. Perhaps your purpose is to be relieved of depressive or anxiety ridden symptoms that drain you of valuable time and energy. Once we define our purpose as being made in the image of God and walk according to His time tested precepts, the elimination of the respective symptoms require skill and mastery. What skills are needed to be relieved of depressive symptoms? I suggest it is important to remember that the time traveler does not return as the same individual. Instead of the defenseless child with only feelings and lacking knowledge with which to express those feelings and catalog the events, we can now return as one infinitely more equipped to process, explain, defend, object, and protect. The adult not only has the knowledge of where the MESSAGES have led but have also gained knowledge regarding the benefits or consequences of choices based on earlier MESSAGES.

The adult returns most importantly with a **voice of his own.** It must be the voice of a compassionate judge that can declare a MESSAGE right or wrong because it helped or hurt. What we are seeking is healing, forgiveness and reconciliation for ourselves.

During the steps involved in journeying home, I am frequently asked about forgiveness. "When should I forgive this or that individual?" But more often a client will relate an event or describe a trip through hell while the tears flow and as they recall MESSAGES from early childhood to present day. Yet surprisingly the individual reflexively announces, "I forgive them." Each time this happens I grieve with the individual not just in regards to the details of the event but in the fact that it can never be laid to rest because the proper mourning has not taken place.

In times past, widows wore black from head to toe. This served as a signal to friends and strangers that an event so affected their lives that a respectable time should be observed before lives could return to normalcy. There was value in this practice. First, those who cared could offer support in appropriate ways. Food would be prepared and brought to the home, words of solace and consolation would be offered and depending on the culture, visitors would lend support simply by their presence. Friends and family appropriately altered their actions toward the grieving widow acknowledging that this process exacted a high price and that the social level of functioning should be different. The body, mind and spirit received appropriate attention.

Today we have lost not only the need for this type of attention but the remembrance that special needs require attention. These practices were instituted in times of apparent and indisputable grief. But what occurs when the tragedy is known only to the individual? What of the gaping wounds that may be ten years old yet unseen. In this scenario we are expected to suck it up and go on. And more than this, we must assume a stoic posture with a smile. As you may recall the example of the hardwood floor must be kept polished and dust free so as not to disturb those around you who appear more distraught than you.

The decision that must logically follow, more precisely the decision that is morally mandated is one of responsibility. Following the very difficult journey back then we are compelled to alter the choices that we make in response to the negative MESSAGES that we once allowed to be presented and perpetuated in our small corner of the universe. This, for some, is a serious day-to day struggle that with practice become easier.

During the paradoxical journey reconciliation is mandated. Not the "I forgive you for the MESSAGES that harmed," but a reconciliation that that begins with forgiving ourselves. In summary, reconciliation is or should be an outgrowth of forgiveness and forgiveness is first and foremost an outgrowth of reconciliation of ourselves.

If we know that the neighborhood bully was frightened, attention-seeking, deprived, and cast aside with little or no hope, then we can understand his efforts to make us feel like-wise. We can rage against the injustice and grieve our victim hood. We can also make the choice to devote not more time and energy in replaying the scene but to remove him from our knapsack.

I purposefully added the subject of forgiveness and reconciliation toward the end of the book because suggesting this action at the outset can be frightening. Might I also mention that this journey is not taken alone? Not just the crusade for reconciliation and healing, but the life journey itself. Our paths may intersect and merge with other roads at various points and for specific lengths of time. But the roads remain separate and distinct even after an apparent merger of two or more. If this concept is disagreeable then consider the very important relationships that we have and have had throughout our lives. The old adage that relationships come about for one of three purposes, a reason, a season, or a lifetime is indeed one that carries truth.

Parent-child relationships will most clearly illustrate this concept. Our children in the prenatal period seem to occupy the same space and time as we do. Yet they grow and are nurtured in a special place inside of us were we can not go. In essence it is part of God's divine plan that a separate space for nurturing and growth is provided for a separate individual. After birth this individual yearns, longs, demands, and gradually seeks that that is rightfully his. It is during this process that our own identity and the right to choose our own path must emerge.

It is this birthing process that I now wish to encourage in you. Various cognitive and philosophical approaches have been offered toward this birthing process. In this context I offer several. In the book entitled *Changing for Good*, the authors suggest the following six stages and corresponding definitions:

Stage 1—Precontemplation: Resistance to change oneself, just the people around them. During this stage the precontemplator may change as long as there is great and constant external pressure. Once the pressure is relieved they quickly return to their old ways.

Stage 2—Contemplation: During this stage the contemplator has indefinite plans to take action within the next six months. Fear of failure (perhaps an old MESSAGE) can keep them searching for a more complete understanding of their problem, or a more sensational solution.

Stage 3—Preparation: Most people in the preparation stage are planning to take action within the very next month, and are making the final adjustments before they begin to change their behavior.

Stage 4—Action: This is obviously the busiest period and the one that requires the greatest commitment of time and energy. Individuals most overtly modify their behavior and their surroundings.

Stage 5—Maintenance: This stage is a critically important continuation that can last from as little as six months to as long as a lifetime. Without a strong commitment to maintenance, there will surely be relapse, usually to the precontemplation or contemplation stage.

Stage 6—Termination: The termination stage is the ultimate goal for all changers. Here, your former behaviors will no longer present any temptation or threat; your behavior will never return.

As a counselor I incorporate these six-stages into each client's treatment plans. However, I am constantly reminded of God's word that plainly states; So that if any one is in Christ, that one is a new creature; old things have passed away; behold, all things have become new." (2Cor. 5:17) The operative words are "in Christ." Matthew Henry further clarifies;

> *For if any man be in Christ,* if any man be a Christian indeed, and will approve himself such, *he is,* or he must be, *a new creature,* Some read it, *Let him be a new creature.* This ought to be the care of all who profess the Christian faith, that they be new creatures; not only that they have a new name, and wear a new livery, but that they have a new heart and new nature.

> And so great is the change the grace of God makes in the soul, that, as it follows, *old things are passed away*—old thoughts, old principles, and old practices, are passed away; and *all these things must become new.* Note, Regenerating grace creates a new world in the soul; all things are new. The renewed man acts from new principles, by new rules, with new ends, and in new company.

I can now look forward because I have looked back. I have looked back and gone back. However, this time I am not bound, I have not been captured, and I have emerged happier, less anxious and more hopeful.

Can you imagine someone offering you a trip forward through a door that only takes you to the past? If you can, then you know how Queen Isabella felt when Christopher Columbus told her that he was sure that he could reach the east by sailing west. And so I have offered to you a trip into a brighter future by traveling through the dark night of the past. Behold the paradoxical gateway.

But can I gain emotional healing if I fail to accept this route? Can I move forward without all of this incredibly difficult and painful work? Or shall I sacrifice my life that has been carefully orchestrated to look and feel a certain way to the world at large as well as to me? The answer is that the paradoxical gateway is but one of the many ways into the future, however, Nicodemus understood the necessity of being born again as did Namaan (2Kings 5:10-14) when asked to return to a place of filth to receive his healing.

> And Naaman, commander of the army of the king of Syria, was a great and exalted man with his master, because Jehovah had given deliverance to Syria by him. He was also a mighty man, but a leper.

> But Naaman was angry, and went away. And he said, Behold, I said within myself, He will surely come out to me and stand and call on the name of Jehovah his God, and strike his hand over the place and recover the leper.

Are not Abana and Pharpar, rivers of Damascus, better than
all the waters of Israel? May I not wash in them, and be clean?
And he turned and went away in a rage.

And his servants came near and spoke to him and said, My
father, if the prophet had told you to do a great thing, would
you not have done it? How much rather then, when he says
to you, Wash and be clean?

And he went down and dipped seven times in Jordan,
according to the saying of the man of God. And his flesh
came again like the flesh of a little boy, and he was clean.

Please be advised that the initial attempts to experience freedom will
be fraught with repulsion, frustration and possible failure. I liken this final
stage to the batting averages in the game considered to be the national
pastime of the United States because of its strong tradition and great
popularity.

For the uninitiated, the game is played on a level field, which covers
about two acres. The playing area is divided into the infield and outfield.
Together these two areas make up fair territory. The rest of the field is
called foul territory. Throughout the game play revolves around the
action between the pitcher and the batter. Pitchers attempt to throw the
ball into the strike zone, an area directly over home plate and roughly
between the batter's armpits and knees. Pitches thrown into this area that
the batter does not hit are called strikes. After three strikes, a batter is out.
Unlike the game of life, the strike rule ends the supposed similarities.
Indeed the batter is alone at the plate surrounded by his team who is
rooting him on. They exemplify the few friends who encourage, cajole
and motivate us to do our best. But there are also thousands of voices who
overwhelmingly distract us in any possible way with hopes of breaking
our focus. No matter the size of our bench members the ultimate test is
what occurs between the batter and the ball thrown his way.

CHAPTER TWELVE

Departing the Text

"Now, I take full blame for all that came next.
For I continued the story...

> ...but departed the text.

Opus from: Goodnight Opus
By Berkley Breathed

A young woman approached me simply jubilant after attending one of my two day workshops. She stated that she was eager to share what she had experienced regarding her decision to "Break Free" by confirming the very heart of my MESSAGE. As she spoke she related the following;

I was at the bookstore, which is a favorite past time of mine, and since I have children, I generally venture into the children's section. While glancing through the colorful display of books all shapes and sizes, I happened upon a children's book written by a cartoonist and satirist whose work appears in the comic section of the newspaper. I decided to peruse his work as I do all printed material before making my final purchase. To my surprise I was so moved by the MESSAGE relayed in the form of a children's story that I purchased the book and placed it on my bookcase. The young woman, barely able to contain herself, continued her story expressing hope that I would share the story's significance and powerful meaning with others in future workshops. She continued, Opus, a strange looking animal part duck and part penguin is the main character in the book. It is bedtime for Opus and his grandmother asks him what story he would like to have read to him before retiring for the evening. Opus requests the "rhyming" book that had been read to him over two hundred times. Grandma agrees but first tells Opus that he must prepare for bed. Obedient and anxious to lie in his grannies warm lap Opus put on his "pink bunny jammies." All settled in grandma starts to read the story in her usual and predictable way. However, midway through the story Opus interrupts now aware that his soul sentinel longs for a different ending that will allow him to start the flow of his creative juices. Still beaming the woman added can you believe that in a children's book the main character decided to change the stories ending read to him by a loving authority figure?

His decision represents the churning feeling that I have had my entire life. From my preadolescence to present day I have felt dissatisfied with the path(s) that was chosen for me yet unconsciously continued to follow. I now know with certainty that just as Opus made a major decision to choose his own ending I too decided to continue my story but with the knowledge and wisdom that I have gained and finally depart the text that had been scripted for me.

Just like the woman mentioned above we too have discussed the scripts at work in our lives. Much like an actor we have been given words and phrases, told to emulate certain gestures, and to respond or act on cue and in concert with prescribed emotions. We have laughed uproariously, suppressed angry feelings or acquiesced when we feared displaying our true feelings would produce rejection from another. The scripted words are powerful MESSAGES given to us with regard to various philosophies, gender assignments, social morays, and traditions derived from our culture and ethnic heritage. Scripts so solicitous of the smallest detail that communication, freedom to articulate and discuss, to experience spontaneity and deliberation with truth as ultimate ends are realms seldom broached. Instead we are compelled to engage in speech and action that demand participation in following the lines of a carefully scripted play or motion picture. The MESSAGE is overt "stay in character."

One example of the scripts we receive can be likened to the following; if I make statement "A" then presumably response "B" must follow or the natural order of things is undeniably upset. For example saying "I love you" to a friend, spouse, child or neighbor is supposed to prompt the recipient to reply "I love you too." It may make us wonder if the initial expression is sincere or if the need for love is so great that this solicitation is sent to signal, prompt, insure and even warn the recipient of the MESSAGE to respond correctly. We will never know, the script does not allow for this. We lack the ability here to assess the dynamics at work and recognize that once again failed MESSAGES prohibit two people from achieving the goal of open and honest dialogue.

The tragedy here is that most of us, seeking to be known, find ourselves role playing. Ellen McGrath states in her book *When Feeling Bad is Good*, that as a whole our society has much disdain for the so called chronic complainer who begins her sentence with "I just don't feel good." Immediately, the listener will respond in one of two ways. The first and most common response is to negate the statement and conduct what is known as one-up-mans-ship. More precisely, my situation is worse than yours and let me tell you about it. The second response may entail reciting by rote that "you should have an attitude of gratitude after all..."

However, McGrath shatters the cultural myth that feeling bad must be negative. And I might add that feelings are God given gifts and help us identify when something has gone awry, they may signal a time for celebration or perhaps a grieving process. The wisdom of King Solomon is evident as we read the third chapter of the book of Ecclesiates;

> To every thing there is a season, and a time for every purpose under the heavens:
>
> a time to be born, and a time to die; a time to plant, and a time to pull up what is planted;

a time to kill, and a time to heal; a time to break down, and a time to build up;

a time to weep, and a time to laugh; a time to mourn, and a time to dance;

a time to throw away stones, and a time to gather stones together; a time to embrace, and a time to refrain from embracing;

a time to get, and a time to lose; a time to keep, and a time to throw away;

a time to tear, and a time to sew; a time to keep silence, and a time to speak;

a time to love, and a time to hate; a time of war, and a time of peace.

Just as we educate our sons and daughters about that "oh, oh" feeling, we too as adults must honor and listen to the internal MESSAGES that protect, warn, direct, and provide insight. The ability to express feelings on any level without feeling the presence or pressure of another's agenda promotes healthy living and intimacy. Further, we should have the ability to risk stating how we feel, be it loves or likes or varying degrees of the two. Instead, we recite a line then throw the script across the room for the other party to answer without deviation, spontaneity or authenticity. The MESSAGE operating here is that "love" means compliance. Romance makes everyone feel better and acceptance makes everything perfect. In part, I do not dispute this. Remembering candlelit dinners, picnics by the lake, and that first kiss of innocence always brings a smile as we begin a sentence with "Remember when we…. But these things should have happened after a session on our own love seat that provided a knowing of self, a loving of self, a forgiving of self, a celebration of self, and a permission of self. If the love of self happened after proper nurturing then when it is time to include someone else or to be included in another's love circle the foundation of love has been laid.

In our lifetime most of us will undoubtedly experience some measure of pain, feelings of rejection and abandonment and an array of various emotions. However, once again sufficient time spent on our own love seat will not allow our foundation to cave in. We brought love into the relationship and when signs of an unhealthy relationship surface we too can take love away. This choice prevents us from being diminished by temporal or limited relationships. Our decision is not meant to lessen the joy felt in a harmonious relationship or negate the pain and grief when there is a departure from a lover, mate or spouse. Real love, which created the world, outlives flesh and blood and does not pale with time.

The difficulty here is to first find a proper definition of the word love. We can never fully describe emotions so deep that they mystify the highest order. Yet our expectations of the emotion or feelings connected with the word "love" are unrealistic. One word can not describe a power that on one hand gives meaning to life yet on the other hand in its absence permits the existence of dark and evil forces. The word "love" has been utilized to exhaustion in all aspects of our lives.

In Scripture the apostle Paul entreats husbands to "love your wives." Although the Apostle was speaking Greek and not English, in this verse he purposely chose not to use other words like Phileo (brotherly love) or Eros (sexual or erotic love). Instead he chooses the word Agape, the kind of love that God has for us all.

Many of us we have not experienced love in any form. But for purposes of clarity Phileo is defined as having affection or personal attachment to someone or simply put to experience brotherly love. Eros means aspiring and fulfilling love often having a sensual quality. For many of us both words are foreign to us. However, the word Agape meaning "love feast, compelled in a moral sense, to be a friend to, one who is fond of, embracing chiefly with the heart until nothing comes between," is the strongest form of love. Who if anyone in your life fulfills this last definition? This lover has been described informally as the "point man." He is described as the one who stands in front of us to receive the first blow, who warns of danger, who consoles and comforts, and who protects at all costs. Just think, Eskimos and other indigenous arctic inhabitants have over two hundred words to describe snow. We have but a few words to describe the pinnacle of a relationship. We have been short-changed by the inadequacy of the script and the MESSAGES that follow.

Polite requests are supposed to yield the desired response. A sneeze is always followed by "God bless you" and even "bad" people are beneficiaries of certain social and religious scripts. Public enemy number can be executed but there are some that would frown at the jubilation that follows. Instead of joining in the revelry, they would ever so slightly bow their heads and speak in hushed Pharisaic tones "God rest his soul."

The exchange of words in a play does not allow for us to make exception or to accommodate the speaker but goes on instead with the same zeal that actors proclaim "the show must go on". The backdrop and the props provide the reality. This makes it very easy for the actors to respond and deliver the lines as written and on **cue.**

Once again consider the story regarding the Christmas ham. The backdrop was the ritualistic family gathering with a warm blazing fire in the fireplace, delicious smells emanating from the kitchen, loving chatter, and the assumption that warm feelings did abound. The ham, sweet potatoes, and green beans are merely the props. The reality was that the dinner was excellent. And because the end had been cut off the ham before it was baked is not a giant leap to deduce that this act was the key to a perfect ham. Never mind that grandmother's pan was too small. However, life is not a play. This chapter is about real life and within these pages we are discussing a precious entity; life with twists and turns, fragile relationships, triumphs, and difficulties. The MESSAGE, the script does indeed shackle us. It can be changed, but only following time, patience, a willingness to explore both past and present events followed by meaningful dialogue.

Any excuse or explanation real or imagined to continue the text can be accepted as long as it negates, softens, or draws attention away from the MESSAGES that failed us. We are entangled by the obvious symptoms that render us incapable of examining or even considering the truth. Rather we are averse to challenging the MESSAGES that fail because in doing so will only result in a backlash, a dismissal and various expressions of disdain, particularly from our beloved parents. When our actions are not evaluated based purely on the MESSAGES we received then we can never hope to get to core issues and truth. Historically our parents, siblings, friends, spouses and other institutions have attempted in every way to tell us, like Jack Nicholson's character in A Few Good Men, that we "can't handle the truth".

The truth, the whole truth...and nothing but the truth

If we dilute every passionate word or act and become ensnared with strategies that guarantee never to offend, disturb, closely examine, or move beyond the prescribed text for the sake of maintaining the status quo, then our life and all corresponding events are indeed regrettable. Is it any wonder that war, persecution, and excommunication have been justified because an individual or group found the status quo incompatible with life?

One example of the above is the recorded event that found inconsistencies with many of the tenets of the Roman Catholic Church. Martin Luther, the German Theologian and one of few known religious reformers, played an integral role in initiating the Protestant Reformation. Luther was moved to write the 95 Theses in opposition to Catholic doctrine and was later investigated, condemned, and excommunicated when he refused to recant his position. To some it would have been safer to retract and renounce his previous position but to Luther going against his own conscience was and is not safe for anyone. He relied solely on a MESSAGE from God.

We must examine yet another hallowed institution, the family, if we are to understand why we have been left so vulnerable. Admittedly this is a heavy encumbrance to place on the institution known as the family but this is the most important entity to which we could ever belong. If the family provides a firm uncompromising steadfast and unconditional foundation of love and communicates positive MESSAGES then we can sit in classrooms that teach little attend religious institutions that misinform us and extract the best of them rather than being victimized by them.

The family that is supposed to provide a nurturing and a protective environment has over-time failed in its mission. Instead of the commitment to view and nurture us as children through early adulthood or when the time is right for us to leave the nest, an arbitrary age of eighteen is the standard that speaks of self-sufficiency. More often it is the age when the parent is off the hook. But what if that child has a special gift? What if the talent or the area of interest takes longer to develop? What if valuable resources needed to promote a special musical, intellectual or athletic gift go beyond the prescribed age?

Our familial institution contributes to generational MESSAGES and becomes an instrument of destruction rather than a fortress against it. Children have minimal external resources or references and are in need of examples, in word and deed, which define right and wrong.

It is my contention that an adoption of the in-spite-of or coincidentally MESSAGE will remind us that it is not what we do but who we are that educates us regarding the specific rights and privileges within the family. The first and most important right being—Love unconditional. Instead of "I achieved in-spite-of adversity," rather," my family gave me the best they had (unconditional love) and therefore I learned how to love myself.

Many would find it frightening to proceed through life without land marks and maps and hazard signs. I submit that certain scripts and MESSAGES provide only the illusion of instruction or warning and guidance, and to follow them is to proceed through life without direction. These MESSAGES often make it impossible to see the hazard signs and consequently we proceed without first examining the consequences of falling rocks, curve in the road, and a blinking yellow light.

Do you recall the cyanide laced Kool-Aide mass suicide at Jones Town? Someone should have told the truth about the MESSAGE-giver very early on so that a whole life-style would be less likely to flourish around someone's psychosexual and psychosocial illnesses. Blaring trumpets should sound when anyone says that you are to disconnect entirely from friends and family or burn the bridges that brought you to your present place. Some bridges though old and unstable have value and worth. Rather than turn away, look closer, delve deeper, dissect even to the smallest cell and review all against the historical backdrop. Like Romulus and Remus, we must return to the place where abandonment and disappointment happened and establish great cities.

Read if you will the following accounting (some suggest a mythical accounting) that provides the need to depart the text.

According to the Roman legend, Romulus was the founder of Rome and Remus was his twin brother. Their story begins when their grandfather Numitor, king of the ancient Italian city of Alba Longa, was deposed by his brother Amulius. Numitor's daughter, Rhea Silvia, was made a Vestal Virgin by Amulius—this means that she was made a priestess of the goddess Vesta and forbidden to marry. Nevertheless, Mars, the god of war, fell in love with her and she gave birth to twin sons.

Amulius, fearing that the boys would grow up to overthrow him, had them placed in a trough and thrown into the River Tiber. At that time the river was in flood, and when the waters fell, the trough, still containing the two boys, came ashore. They were found by a she-wolf who, instead of killing them, looked after them and fed them with her milk. A woodpecker also brought them food, for the woodpecker, like the wolf, was sacred to Mars.

Later the twins where found by Faustulus, the king's shepherd. He took them home to his wife and the two adopted them, calling them Romulus and Remus. They grew up as bold and strong young men, leading a warlike band of shepherds.

One day Remus was captured and brought before Numitor for punishment. Numitor noticing how unlike a shepherd's son he was, questioned him and before long realized who he was. Romulus and Remus than rose against Amulius, killed him and restored the kingdom to their grandfather.

Through their actions Romulus and Remus were unwilling to accept the supposed fate handed them. Upon examination of your family tree you may discover alcoholism, promiscuity, teenage pregnancy and divorce. Statistically it has been suggested that if one parent is an alcoholic their offspring has a fifty-percent chance of following suit. Further, if both parents are alcoholics the child's chance of becoming addicted to alcohol is seventy-five percent. These data are generally known as ones predisposition. Painfully, many of us rely on these old assumptions believing that they had and have no choice.

Opus, our cartoon hero mentioned earlier makes a request to his grandmother. Although he too is certain of the stories outcome he insists that his favorite bedtime story be read, the one with the rhymes that entertained him and made him feel safe. The MESSENGER was someone who we are quite sure loved him very much. But after two-hundred and ten times of hearing about our abusive yet absent father, our drug addicted mother, we like Opus have the option to change the story's ending. Opus chooses to cast aside the routine and predictable in order to see what has been present all the time—the full scope of his life. Historically, we know that Opus, being a penguin, wishes for wings that work. We are not sure, but we might suppose that Opus finally gets his wish. He ultimately flies farther than anyone would imagine possible even for a cartoon character.

I do not suggest that you march single file into the Milky Way behind the satirical penguin. However, as my conference attendees and later my clients attest, being personally moved by his story they do get the MESSAGE…and make a decision to depart the text.

Inertia...a choice

Inertia is defined as the tendency for matter to remain at rest or if moving to continue in the same direction unless affected by some outside force. Inertial forces are at work when we choose a familiar hell rather than chance an unfamiliar heaven. Examples of this phenomenon occur when we fail to pursue the career we have prepared for because of internal and external MESSAGES that suggest "I have so much time on this job despite the fact that my talents have been underutilized." In essence we choose to "remain at rest." We do not challenge injustice in our land because of inertia. "Our justice system may not be perfect, but there is none better". Schools educate with the inertial method and are disinclined to try new methods. As teachers continue to follow the "official curriculum" minds stagnate, creative thinkers are ostracized, and the creative energies are sublimated into negative channels. We may remain connected to individuals who have little or no vision and willfully penalize us, for fear of being ostracized if we depart the text or fail to settle for mediocrity.

Perhaps you may recall the popular television show "Outer Limits." The instructions at the beginning of every show were; "do not attempt to adjust your set! We control the horizontal and the vertical. We have the power to make your reception cloudy or crystal-clear." In robot-like compliance we do not attempt to adjust our set because **they said** that they control the horizontal and the vertical. We passively agree that **they should** have the power to make our reception cloudy or crystal-clear after all they own the station. But the Outer Limits MESSAGE becomes questionable when we surrender our responsibility in defining our own "Inner limits." The decision to change direction is executed only when a stronger external or internal force is applied. The paradox is our refusal to change the channel and depart the text requires more energy to maintain the status quo.

The Clean Slate

Francine had done all the right things and for the right reasons. She obeyed her parents and never missed sending a card on their birthdays. She had always paid attention in Sunday school, and never spent her offering money on candy. She had gotten all A's in grade school, and had been the valedictorian in high school, and senior class president in college. Now she had a more than adequate paying job that offered phenomenal potential for growth. She drove her dream car became a member of the right organizations, recycled every Wednesday, and volunteered her time at the senior citizens center during the holiday season. She had a checking account, a savings account and a pension fund, and four days a week she religiously went to the gym. Francine was at the top of her game, in good physical shape, fairly, no, very attractive yet she complained of still being single. The one thing she couldn't get right was finding a man. Despite all of her material possessions and success to Francine this was the most miserable time of her life. As I reflected on Francine's presenting problem I was reminded of the words written by Iyanla Vanzant who suggests in her book *In the Meantime;* that this is the time; "The one you sit in, stew in, find yourself in when you have done all the right things and gotten the wrong results!"

What becomes of those who "follow the scripts" as all of us do at one time or another and to varying degrees fail to attain our desired outcomes? What must happen in the subconscious, the mind, or the inner self when the lines are recited perfectly, the character portrayed perfectly yet your life is replete with wanting? Francine was miserable and agitated. Anger and feelings of betrayal also come to mind. But there are questions that need to be asked and answered.

Angry with whom?

Betrayed by whom?

Who do we blame for the lines and the script? Who envisioned and then created the character and decided that this is who we should be? Who makes the choice to take the high road or the low, or forego a choice for either? Whatever the answer there is always an ultimate end to the examination process. Closely examining the MESSAGES that failed are the beginning of the process.

The difference lies in the way we view life. Do we exist for the good of society or do we follow certain rules so that all those around us may peacefully coexist? Do we tolerate or accept certain things in relationships so that the relationship may continue (at all costs) or do we bring all to the table and demand acceptance of who we are, so that the relationship may move to the next level or cast aside?

Consider if you will the Blank Slate Theory or Tabula Rosa. This school of thought theorized by John Locke suggests that we enter this world without knowledge or distinct personalities. The theory further suggests that we come ready to receive the many MESSAGES that will direct our lives and control our emotions. However, in truth we are born with personalities that manifest themselves in our genetic code. There is information written on the slate that predates birth. It is God who formed us in the womb and knew and created us from the "foundations of the earth." Jeremiah chapter one verse five affirms this as he records; "Before I formed thee in the belly I knew thee..."

Additionally, at some point we must look back at our own slates replete with MESSAGES and examine the MESSAGES and the MESSAGE givers. This is difficult work but serves as a guide to help us to look forward such that we view our lives, not as a life left with nothing-to-do-but-live-it, but instead as a chance to explore endless possibility. Allow me to paraphrase Georgia O'Keefe, a modern day genius of American art, who spoke of landscapes. "The landscapes [in the desert] look as though they are already painted...until you try to paint them. I looked for someone to tell me how to paint landscapes. They could not. They could only tell me how they painted their own landscapes. I had to try to paint my own."

When Miss O'Keefe asked the question, tell me how to paint landscapes, she probably thought that she could capture the landscapes on canvas based on the way learning is facilitated. She may have started from a reference point, the deserts themselves. She then solicited information from those who had undertaken the task previously. Finally, she searched for instruction which was the right way to proceed in certain circumstances. However, it could be a rather disappointing experience to eat the cake prepared by someone who had no idea of the ingredients, mixing technique or baking time. There is no substitution for the time and effort spent during the information-gathering process. It is absurd and pointless to proceed without a broad knowledge base. When it is time to create and the finished product is an expression of self, then this work must come from a place where no one has or can visit. Therefore, no one can tell you what is there. *"Only a sighted fool asks a blind man to describe a tree."*

A young stage actor said to John Houston, a famous motion picture director, "I am not a movie actor, I do not know how movies are made". This actor was predictably in a very uncomfortable place. Imagine having to portray a role without any knowledge of the mechanism. Mr. Houston told him to look through the eyepiece of the movie camera. He said, "do you see the box?" The actor replied in the affirmative. He said "that is a frame". He further replied "decide what goes there". The young actor has the ability to create from his own vision with skills that he has paid dues to acquire and through his own talent. But what put the actor in this position? Quite simply his honesty in his definition of himself, the acknowledgement of his own limitations, his ownership of his task, and the pause before imposing thoughtless preprogrammed formulas on the character.

Soul Hunger!

After rewriting the manuscript or text of your life and all editorial work has been completed, several questions may come to mind.

What will be my reaction to the text I have just written?
How will be others react to the new text?

The hope is that there would be great anticipation pregnant with excitement when considering the possibilities of writing your own script. Texts can be written and rewritten with knowledge that the outcome can only be determined by the writer. It is the difference between playing in an orchestra and playing with a jazz ensemble. If you have ever had the privilege of hearing Mr. Winton Marsalis lecture then you may have heard his response to the following question. When asked which he enjoyed most playing with the orchestra or jazz ensemble he replied: "When you play with an orchestra there is the joy of playing together and making great music. But when you play jazz, you have both the joy of playing together and the freedom to interpret and express yourself in the framework of the music."

Because we do not live in a vacuum, the above question is very reasonable. We all communally coexist with each person influencing others to varying degrees. As I have so pointedly stated previously there is a profound affect of parent to child to parent, neighbor to neighbor and individual to the rest of the world relationships. Each relationship carries the potential to diminish, augment, and transform us in small or great ways. Therefore, we must respectfully consider the positive as well as the negative impact when we are engaged in our decision-making processes. However, appropriate responsibility is logical and rule once we decide to depart the text. We can not be responsible for the reply and the response or the reaction of others. We must, however decide our posture in the midst of the response.

> *"Those who do not get carried away should be."*
> —Malcolm Forbes

Aside from the familial MESSAGES other MESSAGES come in various forms and from various sources. In my practice I have heard repeatedly "if it weren't for my [sister, mother, teacher, pastor, wife, boss] I could easily manage my life and find fulfillment. But in truth we are made for relationship. Although there is yet no single comprehensive theory of interpersonal relations Warren G. Bennis notes;

> We regard an interpersonal relationship as an irreducible element of reality. Just as we cannot have a line without the

presence of two dots, we cannot have an expression of an interpersonal feeling without the existence of two people.

Essentially, the mandate for interpersonal relationship entails a minimum of two people communicating in supposedly the same language, both verbal and nonverbal. The basis for communication requires a sender who communicates or initiates the MESSAGE and a receiver, who responds accordingly. Further, the communication is cyclical in that the reverse occurs to denote confirmation, clarity, and an understanding of the MESSAGE. Hopefully the cycle continues until time, interruptions, closure, or other matters take precedence. But what occurs when the sender's MESSAGE is not understood and/or the non-verbal cues confuse the receiver?

Marital counseling has become part and parcel of my practice. As a therapist/counselor/social worker I endeavor to unearth the core issues and MESSAGES that evoke painful remembrances that reverberate like heavy bass through the walls of a cheap apartment. I have discovered how remarkable it is and how often the client or in clinical terms the Identified Patient (IP) articulates a MESSAGE to his or her mate using what he or she deems as appropriate, understandable words and phrases. However, as both clinician and observer the non-verbal cues often send contradictory MESSAGES.

During our sessions we note that the difficulty is not in saying "I love you" or "You know I love you, I married you!" but in first defining and then becoming an active participant in intimacy (Into-Me See). The ability to communicate on this level entails sending and receiving different MESSAGES and requires the receiver to abstain from simply hearing the words to becoming an **active listener**. The difference between hearing and active listening is that each requires different skills. Active listening mandates a willingness to do so along with much practice, time and energy.

As young teens we recall hearing a song over and over hearing a few of the words that are repeated yet without a clue as to many of the words being sung. It simply has a nice "beat," and we hum along with the music or "fake it" when the unfamiliar words are heard. But how often have you some time later listened to the words, noted the mood of the singer, listened to the various instrumental accompaniments and been surprised as to what instruments were being played and the words in the song? Active listening does indeed require energy, time, commitment and willingness, actions that we choose to minimize or ignore. Instead, we communicate on levels that suggest to the receiver, "I know best, you listen to what I am saying." The results are two individuals who leave my office resentful or destined to keep their next appointment but determined to maintain the status quo.

Ultimately, the future is one that may lend itself to basic survival in the marriage or relationship for the sake of...the children, the business, the social commitments, or simply friends and family. But according to The "Pyramid of Time/Energy Use" the lowest level, in terms of sending/receiving a MESSAGE is maintenance and survival. The next levels of the pyramid advocate problem solving followed by the involvement, opportunity and permission of each person to create. It has become painfully evident that in dialogues spoken of like the one above their origins can be traced to the individual's prior relationships, experiences or abuses. The result, neither party is willing to actively listen to more than just "the beat."

For Here or to Go?

In discussing those who have progressed through the normal developmental stages making it possible to schedule the pain and pleasure of life I hasten to evaluate other individuals for the sake of completeness. I first speak of those whose primary objective is to avoid even the slightest discomforts of life and live with an attitude of no holes barred or a constant search for ultimate pleasure (hedonism). Second, I must address those of us who allow no outlet or pleasure release referred to as anihedonism. For purposes of accuracy particularly during my initial research, I was adamant about these supposed diametrically opposed personalities or mindsets. But after careful examination and evaluation it appeared that they were more similar than dissimilar. Both suffered from a lack of fulfillment and a void in their lives so deep that it could easily be compared to the absence of light in a darkened room.

Diet is very important to the health and well being of the individual. This MESSAGE once taught in Home Economics class has become irrelevant, meaningless or redundant to most. Picture the triangular shaped drawing posted in every classroom. Its MESSAGE was to emphasize the importance of milk, whole grain foods and the other basic food groups and to encourage proper nutrition that is vital to wholesome living. Today we experience feelings of frustration when we hear the statement that although more Americans are conscious of their weight, fat and caloric intake, and the benefits of regular exercise we are fatter than ever. The mere mention of this fact renders many of us whose gestures of disapproval reveal that healthy eating does not fit into our daily routine. Many admit a knowledge deficit of vegetable preparation. Some will state without apology, "I do not eat vegetables." The designation of heart-healthy is insignificant. Not even the information that green and yellow vegetables have anti-cancerous factors in them suffice to affect a change in behavior. What foods are chosen instead of our life preserving vegetable, whole wheat breads, fish and poultry? Fast food and foods such as pie, cake, and candy that are high in carbohydrates capture the lion-share of dietary choices. The food must be more beautiful and more gratifying or it will not be eaten. Why?

First because the selection of food is driven by the unconscious need to be pleased and satisfied on an emotional level instantly and at all times. Second, it is the only acceptable avenue to squelch that gnawing feeling of emptiness (setting the stage for a variety of eating disorders). It is common knowledge that every afternoon a vast number of teachers, corporate employees, laborers and even those engaged in the medical field choose some form of fast food. We prefer to call it eating on the run. The immediacy to be satisfied on varying levels does not allow for the investment of time required to prepare wholesome meals. The first choice is burgers, then chicken and maybe fish. Of course, the predominant choice is "for here or to go." In summary, food is no longer ingested to "build strong bones twelve ways." Instead its purpose has become a substitute for the ache and hunger of the soul.

Food is not the only aspect where the Olympic motto of higher, faster, stronger, and farther is adopted. Nor does "for here or to go" entail diet/ nutrition. Immediacy in the many areas of our existence has become a way of life. Fun must be more thrilling or other avenues will be sought. The Six Flags organization has long been familiar with this phenomenon. Each year they entice us back to the park, not with the same thrilling rides, but with a roller coaster that goes faster and higher. These rides push us over the brink of excitement and terror. Anything less would mean a decline in attendance at the parks and would reflect negatively on the bottom line.

The Friday the 13th series was met with the challenge of explaining the buckets and gallons of blood needed to capture the target audience again and again and again and again and again. In the past the nightly news endeavored to meet the highest journalistic standard of informational and impartial reporting of the news. Now our local news have adopted a tabloid format to capture more and more viewers. The physical health and mental health care professional as well as other service-oriented professions must be more accommodating and more kowtowing. The rationale whether known or unknown is a need to be taken care of beyond reasonable therapeutic and ambulatory offerings. This by no means is an indictment against the needs of the client. It is the realization that for them the fields of mental and physical services should be defined as "take care of all of me." Vocal and emotional stimuli must be more intense, passionate and titillating or interest will wane. The MESSAGE, if you can't meet the needs that were not provided during my developmental years I will simply find a physician, therapist, psychiatrist, attorney or teacher who can.

Are there more MESSAGES? Obviously the answer is yes! Consider the subject matter of comedians now in contrast to comedians twenty years ago. Subtlety, nuance, and innuendo have been replaced with in-your-face profanity under the guise of humor.

Why the change and why has the tide shifted toward the sensational? The answer, nothing will survive in the realm of deprivation unless it can overcome the numbness threshold and may I add numbness and apathy are the pervasive moods of today.

"But I Just Can't Feel...Anymore"

Departing the text requires more than resolve because for some of us our existence revolves around the omission of **all** pain at all costs. But what of those who have listened to the MESSAGE that said the more pain you endure the greater the gain? Pain in abundance is accepted as merely the prelude to bounteous reward. What individuals have been indoctrinated with the pain MESSAGE such that they can no longer recognize pain and respond *appropriately* to it? If we look at the natural phenomenon associated with the reason for the existence of pain, then we could say that the presence of pain necessarily implies damage. Pain exists to warn the organism to move away from or protect itself from that which is causing the discomfort. Logically, if pain is a protective mechanism, then why are we so bent on displacing it from the forefront of our perception and acknowledgement? Have we endured this injurious state so long that acceptance is our only coping mechanism? Could it possibly be that we are addicted to the physical and emotional endorphins (pain-killers) secreted in our brains and in our environments. Our bodies naturally produce these perfect drugs that keep us pain free and tranquilized but awake. Imagine living a life emotionally and physically pain free...sounds perfect, but do we begin to endure "the life" to get the drug?

In our culture, heroes are defined as those who give the ultimate sacrifice for a cause, a game, a marriage, a job, or an individual. The **approval endorphin** can be a strong motivator. It is important to pause and remember those who fought to save someone from peril, searched for lost children, traveled great distances to aid flood victims, and responded to natural and man-made disasters of all types. Their true selflessness and willingness to take the risk and make the sacrifice in spite of known danger truly makes them deserving of the title "HERO". But is it heroic to endure extreme chronic discomfort until you are incapable of blossoming but instead end up small, tough, compact and thorny. For some of us the feeling of responsibility is so strong for others that we may lack the ability to set boundaries and limitations for ourselves. This ensures that our friends, family members, offspring and spouses will never be appropriately responsible for their own recovery or period of growth. This also insures a parent-child relationship between you the seeker of the approval endorphin and the recipient. Is the **martyr endorphin** at work here?

Perhaps in passing you have heard of VonMunchausen's Syndrome. In any case this emotional malady is an extreme example of the pain endured for the acquisition of attention. Individuals so afflicted will invent a myriad of signs and symptoms so that medical procedures will be performed or medication will be prescribed. In any event the individual is satisfied because "I now have your attention." It is safe to say that the **attention endorphin** levels are elevated in this scenario. And so from the thrill seeker at the amusement park to those of us who lack a fulfilling life and finally the individual in desperate need of attention continue to respond to pain inducing MESSAGES...that fail.

"Just Do It"

Many renowned psychologists, sociologist, philosophers, and religious leaders have offered rationale and solutions for the various emotional maladies and situations we regularly encounter. One contemporary psychologist, author Stephen Covey in his book The 7 Basic Habits of Highly Effective People, suggests that we alone have the power to choose various paths in life and in effect predict their outcome. Conversely, we can spend our lives simply responding to various stimuli in a passive state accepting the hand that is dealt us with little or no thought to the outcome. He further suggests that when we chose the latter we are guilty of approaching life based on a predetermined accumulation of stimuli.

Those who embrace Covey's premise (Predetermination vs. Determininsm) may find themselves convinced that because of the poor choices "they" made early in life, "they" have the responsibility to remain in or change their present status. The results are individuals endeavoring to take **total** responsibility for their behaviors and circumstances who eventually become more frustrated or complacent with their emotional, spiritual, and financial status. At the opposite extreme, they may become belligerent or hostile willing to challenge anyone who suggests that change in their lives can and will produce greater benefit.

Covey notes that in resisting change we often find it easier to justify our behavior with the notion "that's just how I am." Upon accepting this seemingly delusive state of existence, he further suggests that our existence resonates in the following statement; "if you argue [long enough] for your weaknesses, they are indeed yours." Translation the arguments for your behaviors, attitudes beliefs etc. that spew from your mouth or are revealed in your behavior become self-fulfilling prophecies. Covey's remedy for the above is that until we recognize the importance of "taking charge of our lives" we will be doomed to repeat the actions and influences of our parents and generations past. Without a departure from the script that has been written for us by well meaning parents and others, we will maintain our position by the warm fire, unaware of either the need to add our own kindling or carefully monitor its destructive power.

In one of his tapes affirming the ease involved in change Covey cites a detrimental MESSAGE that has indeed failed us. In the scenario a frustrated client shares his concern regarding marital discord. The client is adamant in his assertion that he no longer loves his wife, "the spark is gone." Covey's response to his frustrated client is simply "just love her," and repeats the same statement regardless of the man's pleadings. The client's final retort is that he does not have the capacity to "just love her." Covey continues to implore him to love his wife adding that love is a verb, suggesting the need to take action. Translation, get busy loving someone without examination of your feelings, her feelings, and perhaps the precipitating event or events that led to his feelings.

Upon investigation via the many sessions with struggling clients I find his premise somewhat reasonable. However, as I made attempts to implement his principles in teaching and counseling my suggestion that clients "just do it," as the gym shoe commercial implies, produced feelings of failure, shame, guilt, anxiety, depression and inadequacy. Is it reasonable to propose that individuals no longer have the right to re-examine, outgrow, and undergo metamorphoses relative to those whom they once shared the greatest affinity? In light of my counseling experience I view this proposal as ludicrous and as insensitive as forcing a child to kiss and aunt or uncle who may in times past pinched or emotionally abused them. The intended positive lesson conveyed by dismissing a complaint of no shoes by pointing to the man with no feet may work for those who allow themselves to be plowed under with the argument that "your situation could be worse." Conversely, refusal to acknowledge issues that fail to speak to matters of the heart may lead to greater evils.

My response to Covey comes directly from the Biblical text. Scripture implores us to "love our neighbors as we love ourselves." But in quoting that scripture we overlook an essential element or requirement. And that is the assumption that upon entry into our world we loved and love ourselves. There is truth to the saying that you cannot fully love someone until you first love yourself. Only our Heavenly Father through his son, Jesus Christ, has the capacity to love us unconditionally without the need for reciprocity.

Margaret Mead, after years of extensive research in cultural anthropology and social systems, concludes no decision is irrevocable. She based her premise on observations that prove that growth and therefore success is dependent on the ability to change and adapt. We agree with both Mead's and Covey's premise that encourages us to take responsibility for our actions adding that change is possible. However, the difficulty with their basic premise is that it insinuates that we are consciously aware of the impact that the actions of our parents, siblings, grandparents, academia and society at large have had and continue to have on us. And more vital how we have responded to those influences.

Based on his assumption Covey suggests that we can choose to either negate or embrace those influences. But how does one motivate another or for that matter himself to initiate change without identifying, revisiting, grieving and finally substituting prior negative MESSAGES with the new? Further, we must be consciously aware that the change may entail a change in diet, attitude, relationships, communication style or other behaviors. Any attempt at change will first require knowledge of and an examination of the old MESSAGES followed by dedication and commitment to the new MESSAGES, the ones **you** have created.

Dotson Lawa suggests that if the motivation to change is too low the individual won't do it, the end doesn't justify the means. The motivation is insufficient or the reward is not commensurate with the exertion of energy. Conversely, if the motivation to change is too high, the individual won't do it they are simply overwhelmed by the required demands and discipline. Numerous influences and variables exist that create havoc when decisions to change ones thought processes and behaviors are attempted. Reflect once again on the story about the Christmas Ham and then examine the many changes you personally have attempted to bring about with minimal success.

Finding the perfect level of motivation necessitates a process of trial and error. In light of this assumption, I pose the following question. Will the individual desirous of change, yet failing miserably, experience such frustration that he eventually "throws in the towel" returning to old habits? In my endeavor to bring some measure of emotional health, which ultimately produces wholeness within my clients, I examined the writings, theories, and various therapies of psychologist, psychiatrist, counselors and social workers both past and present. One such contemporary included in my research was David D. Burns M.D. In his book *Feeling Good the New Mood Therapy*, Burns' based his theory on the attainment of emotional health through cognitive reframing and restructuring. Simply put, his approach to therapy is to change one's thinking through "self-talk therapy" which without question influences the individual's feelings and corresponding behavior. He suggests that we must work diligently to uncover the many layers of negative thought patterns until we recognize our cognitive distortions. As noted earlier, Dr. Burns further espouses that uncovering one's cognitive distortions may reveal one or several of the following; all-or-nothing-thinking, overgeneralizing and various attempts at mind reading. He also suggests that there is a need to overcome these cognitive distortions by substituting more positive, objective and rational thoughts. This is done through a series of steps that aid in peeling away the layers of negative cognitive MESSAGES that the individual has received and regrettably continue to embrace. Dr. Burns' approach does offer assistance on the road to emotional health, but only after a thorough examination of the various MESSAGES and their origin. But I must also note that some MESSAGES are so powerful and deeply buried within our psyche that the distortions can only be unearthed through the use of the usual counseling interventions in concert with the ultimate soul-searcher the Holy Spirit. It is through him that we experience an awareness of our need for relationship with our Heavenly Father who literally keeps our tears in a bottle, knows the number of hairs on our head and knows our thoughts a far off or before we know them.

There are additional philosophies regarding the challenge and work involved in making permanent change. For example, a statement supposedly made by a high school custodian suggests that "people change in their own way on their own day" has been passed on and posted throughout schools, offices and the like. At what stage of life must one be or for that matter how desperate must an individual be before there is some willingness for permanent change? Behind the closed doors of pastors, friends, professional and lay counselors, and Twelve-Step meetings, numerous life stories have been shared. For most their stories are recollections of the initial spark that ignited the fire. In our search we make various attempts to extinguish the fire that contains numerous MESSAGES unaware that we will encounter some residual effects.

Despite our actions that entail careful dousing of water the fire continues to smolder long after camp has been broken. For those of you who remember the commercial with Smokey the Bear warning us "remember only you can prevent forest fires," I encourage you to take heed. Because the MESSAGES that pervade our thoughts, beliefs, feelings and actions are like the tiny spark that although now smoldering need only a gentle breeze to re-ignite the flames.

231

Additionally, change for the better is a process and despite our many attempts to avoid it it has the following eight characteristics;

CHANGE IS:
- CONTINUAL
- UNAVOIDABLE
- NECESSARY
- ACCELERATING
- DEVALUATING (the new devalues the old)
- HAS A RIPPLING EFFECT
- CREATES A NEED FOR INTERDENDENCE
- AFFECTS OUR VALUE SYSTEM (makes our current value system obsolete)

The reasons behind our responses to change are varied yet fall in one of four categories. First, if the change impacts our investment of time, money or emotions we are likely to respond in a myriad of ways. Second, our involvement or lack thereof in the planning or implementation of the change will determine our reaction. Third, the environment has a great impact on our response to change. The environment entails people, trust, support and the methods used to initiate the change. Fourth, our perception of the change is unique to each person and is influenced by our past experiences, culture and education.

Generally speaking, on an unconscious level we **think,** feel and long for relationship with God the Father. However, this may require extensive work because the MESSAGES we received from and in our religious institutions are considered sacred and should never be challenged. The first and second steps in the Twelve Step program drive the MESSAGE of change home. After our meager attempts to stop drinking, drugging, overeating we ultimately "came to believe…and [recognize that] we are powerless over… The paradox is that although deep within our souls we thirst for this relationship we consciously choose other things to bring fulfillment. Sadly, we like the deer spoken of in the Psalms, are left with an insatiable thirst that become audible in times of desperation. His panting is not a casual longing or desire but according to the Hebrew definition is a thirst so overwhelming that in his search for satisfaction, the deer makes a noise as audible as the deep sighs we often make when we experience frustration or disappointment. As our souls search for real nourishment we too make a noise perhaps not audible but nonetheless just as gut wrenching as all of nature.

Why is it then that we choose instead to fill our longings with money, cars, alcohol and drugs and things to fill the void? Again the answer can be found in our sinful nature. Within our nature "resides no good thing." And as the Old Testament reports we continue to do what is right in our own eyes. This departure from the God's **True Text** will only lead to our demise. Our only hope is to first acknowledge our sin nature and the true longing of our souls and finally identify the MESSAGES that are the results of these longings.

Departing the text requires dialogue with God. Not the usual bless this and bless that, but a real conversation that permits God to respond in the deepest recesses of our soul. In Neal Donald Walsch's book entitled *Conversations with God* (don't panic his writings are from a metaphysical perspective but contain many profound truths) he writes the following;

I have heard the crying of your heart. I have seen the searching of your soul. I know how deeply you have desired the Truth. In pain have you called out for it, and in joy. Unendingly have you beseeched Me. Show Myself. Explain Myself. Reveal Myself.

I am doing so here, in terms so plain, you cannot misunderstand. In language so simple, you cannot be confused. In vocabulary so common, you cannot get lost in the verbiage. So go ahead now. Ask Me anything. Anything. I will contrive to bring you the answer. The whole universe will I use to do this. So be on the lookout; this book is far from my only tool. You may ask a question, then put this book down. But watch.

Listen.

The words to the next song you hear. The information in the next article you read. The story line of the next movie you watch. The chance utterance of the next person you meet. Or the whisper of the next river, the next ocean, the next breeze that caresses your ear—all these devices are Mine; all these avenues are open to Me. I will speak to you if you will listen. I will come to you if you will invite Me. I will show you then that I have always been there.

All ways.

Be forewarned that it will be a tedious journey as I too struggled with a variety of MESSAGES…that had failed me. It has been through the writing of this book that I discovered a core issues that challenged, directed, infected, held me hostage and took me ever so cunningly to the brink of suicide. Some may say that they only wished not to awaken. But it was I who pondered various plans to take my life.

Oh but GOD!!! As I neared the end of this work, I had my conversation with God who after years of searching, crying out and a refusal to surrender, revealed to me my own personal MESSAGE that screamed rejection!! The knowledge of this MESSAGE that failed me revealed my need for perfection in every aspect of my life, relationship approval, academia, motherhood, wifehood, sisterhood, as a professor, workshop leader, speaker and author.

I encourage you to take the risk…explore the hidden meanings behind your behavior, thoughts and emotions and depart the text that is a result of the MESSAGES that have failed you.

If you always do what you've always done
You always get what you always got.

SELECTED BIBLIOGRAPHY

Allen. P. G. (1986). The sacred hoop. Boston, Beacon Press.

Allender, D. B. (1990). The Wounded heart. Colorado Springs, CO:
Navpress

Allers, R. (Director), & Minkoff, R. (Director). (1994). The lion king
[Motion Picture]. United States: Walt Disney Pictures.

American Psychiatric Association (1994). Diagnostic and statistical manual
of mental disorders (4th ed.). Washington, DC: Author

Anderson, C. (1994). Black labor white wealth. Edgewood, MD: Duncan
& Duncan.

Anthony, S. B. (1874). Making of America. Rochester, NY: Daily
Democrat and Chronicle Book.

Berube, M. S. (Ed.). (1995). Webster's II new college dictionary. Boston:
Houghton Mifflin Company.

Boice, J. M. (1981). Foundations of the Christian faith. Downers Grove, IL: InterVarsity Press.

Bradshaw, J. (1990). Homecoming: *Reclaiming and championing your inner child.* New York: Bantam Books.

Braiker, H. B. (1992). Lethal lovers and poisonous people: How to protect your health from relationships that make you sick. New York: Simon & Schuster.

Breathed, B. (1993) Goodnight Opus

Brown, D. (Producer), & Reiner, R. (Director). (1992). A few good men [Motion Picture]. United States:

Bruner, J. (1977). The Process of education. Cambridge, MA: Harvard University Press.

Burns, D. D. (1980). Feeling good: The new mood therapy. New York: William Morrow and Company.

Chambers, O. (2006) My utmost for his highest. Barbour Publishing Incorporated.

Church, L. F. (ed.) NIV Matthew Henry commentary (1992). Grand Rapids, MI: Zondervan Publishing House.

Cloud, H., J. Townsend. (1992). Boundaries: *When to say yes, when to say no to take control of your life.* Grand Rapids, MI: Zondervan Publishing House.

Coles, J. B. (2001) Dream the boldest dreams: And other lessons of life. Atlanta, GA: Longstreet Press

Coon, D. (1980). Introduction to psychology: *Exploration and application.* St. Paul: West Publishing Company.

Covey, S. R. (1994) First things first. New York: Simon and Schuster.

Crabb, L. (1987). Understanding people: *Deep longings for relationship.* Grand Rapids, MI: Zondervan Publishing House.

Drew, J. M. (1996). Healing the "Mother Wound:" *Dealing with the effects of control, shame, neglect, and overbonding.* American Healthcare Institute.

Estes-Pinkola, C. (1992) Women who run with the wolves. New York: Ballentine Books.

Fairburn, C.G., & Brownell, K.D. (Eds.) (2002). *Eating Disorders and Obesity: A Comprehensive Handbook (Second Edition).* New York: Guilford Press.

Harvey, J.C. with C.Katz (1984). If i'm so successful, why do I feel like a fake?: *The Imposter phenomenon.* New York: St Martin's Press.

Hess, E.H. (2002). Fossil crinoids.

Heyman and Young (1978). When I fall in love

Hulme, W.E. (1981). Pastoral care & counseling. Minneapolis: Augsburg Publishing House.

Joffe', R. (Director). (1986). The Mission [Motion picture]. United States

Johnston, W.B., and Packer, A. H. (1987). Workforce 2000: Work and workers for the 21st century. Indianapolis: Hudson Institute.

Kierkegaard, Soren, Hong, H. V. and Hong, E. H. (1987). Either/or. Boston: Princeton University Press.

Leman, K. (1989). Birth order. Nashville, TN.: Thomas Nelson Publishers.

Leman, K. and Carlson R. (1989). Unlocking the secrets of your childhood memories. Nashville, TN: Thomas Nelson Publishers.

Malloy, J. T, (1988). Dress for success. New York. Warner Books.

Marsden, G. M. (1990). Religion and American culture. Fort Worth: Harcourt Brace College Publishers.

McGrath, E. (1992). When feeling bad is good. New York: Henry Holt and Company.

Meyer, J. (1998) The Battlefield of the mind. Tulsa, OK: Harrison House.

Miller, A. (1979). The Drama of the gifted child: *The Search for the true self.* New York: Basic Books.

Moore, L. How Frog Feels About It

Nash, R.H. (1992). World-Views in conflict: *Choosing Christianity in a world of ideas.* Grand Rapids, MI: Zondervan Publishing House.

Newman, W. R. (1981). The Social impact of television: A research agenda for the 1980's. New York: Rowman and Littlefield.

Nouwen, H. J. (1979). The wounded healer. New York: Doubleday

Peck, M. S. (1978). The Road less traveled. New York: Simon and Schuster.

Proschaska, J. O., J. C. Norcross, C.C. Diclemente. (1994). Changing for good. New York: Avon Books

Ross-Kubler, E. (1969). On death and dying. New York: MacMillan Publishing Co, INC.

Ryan, J. (1994). Seeing God more clearly

Satir, V. (1983). Conjoint family therapy (Third Edition). Palo Alto, CA: Science and Behavior Books, INC.

Satre, J. P. (1940) No Exit. Paris France

Schutz, W. (1958). FIRO-B

Seamands, D. A. (1989). Healing of memories. Canada: Victor Books.

Sheehy, G. (1996). New passages Toronto: Bantam Books.

Sheehy, G. (1981). Pathfinders. New York: Bantam Books.

Sloat, D.E. (1984). Growing up holy & wholly. Brentwood, TN: Wolgemuth & Hyatt, Publishers, Inc.

Vanzant, Y. (1998). In the meantime: Finding yourself and the love you want. New York: Simon & Schuster.

Walsch, N. D. (1995). Conversations with God: *An uncommon dialogue.* Charlottesville, VA.: Hampton Roads Publishing Company, Inc.

Weeks G. R. (1992). Couples in treatment: *Techniques and approaches for effective practice.* New York: Brunner/Mazel, Publishers.

Yalom, I. D. (1985). The Theory and practice of group psychotherapy (third ed.). Basic Books, A Division of HarperCollins Publishers

Zemeckis, R. (Director). (1994). Forest Gump [Motion picture]. United States

Bibles:

King James
New King James Version (NKJV)
American Standard Version (ASV)
The Amplified Bible
New International Version (NIV)

Printed in the United States
72634LV00008B/190